The Changing Soviet Union in the New Europe

STUDIES OF COMMUNISM IN TRANSITION

General Editor: Ronald J. Hill
Trinity College, Dublin

Studies of Communism in Transition is an important new series covering all aspects of communism, but focusing principally on change in communism as a system of rule. At a time when the Stalinist form of socialism is undergoing reappraisal, modification and abandonment in the leading communist-ruled countries, and newly-emergent nations are being led along the communist path, the need to understand this phenomenon and its evolution has never been greater.

The series is edited under the sponsorship of Lorton House, an independent charitable association which exists to advance education in and to promote the academic study of communism and related political concepts.

The Changing Soviet Union in the New Europe

Edited by
Jyrki Iivonen

The Finnish Institute of International Affairs, Helsinki

Edward Elgar

Published by
Edward Elgar Publishing Limited
Gower House
Croft Road
Aldershot
Hants GU11 3HR
England

Edward Elgar Publishing Company
Old Post Road
Brookfield
Vermont 05036
USA

CIP catalogue records for this book are available from the British Library and the US Library of Congress.

ISBN 1-85278-532-2

Printed in Great Britain by
Billing & Sons Ltd, Worcester

CONTENTS

PREFACE

Jyrki Iivonen

It is beyond any doubt that foreign policy has been one of the few fields where *perestroika* has so far proved to be successful. In a relatively short time, a historical transformation has occurred in the nature of the whole international system. Great power relations have rapidly changed from confrontation to cooperation. New steps have been taken in disarmament as well as in negotiating regional conflicts. But it is especially here in Europe that the greatest progress has been made.

In 1985, when Mikhail Gorbachev was elected General Secretary of the CPSU, Europe was divided into two antagonistic blocs. Hardly anyone was able to anticipate the revolutionary events of autumn 1989, when within a few weeks the socialist system collapsed completely in Eastern Europe. This collapse would have been impossible without changes in Soviet foreign political doctrine and practice. The Soviet leadership had rejected the so-called Brezhnev doctrine, thereby making possible the transition to democracy and the market economy.

Throughout the postwar period, Soviet leaders had seen Europe in a politically secondary role. Their main emphasis was on great power relations, while Soviet-European relations were seen in that framework. One of Gorbachev's greatest achievements has been promoting the idea of the 'common European house'. It is not only an expression of the Soviet desire to take a more active role in the making of European policy but also a confession that the era of the bipolar international system is over. It is, of course, possible to argue that the end of bipolarism is mostly due to the declining role of the Soviet Union. But, in spite of that, the concept of the 'common European house' also offers evidence of Europe's new and more visible role in Soviet foreign policy. The aim of this book is to analyse certain aspects of this change.

With the exception of one contribution, this book is based on presentations given at the international conference organized by the Finnish Institute of International Affairs at Tuusula, Finland, on 23-25 November 1990. The articles can be roughly divided into four groups. The book opens with three articles in which wider historical and conceptual issues are discussed. Henry A. Trofimenko of the Institute of United States and Canada in Moscow and Jyrki Iivonen of the Finnish Institute of International Affairs concentrate on historical processes while Neil Malcolm of the Royal Institute of International Affairs, London, analyses the concept of the 'common European house'.

The second part deals mainly with military issues. Gerhard Wettig of the German Institute for East European and International Studies discusses the changes in Soviet military doctrine and Roy Allison from the Centre for Russian and East European Studies, University of Birmingham, considers the recent Soviet debate on the future development of the army. Ksenya Gonchar, of the Institute of World Economy and International Relations in Moscow, has, for her part, taken up one of the most debated issues in Soviet military policy, that of the conversion from military to civilian production.

The third part of the book concentrates on certain economic issues in Soviet foreign policy. Heinz Timmermann of the German Institute for East European and International Studies analyses the changing Soviet attitude towards the European Community and Laszlo Csaba of the KOPINT-Datorg Market Research Centre in Budapest discusses Soviet-East European economic relations.

In the fourth part, some regional issues in Soviet foreign policy are discussed. Priit Järve of the Institute of Philosophy, Sociology and Law in Estonia, for his part, discusses the prospects of the Baltic cooperation. The book concludes with Pekka Visuri of the Finnish Institute of International Affairs on the rapidly changed Soviet attitude towards German unification.

This book is a result of numerous contributions from various individuals and institutions. The Tuusula conference in November 1990 became possible through financial arrangements made by the Finnish Institute of International Affairs and especially its director Paavo Lipponen, as well as by the Finnish Ministry for Foreign Affairs. Special thanks go to Paul Sjöblom, who has gone through all the manuscripts, making them readable for the general public. It is the wish of the editor that this book might give readers new ideas about the complex nature of Soviet-European relations.

List of Contributors

Roy Allison, Lecturer in Soviet Defence Policy and International Security at the Centre for Russian and East European Studies, University of Birmingham, Great Britain.

Laszlo Csaba, Head of Department for the Economies of Eastern Europe, KOPINT-DATORG Institute for Economic and Market Research and Informatics, Budapest, Hungary.

Ksenya Gonchar, Researcher at the Institute of World Economy and International Relations, The USSR Academy of Sciences, Moscow.

Jyrki Iivonen, Senior Research Fellow and Editor-In-Chief, The Finnish Institute of International Affairs, Helsinki, Finland.

Priit Järve, Director of the Institute of Philosophy, Sociology and Law, The Estonian Academy of Sciences, Tallinn, Estonia.

Neil Malcolm, Head of the Soviet Programme, The Royal Institute of International Affairs, London, Great Britain.

Heinz Timmermann, Deputy Chief of the Department of the East-West Relations and International Policy, The Federal Institute for East European and International Studies, Cologne, Germany.

Henry Trofimenko, Chief Analyst at the Institute of the United States and Canada, The USSR Academy of Sciences, Moscow.

Pekka Visuri, Visiting Research Fellow, The Finnish Institute of International Affairs, Helsinki, Finland.

Gerhard Wettig, Chief of the Department of the East-West Relations and International Policy, The Federal Institute for East European and International Studies, Cologne, Germany.

Part I

POLITICAL ISSUES

1 SOVIET POLICY VIS-A-VIS EUROPE: A SOVIET VIEW

Henry A. Trofimenko

1. INTRODUCTION

Generally speaking, Europe ought to be the central concern of Soviet foreign policy. Actually, it has been central for centuries if one looks back into the history of Russian foreign policy. The history of Russia is, precisely, an organic part of the history of Europe. According to the most widespread version, even the creation of Russian statehood was the enterprise of Norse (Swedish) warriors. The rulers of ancient Kiev married their daughters to German kings. But the main uniting force between Russia and Europe became Christianity, which was adopted by Rus' - Russia - as its official faith one thousand years ago. However, during the Tartar and Mongol invasions of the Slavonic lands in the 13th-15th centuries, 'the shroud of barbarity, darkening the horizon of Russia, blacked out Europe from us', as the great Russian historian Nikolai Karamzin remarked.

After the shaking off of the Mongol yoke and the creation of a united Russian state in the 15th century, the fate of Russia and the fate of Europe became inseparably linked. Russian culture as a whole, as represented by the main cultural centres of the Russian Empire, has been essentially European. The rulers of Muscovy restored Russia's close matrimonial

3

ties with the royal houses of Europe, starting in 1472 with the marriage of Tsar Ivan III to Princess Sofia, the niece of the last Byzantine Emperor, Constantine XI Paleologue.

When, in the early 18th century, Peter the Great founded the new imperial capital, St. Petersburg, on the shores of the Baltic Sea, he did not actually open Russia's 'window to Europe'. That window had been opened much earlier. What Peter did was to fling wide a great gate of communications through which strong cultural, trade and political links could be established. The educated Russian nobility in the 18th and 19th centuries used the French language as the main means of communication within its own circle. Thanks to the free flow of educated people between Russia and the rest of Europe, Russian art, literature and philosophy has been an integral part of the general European culture. The three greatest wars of the last two centuries, which the peoples of what used to be the Tsarist Empire and is now the Soviet Union had to endure, were fought mainly on European territory, including the territory of their own homeland. The very success of the Bolsheviks in Russia, who managed to stay in power against all odds after the uprising in Petrograd in October 1917, depended to a great extent on the strong support given by the working masses of Europe, excited by the revolutionary events in Russia.

This is why the gradual separation of the new Soviet state from Europe, which began at the end of the 1920s under the guidance of Stalin, who believed in the autarkic (self-sufficient) mode of economic development, has been somewhat unnatural. But even more unnatural was the creation of the so-called iron curtain between the eastern and western parts of Europe after the Second World War.

As a result of the defeat of Nazism by the Allied powers, the borders of the communist system were moved much deeper into the heart of Europe. The independent countries of Eastern and Central Europe were 'swallowed' by the Soviet Union, the country that undeniably had made the crucial contribution to the victorous outcome of the land battles against the German war machine.

The mainly ideological and imaginary iron curtain, which appeared, however, much more difficult to penetrate than if it had been actually made of iron or steel, was first symbolized by the military division of Germany into the Soviet zone of occupation, on the one hand, and the three zones of occupation by American, British and French troops, and also by the similar division of the former capital of united Germany, Berlin. Then came the two blocs, NATO and the Warsaw Treaty, that consolidated the split. In 1961, the ideological wall and the barbed-wire border fences were reinforced in Berlin by a real wall created of iron and concrete - the Berlin Wall. Like the pompous official buildings that Hitler, the architect, erected in Berlin to symbolize for millennia the eternity of the Third Reich, this wall had to be the palpable embodiment of the permanency of the postwar European settlement - the political division of the continent between the 'two systems'.

The building of the walls after the Second World War, which had been waged not only to eliminate the menace of the militaristic regimes obsessed with an expansionist ideology but also to enhance the democratic way of life and human rights throughout the world, has been regarded with very bitter feelings by the majority of educated people in the Soviet Union. They would have favoured quite a contrary postwar policy: more tolerance, greater openness to the outside world and more intercourse with Western societies.

It was exactly these democratic and humanitarian aspirations of the Soviet people that Stalin's course of enhanced isolation of the Soviet Union from the West aimed to nip in the bud. Stalin probably took his lesson from the mutiny of the Russian military officers against the Tsarist autocracy in December 1825, the so-called Decembrist movement. Most of the officers who had fought Napoleon had been influenced by the ideas of the French Revolution and wanted to establish a democratic regime in Russia. Stalin was afraid that many Soviet soldiers and officers, who had seen with their own eyes that the living standards in defeated Germany and the Soviet satellite countries were much higher than in the victorious Soviet Union, would entertain 'undesirable thoughts' about improving the social system in their own country. That has been one of the reasons for establishing the 'curtain' in the form of stricter separation of the Soviet people from the peoples of the West.

At the same time, a vicious and, in fact, a McCarthy-type campaign was launched in order to find scapegoats to blame for the ills of the Soviet state. This campaign took the form of violent and unsubstantiated attacks against 'rootless cosmopolitans', starting with such extremes as the public vilification of two doctors who dared to send to the West their published book on a new method of treating cancer and ending with such absurdities as renaming a certain brand of white bread 'city loaf' instead of its traditional name 'French loaf'. In this way, Western Europe was effectively closed to Soviet citizens, except, of course, diplomats and certain other officials who were handpicked by the powers-that-be.

2. THE COLD WAR AND EUROPE

Since many European countries lay in ruins after the war, Europe's weight in Stalin's eyes greatly diminished. His main preoccupation in Europe was to install docile governments and regimes in the East European countries, which were forced to build socialist systems of the Stalinist type, eradicating during this process all the forces that entertained the ideas of Western-type democracies. It was especially important to keep East Germany within the Soviet sphere of influence and, to the extent possible, though not with much dedication, to undermine those West European regimes that looked like an easy target for subversion. This explained the open encourage-ment of French communists to vie for power in France as well as the support - via communist Yugoslavia - of the armed struggle of the Greek communists against the democratic government.

The second reason for changing the traditional Euro-pean focus of Russian diplomacy was the emergence of the United States after the Second World War as an unquestionable superpower. It was the only global power in a world whose other main players had been adversely affected by the war. It was a superpower by virtue of its newly acquired economic and military strength and especially by its possession of a new 'absolute weapon', the atom bomb. The third reason, finally, was the partial reorientation of attention to Asia, owing to the victory of communism in China in 1949 and soon after that the war in Korea.

After Stalin's death in 1953, the Soviet attitude to Europe occasionally changed - hence the establishment of diplomatic relations with the Federal Republic of Germany, the playing of the 'French card' in the form of better ties with Paris during the de Gaulle years and, in the mid-1970s, active participation in the Helsinki process. In the last case, the purpose was to finalize and formalize the all-European discussion on the postwar division of Europe.

In reality, however, the whole European policy of the Soviet Union boiled down to the intimidation of the West European countries by the excessive Soviet military buildup. In a way, the Soviet Union treated Western Europe as a hostage in its big power game against the United States. Moscow intimidated Europe in many ways. One of them was the display of strength, such as heavy Soviet tanks and air force formations conspicuously deployed in the GDR and certain other East European countries, or the deployment of several thousands of intermediate, medium- and short-range nuclear missiles specially marked for use against targets in Europe. Moscow also intimidated Western Europe by the actual use of its armed forces in Europe. As is well known, they were used in 1956 to suppress the new, more democratic government in Hungary and in 1968 to oust from power the liberal-minded communist government in Czechoslovakia. Though no encroachment into Western Europe was planned or attempted in either case, the lessons - it can be assumed - have not been lost on Western governments. In view of the Western unity, the idea of pitting Western Europe against the United States has occasionally been entertained in high Soviet diplomatic quarters, with keen theoretical attention being paid to Lenin's postulate of inter-imperialistic contradictions, which ought to be utilized 'in the interest of the world's proletariat'. However, the practical results of some half-hearted attempts to use such tactics in Soviet European diplomacy have amounted to zero.

I was once asked by a Soviet newspaper - after Gorbachev's rise to power - to disprove the frequent allegations coming from the United States that the Soviet Union is 'trying to drive a wedge between the countries of Western Europe, on the one hand, and the United States, on the other'. I answered that nothing would be easier to do, and said that such an allegation is groundless because throughout the postwar years we have actually been driving a wedge between Western Europe and ourselves by pushing the former with soldiers' boots into the embrace of the United States! Regretfully, this observation of the factual state of affairs was somehow not to the taste of one of the most liberal newspapers of the 'new thinking'. So my piece was never published. But obviously this self-evident truth finally dawned on the Soviet foreign policy-makers, who started to change their posture vis-a-vis Europe. That transformation, like most of the other changes, came with the change of the leadership of the CPSU and the Soviet government.

3. *PERESTROIKA* AND FOREIGN POLICY

An important factor in facilitating the change in Soviet foreign policy was the realization that the tactics of 'psychological intimidatory attack' upon European governments, undertaken by Moscow in an attempt to prevent the deployment of American Pershing-IIs and GLCMs in Europe (in a response to the Soviet deployment of SS-20s), had dismally failed and actually backfired. The Soviet ultimatums on this score culminated in Yuri Andropov's announcement on 24 November 1983 that the arms control negotiations with the United States were broken off. Since at the same time the armed intervention in Afghanistan continued, the Soviet Union was actually brought to the dead end of self-isolation. The image of the Soviet government as reasonable in the European context - striving for a balanced solution - had been demolished. As a result, the basic decision reached by the new leadership after 1985 was stop intimidating and start courting.

As is the usual practice in international relations, you start with an idea to be announced for the world to hear.

During the first months after Gorbachev came to power, his message was that Moscow would be willing to improve good-neighbourly relations and cooperation with European countries. Because the relations with the United States were still tense, pronouncements were sometimes made to the effect that the world is big enough for the Soviet Union even without the United States and that the Soviet government might concentrate its foreign political efforts on Europe and Asia. Such statements were not made so much to entice Europe as to impress the White House, to prompt it to be more flexible in its dealings with the Soviet Union. In this connection, the increase in friction between the United States and Western Europe was emphasized.

It is a tradition of Russian - but to a much lesser degree of Soviet - diplomacy that whenever it starts emphasizing the importance of Europe, it turns to its 'natural ally', France, in the spirit of Bismarck's advice that one has to seek friendship not with one's neighbour but with the country beyond one's neighbour. This is the classical balance-of-power principle. The importance of Soviet-French relations is understood by Mikhail Gorbachev as well: 'When we talk about Soviet-French relations, we always stress not only their importance but also their privileged character.'[1]

As known, the first visit of the new General Secretary of the CPSU to a Western country was made to France. It took place in October 1985. During this visit, Gorbachev outlined the agenda of Soviet policy vis-a-vis Western Europe. He mentioned, for example, the necessity of increasing the role of Europe in efforts to improve the international climate. This meant that Moscow was going to revitalize its diplomacy in the direction of Europe. New attention was also paid to the problems of European security, which according to Gorbachev could not be ensured through military means. In his words, 'Europe is simply too small and too fragile to practise power politics'.[2] This meant that, in its policies towards European countries, the Soviet Union would start to place emphasis on political means and solutions. In his speech in the French Parliament, Gorbachev said that 'security in Europe as well as international security in general can only be achieved on the road of peaceful coexistence, détente, disarmament, increased trust and development of international cooperation.'³

The new Soviet attitude towards Europe was seen in certain other ways as well. The Soviet Union was willing to contribute to the success of the Stockholm conference on confidence-building measures and to work constructively in the Helsinki process towards enhancing European security. It was also ready to promote all-European cooperation and to seek new forms and venues for such cooperation and, particularly, to establish business-like relations with the organs of the European Community. Further, the Soviet government had a new, positive and open approach to the problem of human rights, including the increase in cultural, student and other exchanges.

In the field of military relations, the Soviet Union had a desire to establish contacts between the Warsaw Treaty Organization and NATO in order to create a *modus vivendi* that would blunt the confrontation between the two blocs and make possible work towards overcoming the division of Europe. The Soviet Union was also ready to separate the problem of medium-range nuclear missiles in Europe from the arms control talks with the United States on strategic and space weapons and to conclude a separate agreement on this score.

As is generally known, this shift in the European policy of the Soviet Union as well as the radical change in Soviet foreign policy in general was met with disbelief on the part of Western politicians, journalists and some segments of public opinion. Consequently, the only coherent move they could make was to demand concrete proof, proof by deeds. In spite of these suspicions, since 1985 Moscow has proved beyond any doubt that its new European policy is not just a tactical move to deceive the gullible, but a real and profound change in its political course.

The final proof of Moscow's sincerity and realism was provided by the November Paris Summit of the heads of state and governments of the 34 countries participating in the CSCE process. The summit approved the treaty calling for drastic reductions of conventional armed forces in Europe, and it was signed by 22 countries. The signatories also adopted a joint declaration, anticipating a new era of democracy, peace and unity in Europe. It solemnly stated that in the new era of European affairs the signatory powers are no longer adversaries and that henceforth they will maintain only such military capabilities as are necessary to prevent war and provide effective defence.

It is not an exaggeration to say that the Treaty of Conventional Forces in Europe (CFE) became possible as a result of the prior principled decision of the Soviet government to agree to the liquidation of the imbalances in its favour in the conventional armed forces that had existed for a long time in the European region. I not only mean a drastic unilateral cut in conventional armed forces in the European and Asian parts of the Soviet Union by half a million men, implemented during 1989-90: I also mean the initial decision to accept radical and uneven reductions (compared with NATO) in the size of its armoured vehicles and tank forces and artillery, as required by the CFE Treaty.

The Soviet government made other important decisions as well. A new attitude was adopted on the German question. The Soviet Union now had a constructive approach to the unification of Germany. It also dropped its demand that a united Germany should not be a NATO member. One explanation for this change was that the FRG government pledged, for its own part, that the armed forces of united Germany would not exceed 370,000 men and that it would continue to adhere to the non-proliferation treaty.

In accordance with the principle of freedom of choice, the Soviet Union adopted a policy of non-interference in the process of radical change of regimes in Central and East European countries. This included repudiation of the Brezhnev doctrine of the international duty to help like-minded regimes to stay in power - even against the will of their own populations. This kind of new policy included certain military stipulations as well. Substantial unilateral cuts were made in the number of forward-deployed tactical nuclear missiles. The withdrawal of Soviet troops from Hungary and Czechoslovakia, which was to be completed by mid-1991, was started, while Soviet troops were to be withdrawn from the eastern part of Germany by the end of 1994, at the latest.

A new military doctrine, based on the principle of defence, was promulgated. It includes certain practical arrangements inside the Soviet army as well, such as reductions by 20 to 40 per cent in the number of tanks in tank and infantry divisions, the liquidation of armoured operational manoeuvre groups and other measures.

One of the main changes has been the new approach to the problem of human rights, as demonstrated by the contribution of the Soviet delegation to the successful outcome of the Vienna review conference (1986-89). The Soviet role was also prominent in the two follow-up meetings of the CSCE conference on human issues in Paris and Copenhagen and in the preparations for the final meeting to be held in Moscow in September 1991. The basic matter is that now Moscow not only puts its signature to such documents but diligently implements them, as is shown by the release of the remaining incarcerated dissidents and the new laws on freedom of travel, publishing and cultural exchange.

At the level of great power relations, special attention must be paid to the Soviet-American INF Treaty of 1987, which not only started the whole process of dismantling the mental and physical barriers of the Cold War and the most terrible means of warfare on European soil, but actually - through its monitoring provisions - became a tremendous precedent-breaking stride towards military openness across the dividing line of the Western and Eastern blocs of nations.

It is now commonly emphasized in the statements of leaders of Western Europe and the United States that the threat of conventional Soviet arms in Europe is a thing of the past and that now it would take at least two years for the Soviet Union to prepare such a *Blitzkrieg* attack against Western Europe - whereas in the old days of the great Soviet preponderance in conventional forces, two weeks would have sufficed.

4. THE SOVIET UNION AND EASTERN EUROPE

What is the role that the Soviet Union has played in the political developments in Eastern Europe? To answer this question truthfully, one must admit that neither Gorbachev nor anyone else in the Soviet leadership really anticipated the extent of the radical change that has taken place in the countries of Central and Eastern Europe. Two countries, Hungary and Poland, started earlier on this road than the rest of Eastern Europe. The very governments that had been in power in those countries before the recent radical changes took place - the Kadar government in Hungary and the Gierek government in Poland - allowed some form of economic and religious freedom and political debate that were lacking in the other East European countries. It is true, however, that when the activities of the masses started to get out of control, there was a clampdown, as in Poland in December 1981. Nevertheless, the ruling communist parties there had been less dogmatic, a bit more flexible, than the ruling communist parties in the other socialist countries allied with the Soviet Union - with Ceausescu's regime representing the most rigid model of totalitarian rule, comparable only to that of North Korea.

Perestroika in the Soviet Union struck a responsive cord in the hearts of millions of people in the Central European countries, including many dissident intellectuals who had for a long time been advocating 'socialism with a human face' and twice in the postwar period - in Hungary in 1956 and in Czechoslovakia in 1968 - had tried unsuccessfully to establish such a type of socialism. Both of these ventures were crushed by Soviet tanks. The mellowing of the Soviet Union in the process of *perestroika* gave all those liberal democratic forces an impetus to follow suit and to change the regimes in their respective countries in a popular, democratic way.

In all these countries, there had existed an opposition to the established rule. Some of them, like the independent trade union movement Solidarity in Poland, were very strong, with close links with the intellectuals. Even the military government of General Jaruzelski, which had been established for the express purpose of suppressing it, was not able to suffocate the movement. Some of these opposition movements were more like conspiracies of intellectuals, too frightened to take any action. Romania provides an example. Anyway, it is clear in retrospect that in every so-called socialist country of Central and Eastern Europe, there had throughout the years of totalitarian rule accumulated very strong forces of discontent, which had been waiting for their hour to come. Soviet *perestroika* actually triggered the intellectual and political forces that had been longing for a change. This put all those countries on to the road of radical political and economic reform, culminating in most of them in social revolutions that to a greater or lesser extent transformed the existing regimes.

Even after *perestroika* in the Soviet Union had begun to gather steam, the CPSU did not support any of the opposition forces in those countries. At the same time, it was trying to persuade the ruling élites of the countries in question to follow the example of the Soviet Union, to take the course of political liberalization. This was natural enough, in view of the fact that throughout the years all the zigzags in the internal politics of the Soviet Union had unquestionably been repeated in the policies of its satellites. But very soon comrades Honecker, Husak and Zhivkov, not to mention Ceausescu, discovered that this time it was demanding too much of them to follow suit, that in doing so they would be in danger of losing their jobs and power. They understood that what was happening in the Soviet Union very much resembled the Prague Spring, which with the exception of Ceausescu they had been glad to suppress by joint action in 1968.

There are several reasons why the Soviet government has not interfered with the developments in Eastern Europe. The nature of change inside the Soviet Union has been explosive, so that the need to keep it under control has been exceptionally great. There has also been much work connected with the restructuring. It is therefore easy to agree with Renée de Nevers:

> Eastern Europe was initially a low priority for Gorbachev. As a result, Eastern European issues were virtually ignored during the early months of his rule... Gorbachev began to encourage economic changes in Eastern Europe at the same time that he initiated economic reforms at home, but he did not simultaneously advocate political reforms in the bloc.[4]

While advising the ruling autocrats of those countries to be more flexible, the CPSU Politburo did not make a strong effort to steer things its own way. Of course, it started gradually to support to some extent the forces of change, but in such a way as not to offend the ruling camarillas. That is why Gorbachev, during his visits to these countries in 1986-88, was hedging tough questions from popular audiences about their own ruling party élites. However, he was not openly supportive of the forces of opposition; while in Czechoslovakia in 1987, he dodged almost all the questions related to the Prague Spring of 1968. Supporting the official line adopted by the rulers of Prague, he just said that Czechoslovakia had learned the 'correct' lessons from it. More typical of his pronouncements at that time is the following quotation:

> You have something to be proud of. Modern Czechoslovakia stands before the world as an advanced, economically and socially developed state. Its national economy is enviably stable... The living standard of the population, the educational and medical system, the care given the young and the veterans of labour can stand comparison with the highest standards of the world. All these are tangible fruits of socialism, the result of the purposeful work of the toiling masses, guided by the Party of Communists.[5]

But the people of Czechoslovakia as well as those of other Central European countries associated the Soviet *perestroika*, initiated by Gorbachev, with what Alexander Dubcek and his colleagues had started in Czechoslovakia 20 years earlier. In other words, Gorbachev did not encourage the opposition but did not discourage it either. At the same time, old comrades governing East European countries were regularly and publicly assured of complete understanding with them 'on all the key problems of European and world development'.[6] It was only four weeks before the inglorious overthrow of Ceausescu by the inhabitants of Bucharest that the then member of the CPSU Politburo Vitali Vorotnikov, heading the Soviet delegation at the 14th Congress of the Romanian Communist Party (which unanimously reelected Ceausescu), had presented Lenin's bust to Romanian workers as a sign of strengthening ties between Romanian and Soviet communists.

Nevertheless, the crucial contribution to the success of revolutionary developments in Central and East European countries has been made by none other than Gorbachev. That contribution has been the repudiation of the Brezhnev doctrine in the form of abstention from using Soviet troops to influence events in East Europe. More than that, even during the gory events in Romania in December 1989, when Western governments - including the United States - were actually prompting the Soviet leadership to use its troops in support of the popular revolution, the Soviet government stuck to its policy of non-intervention. In this way it confirmed the fact that its position of non-interference was a matter of principle. I, for my part, believe that the attempt by the White House to provoke the Soviet leadership to intervene in Romania was based on an ulterior motive, that of placing the Soviet leadership on an 'equal footing' with themselves, for at that moment US troops were being used in Panama - without much legal ground and in flagrant violation of the Stockholm document of 1986 - to depose Noriega by force of arms.

Strictly speaking, the Brezhnev doctrine, like its earlier American counterpart, the Truman doctrine, had broken its teeth while tackling China at the end of the 1960s. But the Soviet military intervention in Afghanistan - 'to help a friendly government' - revived it. The last minute Soviet decision not to use Soviet troops in Poland during winter 1981 again put this doctrine in doubt.

At the end of 1987, in his book *Perestroika*, Mikhail Gorbachev underscored the principle of the freedom of choice.

> Every nation is entitled to choose its own way of development, to dispose of its fate, its territory, and its human and natural resources. International relations cannot be normalized if this is not understood in all countries.[7]

In June 1989, in his speech to the European Parliament, Gorbachev reiterated the Soviet Union's adherence to a policy of non-interference in the affairs of other countries. He stressed that 'social change is the exclusive affair of the people of that country and is their choice' and that 'any interference in domestic affairs and any attempts to restrict the sovereignty of states, be they friends, allies or any others, are inadmissible'.[8] This was a marked turnabout from his ambivalent call in September 1987 'to exclude any attempts - direct and indirect - to influence the development of countries 'not one's own'.[9] But it was not so much the statements made as the praxis of the Soviet Union during the revolutionary events in the countries of Eastern Europe - including the demolition of the Berlin Wall in November 1989 - that gave tremendous help to the forces of change in those countries. It must be admitted, however, that the results of such change - to state it frankly - did not always correspond to the interests of the Soviet Union, at least as seen from Moscow.

Summing up the changes in Eastern Europe in the spring of 1990, the deputy head of the International Department of the Central Committee of the CPSU, Valeri Musatov, said,

> When more closely and objectively analyzed, the character of change in the countries of Eastern Europe is such that one can speak about the process of altering a social system based on the command and administrative structure of the 'party-state', about the discrediting of the ideological concept of 'real socialism', and, from the foreign policy angle, about the retreat from the postwar division of Europe and the transformation of our alliance system... The revolutions that occurred are the result of a nationwide crisis that had been ripening for a long time. Its basic feature is the crisis of the tenet of state socialism, with its authoritarian-bureaucratic system and dogmatic stand. Such a model, despite all the attempts to modernize it, has revealed in the years up to the 1970s its ineffectiveness in both political and socio-economic aspects... It became clear that without the Soviet insurance net, especially such means of last resort as military interference by the Soviet Union, the reserve of the stability of authoritarian regimes of power has proved to be in actual fact quite insignificant.[10]

Of course, such a realistic analysis of events was not unanimous in the Soviet Union. There are voices and forces that consider 'loss' of Eastern Europe as the greatest blunder, if not outright betrayal, by Gorbachev of the idea of the international socialist system. Partly, it is the backlash of the hegemonic mentality that has been inculcated into the Russian people for ages.

Vladislav Anufriev, at that time second secretary of the

Central Committee of the Communist Party of Kazakhstan, in his speech at the plenum of the CPSU in February 1990, opened the taboo subject and frankly stated his apprehensions:

> Someone has to answer, comrades, for the events in Eastern Europe, about which nobody wants to talk here. Our buffer zone has been demolished.[11]

The same question was later raised by General Albert Makashev. Paradoxically, some representatives of the non-Slavic nations of the Soviet Union, who feel themselves oppressed by the Russians, would nevertheless regret the 'loss of Eastern Europe'. Many Soviet people, of course, have not fully realized to what extent the 'eternal friendship' of the peoples inhabiting the 'socialist camp', as it used to be called for dozens of years, was based on unequal political relations between Big Brother and the East Europeans, on the ever-present threat of force, which has been amply demonstrated for the 'locals' by the deployment of large contingents of Soviet troops in Poland, Hungary, the GDR and Czechoslovakia. At the same time, many people in the Soviet Union feel that they or their fathers and grandfathers paid with their blood in the Great Patriotic War for the creation of the belt of friendly states. Accordingly, 'to give it away', as the popular saying goes, would mean to annul, in a way, all those sacrifices.

But at the same plenum of the CPSU Central Committee where Anufriev aired his regrets about the events in Eastern Europe, the Central Committee was given an explanation of the reasoning of Gorbachev and his like-minded colleagues when they acquiesced in the course of events in Eastern Europe. Foreign Minister Shevardnadze said there:

> Let them stop blaming *perestroika* for the demolition of the political structure of Europe. That structure has been destroyed by the will of the people, who no longer want to reconcile themselves to violence. And violence - and somehow this has been forgotten - was committed at the end of the 1940s, when the structure of the people's democratic governments emerged after the Second World War. The democratic forces that cooperated with the communists for

the sake of victory over fascism were thrown out of the coalition governments in the countries of Central and Eastern Europe. Regimes of personal power were established, although they were labelled as regimes of the dictatorship of the proletariat... It was then, not in 1985, that the belief in socialism based on suppression and violence started to be undermined.[12]

It must be added that the rapid deterioration of the economic and social situation in the Soviet Union blunted to a great extent the debates about the merits of the Soviet government's abstention from active interference in East European affairs and about the apportioning of the blame for the 'loss' of Eastern Europe. Many people rethought their former negative evaluations of the events, especially when they were themselves able to see - through personal travel as well as in TV reports - that the people in those countries were now happy and that, despite all the common hardships, the economic situation there was much better than in the Soviet Union. The focus of attention of the Soviet people has simply shifted to what is happening inside their own country.

Nevertheless, a great amount of scepticism, which sometimes presents itself as an open hostility towards the events in that part of Europe, still remains. And the proof of this is the largely sceptical reporting by quite a few Soviet journalists from those countries. This is to a certain extent paradoxical: at the same moment when those avant-garde representatives of the new thinking in Soviet journalism started reporting about anything from inside Central and East European countries, they turned from objective observers into prophets of doom, predicting ever new difficulties and immeasurable obstacles facing the governments of those countries. For their peoples' misery and poverty have been predicted. There was not a single dark spot on the horizon that would have been missed and not preached about and lamented upon by the self-appointed guardians of truth. At the same time, other international and domestic events were reported in a very sophisticated way. It seems as if the correspondents dispatched by some of the Soviet central papers (*Pravda* and *Sovetskaya Rossiya* being foremost among them) to report events in

Eastern Europe, had to give a prior pledge similar to the oath taken in American courts but with a negative meaning: I swear to report the untruth, the whole untruth and nothing but the untruth. So strong are the national jealousies, stereotypes and hegemonic tradition.

While concluding this subject, I would like to concur with the succint summing up of Gorbachev's policy vis-a-vis the countries of Eastern and Central Europe given by Henry Kissinger in June 1990.

> I have yet to meet a Soviet personality in a position to know who believes that Gorbachev's purpose in 1989 was to start dismantling the Soviet empire. What he appears to have sought was to foster growing access to Western resources and technology by putting in place in Eastern Europe reformist Communists capable of liberalizing, not over-throwing, existing institutions. But when matters got out of hand, Gorbachev displayed extraordinary fortitude. He confined the Soviet Army to its barracks even while Communism was being dismantled all over Eastern Europe. Gorbachev would not be the first revolutionary to set in motion events that sweep beyond his design. But since history judges results more than intentions, it will be kind to Gorbachev.[13]

5. THE SOVIET UNION AND GERMANY

It is unnecessary to recapitulate here the long history of the German question after the Second World War or the division of Germany by the wartime allies in accordance with the Yalta and Potsdam agreements. Some historical facts must be mentioned, however.

It is quite certain that, during the first dozen years after 1945, the so-called support given by the allies to the wartime anti-Nazi coalition for the unification of Germany was to a large extent demagogic by nature. In spite of numerous sessions of the Council of Foreign Ministers representing the five great powers, in spite of the top level meetings of the political leaders of the respective countries looking for a 'solution' to the German question, actually nobody either in the East or in the West was eager to see Germany united. But with this fact taken into account, one has to admit that the Soviet Union was the last country among the former allies to refrain from giving formal support to the idea of German unification.

The division of Germany into two halves, West and East, was first and foremost the logical consequence of the separate monetary reform carried out in the Western occupation zones by the United States, Great Britain and France on 20 June 1948. This step was a sort of death warrant for German unification. In the same way, the financial unification of the FRG and the GDR on 1 July 1990 meant *de facto* unification of the country. All further steps have just been acts of formalization of that seminal event. My point here therefore is that the real wall in Germany was erected in July 1948, not August 1961.

The signing of the Helsinki Final Act in August 1975 by heads of states and governments was considered by the majority of statesmen throughout the world as drawing the final line under the Second World War, formally recognizing and, in a way, legitimizing the 'realities' of the postwar arrangements in Europe, and first and foremost its division into two incompatible 'systems'.

Since that time, the solution of the German question has been postponed to an indefinite future. It is interesting to note that in the Soviet *Diplomatic Dictionary*, published in 1960, the article on the German question was probably the longest, occupying 20 pages. In the 1984 edition of the Dictionary, there was no such article at all. The German question was considered non-existent, probably solved for ever.

The importance of the German question was understood by Mikhail Gorbachev. In 1987, he wrote,

> Let me say quite plainly that all these statements about the revival of 'German unity' are far from being '*Realpolitik*', to use the German expression. It has given the FRG nothing in the past forty years... No matter what Ronald Reagan and other Western leaders say on that score, they cannot actually offer anything realistic to the FRG as regards the so-called German issue... For the time being, one should proceed from the existing realities and not engage in incendiary

speculations.[14]

Similar sceptisim could be found on the German side as well. Theo Sommer, one of the leading West German columnists, has admitted,

> Not many Germans expected the reunification to happen in their lifetime. Like many of my countrymen, I thought that with luck the Berlin wall might come down before the end of the century and that the German Question might be placed on the world agenda by 2030 or 2050.[15]

As recently as December 1989 - after the opening of the Berlin Wall President Gorbachev was saying that it is for our grandchildren to try to reopen the problem of unification, but not for the present generation of politicians. He declared,

> With all decisiveness, we underscore that we shall be able to stand behind the GDR. This country is our strategic ally and a member of the Warsaw Treaty. It is necessary to proceed from the realities that have been in place since the war - the existence of two sovereign German states, both members of the United Nations. Departure from that is fraught with the destabilization of Europe.'[16]

Why did Gorbachev initially take such an irreconcilable stand regarding the unification of Germany? Several factors must have been at work. First of all, there was the natural difficulty for a Soviet person, not to speak of a Soviet leader, to reconcile himself to the restoration of the *status quo ante bellum*. Things were going bad for the Soviet Union: agriculture was in an awful state, industry was not working properly, government authority was about to collapse and so on. In such a situation, it was impossible to stomach such an offence as the desertion of the GDR from the 'socialist camp'. Whatever divisions of opinion among the population there might have been regarding the current troubles of the country, past injustices and the crimes of Stalin and his henchmen, there was one glory, joy and consolation uniting the whole Soviet people (excluding the Baltic republics) irrespective of nationality, social status or religion. That glory was the sacred victory in the most horrible war in the history of Russia. It was a victory for which many Soviet people - those who perished in the war as well as those who are still alive - had shed their blood. Now this victory seemed to be taken away from them by those who had been defeated and divided to prevent the tragic history from being repeated. Victory in the Great Patriotic War against fascism was the only bright star on the dark horizon of the country's destiny and it was now being blackened by hostile forces. That was how it was felt throughout the Soviet Union, and no leader of the country could easily dismiss these feelings. It was difficult enough for a Soviet man or woman to become reconciled to the drastic changes in Poland, Hungary and Czechoslovakia, changes characterized *inter alia* by open expressions of anti-Soviet emotions in those countries, but to acquiesce - on top of that - to the departure of the GDR was simply too much.

One should also understand the feelings of the Soviet military officers. They had been brought up in their military schools and academies according to the strategic and tactical lessons of the battles against German forces. In other words, they had been theoretically fighting the 'German menace' throughout all their conscious lives and now, in a very short time, they had to swallow the fact that the Germany of their lessons would be revived again (what is meant here is the economic and military potential of the country, not the social set-up of the reunited society). As of the end of 1989, there were a few hundred Soviet Second World War veterans still serving in the armed forces. But the bulk of them had already gone, including most of the old marshals. They perhaps would have wanted to stonewall any compromise on Germany.

Fear of the resurgent Germany is not confined to the Soviet Union alone. Many people in the United States, not to speak of other European countries, are awed by the critical mass of the united Germany. This awe is nowhere so evident as in France, which was one of the 'best friends' of the then Federal Republic of Germany. There are therefore grounds to argue that the French influence has been one of the factors that for a while inhibited the flexibility of the Soviet Union concerning German unity.

In the first days of December 1989, President Mitterrand rushed in panic to Kiev (a city that had undergone the Nazi occupation rather than to Moscow that had not) to plead with Gorbachev to foil the developments in Germany. It looks as if he initially succeeded in using Soviet hands to block the unification. As soon as the leaders of France became convinced that the Soviet Union would try to do the nasty job, they washed their hands and started courting Bonn, issuing joint declarations demanding speedier formation of a common EC defence policy.

It took a lot of soul-searching in Moscow and a deep analysis of events (including the popular attitudes in both parts of Germany) to come to the realization that the only way to prevent German unification, as demanded by popular forces, was to prevent it physically, by using armed troops. But that was out of the question, taking into account the stakes the Soviet government had in the new international environment and the plethora of unsolved problems at home. By the beginning of February 1990, the Soviet Union dropped its opposition to the unification and started to work closely with the United States, Britain, France and the two Germanys to solve all the problems pertaining to the external aspects of the unification process.[17]

While accepting in principle the unification of Germany, the Soviet government resurrected the old Soviet stand that the united Germany should become neutral; and it started to sell this thesis to both Germanys and to the West, but met with a firm refusal to accept it by all concerned. The governments of the FRG and GDR as well as of the United States, Britain and even France insisted that a united Germany should become a member of NATO, or that at least it should be allowed to decide for itself its affiliation (though it was clear right from the beginning that its choice would be joining NATO).

For the majority of Soviet specialists in international relations, it was also clear that the inevitable solution - if one stuck to the principle of freedom of choice - would be for Germany to join NATO or, to be precise, for East Germany to merge with the stronger West Germany and thus be incorporated into NATO. The solution was not only inevitable but actually advisable, even from the point of view of the Soviet Union's long-term interests in Europe.

If Germany had been declared neutral and kept that way by force (though probably it would have been a futile attempt), the flames of German nationalism would have been ignited and the mistakes of the 1919 Versailles settlement repeated. On the other hand, a plain declaration of pro-forma neutrality, without any enforcement, would have given the new European colossus *carte blanche* for its military build-up and planning. Germany could not have been incorporated in the Warsaw Treaty either, not only because the Warsaw Treaty itself was at death's door but also because, evaluating the situation in the *Realpolitik* terms of the main thrust of divergent influences, the possibility of such an outcome in such a situation was equal to zero. The only realistic alternative was therefore to insist on some *sine qua non* conditions for the unification of Germany with its NATO membership granted, the absence of such conditions being reason enough for the Soviet Union to go the whole hog in its efforts to prevent it.

But instead of such a pragmatic approach to the problem, Moscow started to reinvent absolutely unrealistic 'alternative solutions' designed to bar German membership of NATO. Among these were suggestions that Germany should join both NATO and the Warsaw Pact, that Germany might join NATO's political but not military organization, that the Soviet Union should join NATO, etc. All such proposals - which really amounted to a waste of time - only amply demonstrated, as Henry Kissinger has noted, that the Soviet Union was 'shackled by the categories of the past'.[18]

Nevertheless, such delaying tactics seemed to have worked in the sense of making Western leaders realize that they had to pay a price for the unification of Germany on their terms. This was understood best by the leaders of the Federal Republic, who started intensive consultations with the Soviet government on the terms and conditions of the unification within the NATO membership.

On the other hand, it was soon understood in Moscow that the Soviet Union might be put into a position where it would become the only country blocking German unification without reasons that world public opinion could accept. President Gorbachev put it this way,

> It seems to me that some in the West pretend to be more enthusiastic about German unification than they really are. They even hope to use us to put a brake on unification so that we would get the blame and end up at loggerheads with the Germans.[19]

As a result of constructive shifts in the positions of both sides, the compromise on the German question was finally worked out during the meeting between President Gorbachev and Chancellor Kohl in the Caucasus in July 1990. On the Western side, the seminal step was the London declaration, issued by the leaders of the NATO countries, on a transformed North Atlantic alliance in which they pledged, among other things, to reduce their reliance on nuclear weapons and to adopt a new NATO strategy, making nuclear forces truly the weapons of the last resort.[20] Also very important from the Soviet point of view was the establishment of a ceiling for the numerical strength of Germany's armed forces (370,000 men) and the German commitment to renounce nuclear, chemical and biological weapons. Such steps allowed Moscow to lift its objection to Germany of joining NATO.

Ratified at the Moscow meeting of the foreign ministers of the six countries in September 1990, these and commonly agreed terms and conditions of the German unification opened the way for the signing of the Treaty on the Unification of Germany and for the formal recognition of the unification on 3 October 1990. As a result of the parliamentary elections held in united Germany in December 1990, the Christian Democratic Party with its ally, the Party of Free Democrats, which were the main architects of German unification, stayed in power by gaining an overwhelming majority of votes.

NOTES

1. *Pravda*, 8 December 1989.
2. M. S. Gorbachev, *Izbrannye rechi i stati*, vol. 2 (Moscow: Politizdat, 1987), p. 435.
3. ibid., p. 465.
4. Renée de Nevers, 'The Soviet Union and Eastern Europe. The End of an Era,' *Adelphi Papers*, no. 249, 1990, p. 23.
5. *Pravda*, 11 April 1987.

6. *Pravda*, 28 September 1988.
7. M. S. Gorbachev, *Perestroika: New Thinking for Our Country and the World* (New York: Harper & Row Publishers, 1987), p. 177.
8. *Pravda*, 7 July 1989.
9. *Pravda*, 17 September 1987.
10. *Pravda*, 14 May 1990.
11. *Materialy plenuma Tsentralnogo Komiteta KPSS 5-7 fevralya 1990 g.* (Moscow: Politizdat, 1990), p. 187.
12. ibid., p. 192.
13. *Newsweek*, 18 June 1990.
14. Gorbachev, *Perestroika...*, pp. 199-200.
15. *Newsweek*, 9 July 1990.
16. *Pravda*, 12 December 1989.
17. This 'Two plus four mechanism' was formally adopted at the meeting of foreign ministers in Ottawa, Canada, in February 1990.
18. *Newsweek*, 18 June 1990.
19. *Time*, 4 June 1990.
20. *New York Times*, 7 July 1990.

2 NEW THINKING IN PRACTICE: GENERAL CHANGES IN SOVIET POLICY TOWARDS EUROPE

Jyrki Iivonen

1. INTRODUCTION

The purpose of this chapter is to present some general conclusions on the main changes in Soviet policy vis-a-vis Europe,
mostly seen in historical perspective.[1] Soviet foreign policy
has here been understood both as a conceptual framework concerning the Soviet perceptions of the international system and
as a totality of the activities concerning the relationship of the
Soviet Union towards that system and its components. Europe,
for its part, has been understood as a territorial concept; it
covers both the West European democracies and the former
East European socialist states that only recently embarked on
the course to political democracy and the market economy.

The discussion is divided into four parts. It starts with
an analysis of Europe's role in Russian and Soviet history.
After that, the priority system in Soviet foreign policy is
discussed. Of particular concern is whether the structure of
the international system, be it bipolar or multipolar, has influenced Europe's role in Soviet foreign policy. Third, the
new European policy in the framework of the new foreign
political thinking (NPT) - both its content and its practical

28

implications for Soviet activities - is analysed. Especial attention is given to the question whether the new thinking has affected Soviet relations with various parts (Western, Eastern and neutral states) of Europe. Here the idea is, in particular, to draw some conclusions about the real functions of the new thinking. That is, does the new thinking represent only a doctrinal change or does it have other aspects as well? Finally, some questions about the future are also discussed. From today's perspective, the international situation is rather complicated, because no one can say for sure what the future development of the Soviet Union will look like. One of the main questions for the future is: are the inter-state relations in Europe losing their position to international relations? The probable dissolution of the Soviet Union certainly gives new momentum to this process. Already, the emergence of a number of republican foreign policies inside the Soviet federation can be foreseen, in spite of the opposition of the central administration.[2]

2. FROM MULTIPOLARISM TO BIPOLARISM

The question of Europe has traditionally been one part of a wider Russian and Soviet social and philosophical debate. The controversy has concerned the best road of development that backward Russia, located historically between Europe and Asia, should choose. In other words, should it follow Europe's example or lean on its own traditions and possibilities? This dilemma was first widely discussed during the first half of the 19th century. Now this subject has become topical once again.

At the beginning of the 19th century the discussion on Russia's future led to the emergence of two schools of thought. The Slavophiles argued that Russia should be developed on the basis of its own resources and traditions. According to them a particular Russian course of development existed, based on the ancient Russian village community, *mir*.[3] The representatives of the other school, the Zapadniks, argued that Russia lagged behind Europe in both social and economic development and that therefore the only way to overcome its backwardness was to build a new society based on the Western example, with its political values and institutions.[4] Socialism, and especially its Marxist variant, was originally one of the numerous Western solutions to Russia's problem of backwardness. The task of Lenin and Stalin as political thinkers and actors was to elaborate for Russia a socialist application in which a modern technological society could be combined with Russia's economic and social structures.

The old controversy over the course of Russia's development has become topical again since *perestroika* was launched in the mid-1980s. Numerous political and economic reforms carried out in the name of *perestroika* have been interpreted as conscious efforts to make the Soviet Union a modern Western society by abandoning the constraints inherited from the past, both Soviet and Russian. Simultaneously with the effort to Westernize the Soviet Union, a number of national movements in the traditional Russian spirit have emerged.[5] Some of them emphasize the negative effects of Westernization, to be prevented only by returning to traditional Russian values, such as the Orthodox religion, the Russian national spirit and the revival of the village community, *mir*.[6] The new political role of the Russian Federation as a competing force among the All-Union Soviet institutions provides convincing proof of this new trend.[7]

In the October Revolution of 1917, modernization along socialist lines was the course chosen. The task of socialism was to make Soviet Russia an industrialized great power. To achieve this, all sectors of society had to serve the demands of socialist construction. One of these sectors was foreign policy, where the basic doctrine remained unchanged from the early years of the 1920s up to the 1980s.[8] The doctrine was based on the materialist view of history (historical materialism), on the belief in progressive human evolution from a lower level to a higher one, from capitalism to socialism. The goals of foreign policy have usually been dictated by domestic factors; in other words, the task of foreign policy has been to serve the aims of the socialist revolution.

The basic doctrine of Soviet foreign policy was adopted during the first years following the October Revolution and the Civil War and underwent only minor changes during the following decades. It was *perestroika* that first changed the situation. And even then, it first looked as if only the methods and instruments of foreign policy had changed, but not the doctrines.[9] As for the foreign policy doctrine, it first began to change in 1987.

The traditional foreign politicy doctrine of the Soviet Union has been characterized by the view of a global struggle between capitalism and socialism. In the framework of this doctrine, Soviet relations with the capitalist states have been guided by the action programme of peaceful coexistence.[10] Its starting point is the idea of the uneven development of capitalism, owing to which socialism cannot win simultaneously in all the developed countries. During the transitional period, antagonistic social systems must live side by side. The final victory of socialism has not been questioned, although it is admitted that it is most profitable for the mankind as a whole, provided the inter-systemic competition takes place through peaceful means, that is, in the form of economic competition. Already in 1921, Lenin was quite convinced that this competition would demonstrate the superiority of socialism and make possible a peaceful transition from capitalism.[11]

While Lenin still saw Europe in a decisive role as regards the future of socialism, Stalin openly declared that the Soviet Union and the United States, as true world powers, would dictate the direction and rate of global development.[12] For him, Russia's peaceful coexistence with Europe was only a 'temporary balance of power', where socialism became ever stronger. The main task of peaceful coexistence was therefore to prevent war and guarantee profitable conditions for the continuation of the economic competition between socialism and capitalism.[13] The concept of peaceful coexistence was first reformulated in the 1950s. At that stage, economic competition was no longer seen to be as important as before; instead, the necessity to avoid war and especially nuclear war was emphasized. It was also pointed out that the principles of peaceful coexistence were connected to the basic principles of international law.[14]

In the Second World War, the United States had abandoned its policy of voluntary isolation and had become a world power in the true sense of the word. Its alliance with the Soviet Union against Germany and Japan gave new impetus to the bipolar thinking in the Soviet Union. Its foreign policy became more and more based on the bipolar view of the international system. It was believed that the future of world politics depended on the will of the two great powers, who were in possession of nuclear weapons. That their mutual relationship changed from cooperation to hostility does not change anything from our point of view; the fact remains that the Soviet Union saw the great powers as united, both in good and in bad.

For over four decades, the international system has been understood as being dominated by the two great powers. Numerous political crises in Europe as well as in the Third World have been interpreted as expressions of the antagonistic political conflicts between them. Europe in this system has been a modest borderland between East and West, an area that could be used by the United States in launching an attack against the Soviet Union. The basic motive of Soviet policy towards Europe has therefore been to control that area as effectively as possible and to eliminate in advance the growth of American political, economic and military influence there. Although many Soviet foreign politicy measures involved neighbouring Europe, in the background there remained the global competition with the United States. It can therefore be concluded that for a rather long time Europe stayed in the background in the Soviet foreign politicy priority system.

3. PRIORITIES IN SOVIET FOREIGN POLICY

The priority system refers here to the way a country manages its central foreign politicy activities within a certain period. When the priority system of a country's foreign policy is examined, it is also possible to name the countries that are seen as friends and foes. In Soviet foreign policy, the priority system has changed to only a limited degree. The most radical change was brought about by the Second World War. In the interwar period, Soviet foreign policy was still directed towards Europe. Europe, Germany in particular, was believed to play a decisive role in the future of socialism. In spite of certain of Stalin's positive statements, the United States was not seen as the cradle of the socialist revolution but rather as the highest stage of capitalist development. The working-class movement did not play any important political role there, while in US foreign policy a rather isolationist strategy was adopted.[15] The official attitude towards the Soviet Union was also highly negative; diplomatic relations between these two countries were not established until 1933.

After the Second World War, a profound change took place in the Soviet priority system. The United States had turned into an active global power. Its position was further strengthened by possession of nuclear weapons. Stalin quite rapidly took note of the changing role of the United States. The possibility of war was prominent on the agenda. Stalin spoke of the possibility of avoiding war between capitalism and socialism, while simultaneously arguing that inter-capitalist wars were still unavoidable. In this way, he admitted that the role of the United States in the Soviet priority system had become more central than before.[16] When the Soviet Union at the end of the 1940s started to develop its own nuclear deterrence, the foreign politicy importance of the United States only increased, because now Stalin's strategic solutions were based on the aim of making the Soviet Union militarily as strong as the United States. The aim of the Soviet Union to control the East European countries was connected to its fear of the United States. On the basis of strategic reasons alone, the Soviet Union needed a security zone in Central Europe, because in that way it could effectively contain the possibilities of a surprise attack against it.

The transition from the original Cold War to the détente of the 1970s and after that back to the new Cold War did not affect the Soviet postwar priority system to any considerable extent. Europe as well as the growing number of Third World countries was further analysed in the framework of great power relations. The first break in the wall of bipolarism appeared at the beginning of the 1970s, when the United States normalized its relations with China. But even that event was generally interpreted as an American effort to improve its position towards the Soviet Union, which for its part had been more than successful in its foreign politicy and domestic efforts in the Third World as well as in Europe. During the years of *perestroika* the United States has continued to keep its priority position in Soviet foreign policy. Nevertheless, the situation is now completely different from what it used to be.

Gorbachev's rise to power in March 1985 did not immediately affect the foreign politicy priority system. The new leadership made it immediately clear that the most important foreign political goal of the Soviet government was to improve relations with the United States, which was designated as both the 'main opponent' and the 'most important partner'.[17] World peace could not be secured without the normalization of great power relations, but in addition it was believed that cooperative great power relations were a necessary condition for solving the crisis in the Soviet economy. The Soviet leadership realized that military competition was one of the main factors that had ruined the Soviet economy. One of the best ways to increase the resources of the civil sector is to cut military expenditures. And that could not be done without normalization and mutual understanding on arms cuts. In this way, foreign policy served domestic needs and gave new support to the argument that the ultimate reasons for the changes in Soviet foreign policy could be found to stem from the domestic scene.

4. THE NEW EUROPEAN POLICY OF THE SOVIET UNION

Although Soviet foreign policy focused its main attention on the United States, relations with the European countries have also become gradually more and more important. Normalized great power relations have paved the way for new relations with Europe, socialist and non-socialist alike. But it is still clear that Europe's importance remains secondary; good relations with Europe are not possible without improved great power relations, while great power relations had started to improve independently of the state of Soviet-European relations. On the other hand, Europe's position in the Soviet priority system was always higher than that of the Asian countries; whereas Gorbachev has rather rapidly visited all the important European countries, in Asia he has so far been only to India and China and in April 1991 to Japan.[18] On the other hand, it is good to remember that the order and number of visits does not necessarily depend on the priority system; in the future the military and economic importance of Asia, especially Eastern Asia (countries like China, Japan and Korea), will grow, as Gorbachev in his speech in Vladivostok in August 1986 has already predicted.[19]

Since 1987, Soviet-American relations have become firmly established. While bipolarity was strengthened in this way, it simultaneously became possible for the Soviet leadership to pay more attention to Soviet-European relations as well. A new, more positive atmosphere for improving East-West relations in the European framework can be seen in many cases. The Soviet Union, for example, no longer saw the European Community (EC) as an economic-political cover organization of NATO. To confirm its new attitude, the Soviet Union in 1989 established diplomatic relations with the EC.[20] In the same way, among Western governments, the Soviet attempts to approach West European countries are no longer seen as an attempt to split them away from the United States. On the contrary, the Soviet Union has gradually cultivated the idea that the existence of NATO and the presence of United States forces in Europe are factors that tend to stabilize the European situation. Especially after German unification had become a foregone conclusion, the Soviet Union no longer opposed German membership in NATO, because in that way other West European countries could more effectively contain German expansionist tendencies. Further, because the United States had as early as the 1970s taken part in the CSCE process, its participation in the future arrangements would be completely legitimate as well.[21] There are other problem areas where mutual understanding among the great powers is obvious. One of them is the peaceful settlement of the Third World regional conflicts, which, especially since the Iraqi invasion of Kuwait, have become one of the main results of the great power normalization.[22] The war of the United States-led alliance against Iraq in January-February 1991 was openly supported by the Soviet Union, showing that great power co-operation can emerge in the field of military activities as well.

In its relations with West European countries, the Soviet Union has been able to construct a new bilateral as well as multilateral network. Gorbachev's and Shevardnadze's many visits abroad have led to a situation in which numerous intergovernmental agreements have been concluded. All the agreements are not of the same type, however. While in Soviet-American relations the main concern has been security issues, in Soviet-West European relations the main concern has been economic. Soviet dealings with countries like Germany, France and Italy are important, especially in the sense that they have opened up new possibilities for wider economic cooperation and in that way made it easier to carry out necessary economic reforms in the Soviet Union. In addition to the EC, new contacts have been established with such multinational organizations as NATO, the Council of Europe and the Nordic Council.[23]

Some concrete elements in Soviet-European relations will be discussed in other chapters in this book. It therefore suffices to point out that the real turning point in Soviet-European relations took place in 1987. From the theoretical point of view, Gorbachev's book *Perestroika: New Thinking for Our Country and the World* has been especially important.[24] There he presented his idea of the common European house' (similar ideas had earlier been presented by President Charles de Gaulle and certain West German politicians[25]). He also spoke of the need for new security arrangements in Europe and pointed out that the growing interdependence of European nations had made cooperation more and more important. Theoretical articles on 'new political thinking' by prominent Soviet experts like Yevgeni Primakov and Alexander Bovin appeared during the same year.[26] In all of them, the necessity for new approaches was emphasized.

Dramatic changes have also taken place in Soviet relations with Eastern Europe, changes that would not have been possible without Gorbachev's contribution. After March 1985, it took quite a while before it became evident that the East European socialist countries were ready to follow along the lines of *perestroika*.[27] Gorbachev travelled extensively in the area, speaking of the necessity for economic and political reforms. But his approach was at that time still rather cautious. It was in 1988 that for the first time his tone became sharper and more critical. He started to speak, for example, about free political choice for all countries, including those of Eastern Europe.[28] By that he did not refer to the right of small socialist states to continue their policy of stagnation but rather to the fact that so far Soviet-East European relations had been based on erroneous premises, creating an obstacle to internal reform there.

In 1985, when *perestroika* was launched in the Soviet Union, political liberalization had started for practical purposes only in Poland and Hungary and even there on a very limited scale. Other East European leaders maintained a very suspicious attitude towards changes connected with *perestroika*, especially those of a political nature. They tried to explain the Soviet reforms in the light of Soviet domestic problems and argued therefore that there was no need for similar changes in their own countries. Soviet leaders, for their part, considered it important to have similar reforms carried out in the East European countries. They were unwilling, however, to take any special measures to achieve this; that would have violated the principles of the new foreign politicy, where non-intervention in the internal affairs of others was strongly emphasized. Direct intervention was not even necessary, because already the emergence of a prominent political example was enough to stir up a popular movement demanding far-reaching reforms. This new non-interventionist policy was later renamed by Gennadi Gerasimov as the 'Sinatra doctrine', which declared that every socialist country had the right to work out its solutions 'in its own way'.

Soviet relations with the other socialist countries had been earlier based on the Brezhnev doctrine. According to this, the right and duty of each member state of the socialist community was to launch active measures if the achievements of socialism were endangered in any of the member states. When in 1987 Brezhnev's foreign policy began to be censured in the Soviet Union, critical attention was drawn to the application of this principle in the Czechoslovakian crisis of 1968. To prove that the rejection of the Brezhnev doctrine was real, the Soviet leadership made numerous decisions in 1988-

89, the most important being the announcement by Eduard Shevardnadze at the end of 1988 that the Soviet Union was ready to start withdrawing its troops from Eastern Europe. This decision meant that the conservative leaders of Eastern Europe had lost the force on which they had based their absolute rule, namely, the Soviet military presence.[29] Revolutionary political change in these countries was therefore only a question of time. On the other hand, one should remember that similar, earlier measures have not been eradicated: for example, the annexation of the Baltic states, carried out in 1940, has not been annulled so far. On the contrary, the separatist demands based on the illegal nature of the annexation have been vigorously condemned by the CPSU leadership.[30] In his speech in March 1991, President Gorbachev finally declared that a certain variant of independence could be possible for the Baltic states as well as for other Soviet republics striving for separation, resembling that of East European countries before the adoption of the Sinatra doctrine.

From the Soviet point of view, the absolute military control of Eastern Europe was, owing to the great power détente, no longer as crucial as within the international system produced by the Cold War. When the uprisings started, first in the German Democratic Republic and soon after that in Bulgaria, Czechoslovakia and Romania, the Soviet Union did not publicly show willingness to contain the erosive development. At the beginning of 1990, a new situation had therefore emerged, where neither the military nor the economic community of the socialist states any longer existed except formally. At the end of 1990, it was announced that the role of the CMEA would change and in February 1991 that even the activities of the Warsaw Treaty Organization would be rearranged. The Soviet Union is therefore already aiming at wider all-European arrangements: in the economic field, in cooperation with the EC and in foreign and security policy in the framework of the CSCE process.

Some mention of the changed Soviet attitude towards neutrality must also be made in this connection.[31] The Soviet stance has had two dimensions. On the one hand, the Soviet Union has traditionally understood neutrality in the framework of the Cold War structures. Finland's neutrality, for example, has been understood as an effort not to get involved in the great power conflicts. For quite a long time the Soviet Union saw neutrality as a corrupted choice; it was believed that in a serious political crisis the neutral countries would in any case take the side of the West. Consequently, neutrality was not seen as a credible choice. For a long time, even Finland's neutrality was analysed in a critical light, although it at the same time was presented as some sort of an example for other European states.[32] Now when the Cold War structures have more or less disappeared, it would be only logical to conclude that there no longer existed a similar need for neutrality; without the great power conflict, neutrality has, in other words, become unnecessary. On the other hand, along with détente, the Soviet Union has been willing to admit the genuineness of neutrality, especially in Finland's case. Such an admission was made during Gorbachev's visit to Finland in October 1989.[33] But it is ironical that the country's neutrality should be accepted and publicly recognized by the Soviet Union first at the moment when it is no longer necessary as a political solution for the neutral countries.

Finally, a few words should be said about the political functions of the new foreign politicy changes as well as about the functions of the reform of Soviet foreign politicy doctrine, methods and instruments. Within the whole body of socialist thought, Gorbachev has so far tried to act as some sort of a modern socialist Martin Luther. His *perestroika* has amounted to some sort of a '*Reformation der Realsozialismus*', which aims at regaining the original pure content of socialism, free of corruption and selfishness.

In the field of foreign policy, the socialist '*Reformation*' seems to have three different aims. First, there is the aim of rationalizing the foreign political activities of the Soviet Union. When old goals, such as world revolution and complete nuclear disarmament, were no longer within reach, they had to be redefined. And when the goals were redefined, the instruments and methods of the foreign policy had to be re-evaluated as well. Second, the new thinking about foreign affairs seems to aim at a more realistic approach to realities. There has been, for example, lively discussion on the image presented of the capitalist system, raising the question: does it really correspond to the truth? It has similarly been admitted that quite frequently Soviet foreign policy has been based on incorrect premises. Third, the new foreign politicy thinking has also had the function of a new image builder. The Soviet leadership wants to show the rest of the world that the basic quality of the Soviet state apparatus has profoundly changed and that therefore there are no further political or moral obstacles to the development of closer economic and other relations with it.

5. QUESTIONS FOR THE FUTURE

So far, the main question in discussing the development of Soviet foreign policy has been the quality of various doctrinal and practical solutions. In the future, new and much more burning questions are, however, emerging. When we today consider the role of the Soviet Union in the new Europe, we must also ask: what kind of a Soviet Union are we talking about? Conflicts between different national groups in the country since 1987 have led to a situation where even the existence of the Soviet Union in its present form is more and more questionable. While different Soviet republics, and even smaller regional units, have striven for wider autonomy and independence, they have simultaneously questioned the legitimation of the All-Union organs to have a monopoly in international relations and foreign policy. Constitutionally, the Soviet republics are sovereign states, which have voluntarily joined together, creating the Union of Soviet Socialist Republics. In this way they have given up some of their sovereign rights: foreign policy and military issues are sectors where the decision-making power belongs to the All-Union instead of the republican organs.

Nearly all Soviet republics have now questioned this monopoly of the All-Union organs. All 15 Socialist Soviet Republics (SSRs) plus a number of Autonomous Socialist Soviet Republics (ASSRs) have issued their declarations of sovereignty, whereby they have demanded, among other things, the right to exercise independent foreign policy; to conclude diplomatic relations with other states; to have their own diplomatic apparatus abroad as well as in Moscow; to conclude treaties with other states, and so forth. It is not only the Baltic republics that demand this but also Russia and other Slavic republics. If Russia, for example, starts to adopt its own foreign policy line independently of the Soviet administration, there is very little that the Soviet foreign ministry can do. So far, its only concrete measure has been the formation of the separate department of Soviet republics.[34]

What the individual Soviet republics actually want is to change their present hierarchical centre-periphery relations to equal relations between different nationalities, this also being one sign of the emergence of a civil society in the Soviet Union. The recent reluctance of Western governments to support these moves on the international agenda shows, however, that they are still rather unwilling to make the position of the Soviet leadership (or actually that of Gorbachev) more difficult by encouraging separatist republican demands inside the country.[35] But in the long run, it appears more and more probable that the breakup of the anachronistic Soviet administrative system cannot be avoided. One evidence of this is the growing demand of the Soviet republics to separate their foreign and military policies from the All-Union decision-making, especially because the power of the central administration is becoming weaker and weaker.

NOTES

1. An earlier version of this article is Jyrki Iivonen, 'Kohti uutta Eurooppaa: Länsi-Eurooppa Neuvostoliiton Euroopan-politiikassa' (Towards a New Europe: Western Europe in the Soviet Policy vis-a-vis Europe), *Ulkopolitiikka*, vol. 27, no. 2, 1990, pp. 33-42.
2. *Izvestiya*, 20 November 1989.
3. On Russian village community, see Andrzej Walicki, *The Slavophile Controversy: History of a Conservative Utopia in Nineteenth Century Russia* (Oxford: Clarendon Press, 1975), pp. 169-76.
4. Timo Vihavainen, 'Russia and Europe: The Historiographic Aspect' in Vilho Harle and Jyrki Iivonen (eds), *Gorbachev and Europe* (London: Frances Pinter, 1990), pp. 3-6.
5. Thomas Parland, 'Rysk nationalism - förr och som en kraft i framtiden' (Russian Nationalism - Earlier and as a Power of the Future), *Finsk*

Tidskrift, nos 9-10, 1990, pp. 560-81.

6. On the Russian national conservatism today, see Roman Szporluk, 'Dilemmas of Russian Nationalism', *Problems of Communism*, vol. XXXVIII, July-August 1989, pp. 15-35.

7. This was especially emphasized by the Russian Nobel-writer Alexander Solzhenitsyn in his article 'Kak nam obustroit Rossiyu?', which appeared in *Literaturnaya Gazeta* and *Komsomolskaya Pravda* (18 September 1990) and which led to a lively dicussion both in the Soviet Union and abroad.

8. On Soviet theory of international relations, see, e.g., V. Kubalkova and A. A. Cruickshank, *Marxism-Leninism and Theory of International Relations* (London: Routledge & Kegan Paul, 1980) and Margot Light, *The Soviet Theory of International Relations* (Brighton: Wheatsheaf Books, 1988).

9. During the first years of Gorbachev's rule, extensive personnel changes took place in the Soviet diplomatic apparatus. Between March 1985 and August 1988, for example, over 80 per cent of the Soviet ambassadors were changed. Day-to-day diplomatic activities also became more open during the same period: see Jyrki Iivonen, 'Gorbachev's Personnel Policy' in Ronald J. Hill and Jan Åke Dellenbrant (eds), *Gorbachev and Perestroika* (Aldershot: Edward Elgar, 1989), p. 163. Although the rapidity of the changes has decreased since then, some important events have taken place later on. The most important has been the resignation of Eduard Shevardnadze in December 1990. He was succeeded in January 1991 by former ambassador to Washington, Alexander Bessmertnykh.

10. On the action programmes of Soviet foreign policy, see Jyrki Iivonen, *Independence or Incorporation? The Idea of Poland's National Self-Determination and Independence within the Russian and Soviet Socialism from the 1870s to the 1920s* (Helsinki: The Finnish Institute of International Affairs, 1990), pp. 15-16.

11. V. I. Lenin, 'Rech pri zakrytii konferentsii, 28 maya 1921. X vse-rossijskaya konferentsiya RKP(b)', *Polnoe sobranie sochinenii*, 43, pp. 340-1.

12. In his article 'Fundamentals of Leninism', published soon after Lenin's death, Stalin wrote of the possibility of combining the Bolshevik dedication with the American spirit of entrepreneurship (I. V. Stalin, *Sochineniya*, 6, p. 186).

13. Light, op. cit., p. 32.

14. Light, op. cit., p. 47.

15. That United States foreign policy in the interwar period would have been completely isolationist is a doubtful argument. Although this argument has been true at the diplomatic level, American influence was clearly felt in the economic sphere, where the United States took active part in the recovery efforts of the world economy. It was only after the great depression that the situation changed: see Paul Johnson, *Modern Times: The World from the Twenties to the Eighties* (New York: Harper & Row, 1989), p. 232.

16. Light, op. cit., p. 216.

17. Heinz Timmermann, 'Sowjetunion und Westeuropa: Perzeptionswandel

und politische Neuausrichtung' in Hannes Adomeit, Hans-Hermann Höhmann und Günter Wagenlehner (eds), *Die Sowjetunion under Gorbatschow* (Stuttgart: Kohlhammer, 1989), p. 332.

18. Already during his first years in power, Gorbachev visited all the European socialist counties except Albania. As for other European countries, he has been to France, Switzerland, Iceland, Great Britain, Ireland Germany, Finland, Italy, Malta, Spain, Norway and Sweden. In addition, he has visited the United States several times and Cuba once.

19. *Pravda*, 29 July 1986.

20. On the development of Soviet-EC relations, see Heinz Timmermann, 'The Soviet Union and Western Europe: Conceptual Change and Political Reorientation' in Harle and Iivonen, op. cit., pp. 103-29.

21. Sergei A. Karaganov, 'Towards a New Security System in Europe' in Harle and Iivonen, op. cit., pp. 48-9.

22. See the statements by foreign ministers James Baker and Eduard Shevardnadze in *Ulkopolitiikka*, vol. 27, no. 4, 1990, pp. 4-5.

23. A new approach to Soviet-Scandinavian relations was described in Mikhail Gorbachev's speech in Helsinki in October 1989: see Jyrki Iivonen and Pertti Joenniemi, 'Gorbatshovin Finlandia-talon puhe: Uuden ajattelun sovellutus' (Gorbachev's Speech at the Finlandia Hall. Application of the New Thinking) *Ulkopolitiikka*, vol. 26, no. 4, 1989, pp. 49-51.

24. Mikhail Gorbachev, *Perestroika: New Thinking for Our Country and the World* (London: Collins, 1987).

25. According to Ole Nørgaard, such concepts as 'common security' and 'security partnership' were used by the West German Social Democratic Party at the end of the 1970s and the beginning of the 1980s: see Ole Nørgaard, 'New Political Thinking East and West: A Comparative Perspective' in Harle and Iivonen, op. cit., p. 57.

26. On the content and concepts of the new thinking, see Gerhard Wettig, ''New Thinking' in Soviet Foreign Policy', *Berichte des Bundesinstituts für ostwissenschaftliche und internationale Studien*, no. 67, 1989.

27. See Jyrki Iivonen, 'Perestroika ja pienet sosialistiset maat' (Perestroika and the Small Socialist Countries), *Ulkopolitiikka*, vol. 25, no. 3, 1988, pp. 33-43.

28. Heinz Timmermann, 'Die Sowjetunion und der Umbruch in Osteuropa', *Berichte des Bundesinstituts für ostwissenschaftliche und internationale Studien*, no. 51, 1990, p. 7.

29. The withdrawal of Soviet troops from Eastern Europe has proved to be a difficult technical and political problem. One of the problems is the relocation of the troops within Soviet territory. As to technical difficulties, it might be mentioned that the operation itself takes time from three to four years and has therefore caused some suspicions among the new governments in Eastern Europe, Poland in particular: see Douglas L. Clarke, Poland and the Soviet Troops in Germany. *Report on Eastern Europe*, vol. 2, no. 4, 1991, pp. 40-4.

30. See the declaration of the CPSU Central Committee on the situation in the Baltic Republics (*Pravda*, 27 August 1989).

31. On the changing Soviet attitude towards neutrality in the European

44   *The Changing Soviet Union in the New Europe*

framework, see Bo Petersson, *Sovjetunionen och neutraliteten i Europa* (The Soviet Union and Neutrality in Europe) (Stockholm: Utrikespolitiska institutet, 1989) and Bo Petersson, *The Soviet Union and Peacetime Neutrality in Europe: A Study of Soviet Political Language* (Stockholm: The Swedish Institute of International Affairs, 1990).

32. Jyrki Iivonen, 'Finland som model: Det finsk-sovjetiske forhold som et eksempel på fredelig sameksistens' (Finland as an Example: The Finnish-Soviet Relationship as an Example of Peaceful Coexistence) in Christian Mailand-Hansen and Ole Nørgaard (eds), *Sovjetunionen og freden - en debatbog* (The Soviet Union and Peace - a Discussion Book) (Esbjerg: Sydjysk Universitetsforlag, 1983), p. 162.

33. *Pravda*, 26 October 1989.

34. *Izvestiya*, 20 November 1989.

35. During the conference of European governments in Paris in autumn 1990, the major European governments did not oppose the Soviet demand to have the Baltic delegations to be excluded from the conference.

3 THE SOVIET CONCEPT OF A COMMON EUROPEAN HOUSE

Neil Malcolm

1. INTRODUCTION

Russia has never been able confidently to assume 'European status'. Because of its peripheral situation, its cultural specificity and its size, it has tended to be regarded with a special apprehensiveness by its Western neighbours. A large amount has been written about Russian 'expansionism' and its roots - whether in geography (the absence of natural boundaries), in the nature of the patrimonial, despotic state, or in quasi-theocratic, quasi-socialist messianism. It is clear that Russia's economic backwardness and cultural isolation generated conflicting attitudes to Europe among its own leaders and élites. On the one hand there was a sense of vulnerability and mistrust, on the other a desire to 'catch up', and in particular to acquire the technologies needed for self-defence. This conflict tended to express itself in a cyclical pattern of isolationism and stagnation, military defeat, reform and Westernization, followed by a return to isolationism. Constant throughout, however, has been an emphasis on state power and military strength. Russia's relations with the rest of Europe have been predominantly military relations. During the 20th century the Soviet Union's enormous armed strength,

its expansion into Central Europe, and its ostensibly 'revolutionary' ideology served to entrench its image as an outlaw
in the society of European nations.

The world could perhaps be forgiven, then, for reacting
with a certain scepticism when a Soviet leader emerged in the
second half of the 1980s who expounded a thoroughgoing
internationalist, idealist and increasingly liberal vision of
international relations, who declared that 'the criteria of
justice, equality, respect for human life as such, that existed in
theories, sermons and dreams, are beginning to take effect in
real world politics, driving back militaristic and great power
approaches', and who called for the creation of a 'common
European house', 'an inter-state and inter-ethnic community,
constructed on the basis of universally shared values', 'an
integral political, legal, economic and cultural space, an
alliance of states with common structures maintaining military
and ecological security and ensuring a high level of
multifarious interaction'.[1] Such a radical turnabout, with such
far-reaching implications, demands the closest attention. This
chapter focuses on those elements of Gorbachev's new thinking
that relate to Europe, and in particular on Soviet conceptions
of the future shape of the European house. It tries to explain
why they came to the fore when they did, what their relation is
to policy, and how they have changed since 1985. Finally, it
offers some considerations on how Soviet relations with
Europe are likely to develop in the future. What does the
current Soviet leadership want when it says that it would like
the Soviet Union to be accepted as a 'normal' European power,
and how realistic are its aspirations?

2. SOVIET ISOLATION

Like the overwhelming majority of the Russian intelligentsia at
the beginning of the 20th century, Lenin looked to the West for
enlightenment and for models of social progress. The revolution of 1917 was conceived by him principally as the first
step in a chain reaction which would lead to the emergence of
socialist regimes in the advanced countries. An internationalist
Europe would come to the aid of progressive Russia and help

to drag the country out of its 'Asiatic' backwardness. But the 'Europe without frontiers' of Lenin's vision was a post-capitalist Europe. As things were, he maintained, national concentrations of capital would retain their local identity, work more and more closely with their increasingly militarized national states, and wage merciless war for markets and resources. A 'United States of Europe' constructed on the existing social order, Lenin argued, would be 'impossible or reactionary': only a shared murderous hostility to socialism could hold it together, and then only on a temporary basis.[2] The task assigned to the new Soviet diplomacy in Europe, then, was a challenging one - to secure the country's survival in an increasingly dangerous, violent environment, in which the Soviet Union was at once one of the weakest and the most hated of the participants. To do so it had to play the game of power politics as ruthlessly and determinedly as the encircling capitalist states. In such circumstances it is not surprising that during the Stalin period traditional Russian militaristic, isolationist, and even outright xenophobic values soon began to gain the upper hand.

After the Second World War the Soviet Union acquired a less insecure position. It was less necessary for it to create splits among its potential enemies. For all its anathematizing of NATO, Moscow undoubtedly saw solid advantages in the predictability it brought to European politics, in the division of Germany which it enforced, in the opportunities which it offered for influencing America's policy through its allies, and in the sanction it provided for the Soviet Union's own domination of the eastern part of the continent. The other European states played an essentially secondary role in the new bipolar super-power system.

The experience of the war and its aftermath also sparked off a new line of development in Soviet thinking about international relations. From 1941 to 1945 the Soviet Union had after all fought successfully in an alliance alongside powerful capitalist states. It had even seemed at one stage that the United States might be ready to provide assistance to Moscow for the postwar reconstruction effort. Subsequently, rapid economic recovery in Europe, social reforms, and sustained international cooperation in the EEC and NATO, encouraged Soviet international affairs experts to articulate bolder new perceptions of the West. By the 1950s and the 1960s it was being suggested more or less explicitly in the specialist press that the capitalist world, far from descending into a spiral of conflict and decline, offered opportunities for collaboration, as well as threats, that it was moving ahead towards greater prosperity and integration.[3]

Under Khrushchev and Brezhnev, some of these ideas found partial expression in official foreign policy doctrine and practice, in attempts to promote 'peaceful coexistence', 'détente', and the 'European process'. But the revisionist groups and factions were politically weak, and their preferences were implemented in a half-hearted and ineffective way. The Helsinki Conference on Security and Cooperation in Europe, of which the Final Act was signed in 1975, was accompanied by Soviet appeals for a new system of collective security and intensified pan-European economic cooperation and cultural contacts, but such calls were not new to Western ears, and there was no significant change of policy. It was clear that the Soviet Union's primary concern was to entrench its defensive position in Europe by eliciting formal recognition of postwar boundaries in the eastern part of the continent. Old barriers to East-West communication in Europe remained firmly in place. Soviet spokesmen complained that American influence and 'Atlanticism' in Western Europe were blocking progress towards deeper collaboration. Such an approach to the matter was scarcely likely to encourage a cooperative attitude in London, Paris or Bonn. In any case, the old barriers to East-West communication on the continent remained in place.

In 1977, negotiations were started between the EC and the CMEA, but the talks foundered when it emerged that Brezhnev refused to countenance the establishing of direct links between Brussels and individual Eastern bloc states. The Soviet state monopoly on foreign trade remained intact. It was obstinately maintained that just as there were two world economies so there were two distinct systems of economic integration in Europe. As for the security dimension, here the superpower competition was pursued with the previous disregard for European sensitivities. Soviet handling of the controversy over SS-20 and Cruise and Pershing-II deployment at the end of the 1970s was particularly clumsy. As often as not, the outcome was to drive the European allies further into the arms of the United States.

By 1985, it was no longer possible to ignore the failure of the Soviet Union's foreign policy strategy towards Europe, and the West in general. The country was rapidly losing ground in the East-West competition - in economic terms, military-technological terms and political terms. Despite the presence in Washington of the most confrontational administration since the Second World War, 'Atlanticism' was rife in Western Europe. In Eastern Europe economic and political decay was advancing, most spectacularly in Poland. The new generation of leaders which came to power in Moscow had many reasons to institute a radical review of policy. This disposition was encouraged by the personal contacts many of them enjoyed with particularly Western groups in the Soviet élite. There were employees of the party and state apparatus, and the foreign policy research institutes, who had for decades been covertly disseminating among the intelligentsia liberal and social democratic ideas which shed doubt on the fundamental premises of Leninism about international relations, and in particular about the weakness and aggressiveness of capitalist states.[4] This long period of preparation explains the suddenness with which notions such as interdependence, global economic integration, the viability of reformist socialism, mutual security and 'sufficient defence' bubbled to the surface of the official discourse in the middle of the 1980s. What was going on was not a calculating assumption of Western progressive phraseology, designed to lead world liberal public opinion by the nose, although no doubt Soviet foreign policy professionals appreciated the particular effectiveness of Gorbachev's and Shevardnadze's high-sounding language. It represented the culmination of a long-running organic process in Soviet postwar intellectual life, rooted in a revulsion against Stalinist and neo-Stalinist nationalism and isolationism, something which with the wisdom of hindsight seems perfectly predictable.[5]

The post-1985 shift in foreign policy doctrine was reinforced by linkages at several levels with the internal reform process - in terms of economic conditions (internal marketization and external 'opening up' are complementary), in terms of social-political supports (using the intelligentsia as allies against officialdom), in terms of political values (compromise, the rule of law, and an appeal to 'universal' values), in 'mind-set' terms, and so on.[6] Among the various international systemic and internal societal factors which have played a part in the genesis of Soviet new thinking, there are some which fit into a cyclical pattern of the kind referred to at the start of this chapter, but there are others (changes in the nature of the international system and deep-running social changes inside the Soviet Union - and the new perceptions which these two kinds of change generated) which suggest a more permanent shift - or at least the promise of one. We shall return to this question in the final section

3. THE COMMON EUROPEAN HOUSE - THREE TRANSITIONS

The Soviet common European house project has been treated with caution, and frequently with scepticism in the West, not simply because of the novelty of the underlying concepts in the context of postwar Soviet foreign policy. The content of the common European house idea has altered substantially even since 1985, as Moscow has reappraised its relationship with Europe. In broad terms three stages can be distinguished. The first reappraisal occurred during 1985-89. It involved breaking with the post-1945 approach to Western Europe principally as a subordinate element of a US-dominated alliance, to be used to manipulate US policy, whether by encouraging anti-Americanism in Western Europe or by using countries in the region to set examples of détente and closer East-West relations. This was replaced by a view of Europe as increasingly a 'power-centre' in its own right, but one closely attached to its transatlantic partner. In relations with such an entity, old-style tactics of forceful 'leverage' would be quite inappropriate.

The second reappraisal occurred in 1989-90. It meant abandoning Gorbachev's initial 'one Europe, two (slowly converging) systems' view, and accepting that the countries of the old Eastern bloc would inevitably fall into the West European orbit. It was accelerated by the changes in the status of East Germany and consequent changes in military balance, and involved an urgent search for a new security relationship with the West. The third reappraisal is now under way. Set in train by revolutionary domestic processes, it concerns less the changes which the country's leadership might envisage occuring in Europe as a whole, and more the 'Europeanization' of the Soviet Union itself, conceived of by many Russians as an essential condition for its inclusion in the common European house.

TRANSITION I: ACCEPTING AN 'ATLANTICIST' WESTERN EUROPE

Anti-American Europeanism

Gorbachev's European diplomacy began with a flourish, with his visit to Paris in October 1985. He declared that Western Europe was 'at the centre of attention in Soviet policy', and that it was a priority of his government to overcome the division of the continent and encourage better cooperation. Moscow would henceforth deal with the European Community as a 'political unit'. EC-CMEA talks were restarted, this time on the explicit understanding that direct ties could be established between Brussels and the East European capitals.[7]

It rapidly became clear, however, that policy had been adjusted rather than fundamentally changed. The way Gorbachev used the phrase common European house was reminiscent of the way Brezhnev used it in Bonn in 1981, namely, as part of a plan to emphasize policy differences inside the Western alliance, in this case over Washington's strategic defence initiative.[8] *Pravda* declared that as far as the Americans were concerned, Europe was 'someone else's home'. Gorbachev argued that the continent must be protected against becoming 'a testing ground for the Pentagon's doctrine of a limited nuclear war'.[9] Officials and journalists warned that European culture was at risk not only from extermination in war, but also from 'elements of degradation...and the growth of cultural expansionism, primarily from the United States of America'.[10] At the 27th Party Congress, Gorbachev's report predicted the rapid collapse of bipolarity and American dominance in Europe. The NATO allies, he asserted, were 'coming increasingly to question Washington's diktat'.[11]

As in the past, this crude 'wedge-driving' had limited results, and did little for the credibility of new political thinking in general, and the concept of the common European house in particular. It was in any case apparently conceived as a part of an essentially US-Soviet negotiating process. Alexander Bovin wrote bluntly in *Izvestiya* in September 1985: 'We would like to make use of Western Europe's potential via the transatlantic channel in order to meet the evident deficit in common sense among the current administration in the United States.'[12] It was that superpower dialogue which took the lion's share of Soviet diplomatic attention in 1985-86. In the drive to preserve START and the ABM treaty, and to achieve progress in talks on arms reduction and confidence building, the role of the West European allies was spelt out quite explicitly in Moscow. They were to 'speak more definitely and confidently' on East-West security issues, to 'suggest realistic assessments', to fulfil their 'special mission' of rebuilding détente.[13]

Rethinking Europeanism

When the Soviet Union relaunched its European diplomacy in 1987 (the 'year of Europe' as it was called in Moscow), the common European house slogan was resurrected, but the concept had been fleshed out and modified in a way which suggested that a genuine rethinking was taking place about how to approach building a more solid relationship with Western Europe. First and foremost, this meant discarding the old scheme which opposed Europeanism and Atlanticism, and which implied that Western Europe faced a simple choice between alignment with the United States and normalizing relations with the Soviet Union. It meant adopting, in other words, an approach calculated not just to appeal to opposition and radical groups which might put pressure on West European governments, but to attract the interest of governments and establishments themselves.

That a fresh start was needed had been made painfully clear by reactions in France and West Germany to aspects of the Soviet-American talks on removing ground-based medium-range nuclear missiles from Europe. There were loud expressions of concern about the risk of decoupling the United States from European defence, and demands for 'compensatory measures'. There seemed to Soviet eyes a real possibility that confrontation with the United States might in the end merely be replaced by confrontation with an increasingly united West European military entity. It became a matter of urgency to deal with European perceptions of a Soviet threat - by devoting greater attention to conventional disarmament on the continent, and by dispelling suspicions of a conspiracy to split the Atlantic alliance.[14] Deepening economic problems in the Soviet Union and East European countries also exerted pressure on Soviet policy-makers. It became imperative to bring to a conclusion and begin to exploit the new agreements being worked out with the European Community, which appeared to be moving ahead to closer integration. Here, as in the security sphere, West Germany had to play a central part, and it was in 1987 that relations between Moscow and Bonn, which had remained cool until 1985, finally began to warm up.

The common European house concept was relaunched by Gorbachev in a speech in Prague in April 1987, and expanded in his book *Perestroika*, published later in that year. Europe, he declared, possesses 'a certain integrity, although the countries involved belong to different social systems and are members of opposing military and political blocs'. It faces common tasks: it has to dispose of a dangerous accumulation of armaments, to reduce environmental pollution, to devise means of coping with pressures for economic interdependence, and to work towards a solution to 'global problems' - debt, under-development, regional conflicts, terrorism, AIDS and drug addiction. At the same time, it has great resources at its disposal - a common dedication to the avoidance of war, accumulated experience in the practice of international relations, an impressive network of international agreements and organizations, and the economic and technological potential which would be unblocked by closer pan-continental cooperation.

The Soviet leader also outlined the first practical steps to be taken in building the 'common house': eliminating force imbalances between NATO and the Warsaw Pact, removing all nuclear weapons, adopting 'non-offensive defence' and 'reasonable sufficiency' in armaments, increasing the number of joint ventures in industry and services, abolishing restrictions on the export of 'sensitive' technology to the East. He proposed, too, that the human rights dimension of the Helsinki process should receive more emphasis, repeating an earlier offer to hold a conference on the subject in Moscow.

The trouble with this catalogue was that apart from the human rights initiative, and the suggestion for changes in military doctrine, none of it was particularly new. There was little to indicate that the Soviet Union wanted to see a real erosion of the blocs - indeed, its determination to preserve two German states for the foreseeable future was made quite explicit. The old 'impossible' demands were still there - rapid denuclearization, sweeping away trade controls - and there was the same reluctance to allow the United States into the game on equal terms:

> Our idea of a common European house certainly does not involve shutting the doors to anybody. True, we would not like to see anyone kicking the doors of the European home and taking the head of the table in somebody else's apartment. But then, that is the concern of the owner of the apartment. In the past the socialist countries have responded positively to the participation of the United States and Canada in the Helsinki process.[15]

Few West European readers of Gorbachev's *Perestroika* were likely to feel confident about the implication that whereas the Soviet Union occupied a chair at the European table because of a shared European heritage, the United States was only there by invitation. Gorbachev's appeal to culture and geography, one might suspect, would carry little weight with an audience who felt considerably more kinship with the world of Hollywood and Jack Kennedy than with the world of Mosfilm, socialist realism and Konstantin Chernenko. This was an audience, moreover, who was inclined to perceive the Soviet Union as a threat by virtue of its sheer size and military capability, and who had been accustomed to regard the powerful American presence in Europe as the ultimate guarantee of its security.[16] Anti-American Europeanism was well tailored to the preconceptions of the traditional left and the neo-Gaullist right, but these were fading forces in the Europe of the 1980s.

Be that as it may, by 1987 it appeared that the Soviet foreign policy machine had acquired the capacity to recognize, and act on these elementary truths. It was repeatedly stated in Moscow that the future shape of the European house would be determined 'by the creative endeavour of all European countries'. Hans-Dietrich Genscher and other visitors to the Soviet Union were drawn into animated discussions about possible 'architectures'.[17] A start was made on the task of rendering the common European house prospectus at once more concrete and less alarming. Negotiations with the EC were making good progress. Hungary was allowed unprecedented latitude in reaching its own agreement with Brussels, and the Soviet press occasionally cited Hungary as a model in its combining of domestic economic reform and widening ties with the West. German business leaders were encouraged to explore possibilities for investment and cooperation in the Soviet Union. In March 1988, Gorbachev spoke in Yugoslavia of the need to build 'a really all-European market'.[18]

The Soviet Union moved swiftly to calm British and French fears. The two countries' strategic forces were excluded from the Intermediate Nuclear Force negotiations, large conventional arms cuts were promised, and big concessions were made in the fields of verification and confidence building. At the beginning of 1988, Shevardnadze assured Geoffrey Howe that the Soviet Union was not advocating nuclear disarmament in isolation from reductions in other categories of weaponry.[19] He also made it clear that his government understood the logic of the United Kingdom's attachment to deterrence. It was not, he acknowledged, 'based on fetishing nuclear arms, but on a definite interpretation of the existing realities and an idea of the nature and degree of the potential threat'.

The next step was to clarify the relationship of the

common European house to the existing pattern of alliances. Gorbachev had always denied any intention to drive wedges between the United States and its European partners in NATO. Indeed, it was characteristic of Soviet new thinking to aspire to build new international institutions rather than to destroy old ones. Shevardnadze was no doubt quite sincere when he remarked to the West German Foreign Minister in July 1986 that 'given all the alliances that have taken shape, it is essential to strengthen those threads whose severance is fraught with danger of severance of the world fabric'.[20] Such a view of things is likely to have been encouraged by Soviet concern about how to preserve intact the Warsaw Pact structure amid the unsettling effects of economic realignment in Europe. By 1987, it must have seemed that there was a great deal to be gained by toning down the inspirational theme of the melting away of the blocs, especially since it was clear that NATO was in no danger of vanishing first. In an interview with the PCI newspaper *l'Unita*, Gorbachev stated unequivocally:

> The historical relationship between Western Europe and the United States, or say, between the Soviet Union and European socialist countries, is a political reality. It may not be ignored if one pursues a realistic policy. A different attitude would upset the equilibrium in Europe.[21]

If the common European house was ever to be accepted in Western Europe as having any meaning in security terms, it had to include all the CSCE participants, including the transatlantic ones. By 1989, the Soviet leadership was coming to accept this quite explicitly and openly. In the joint Soviet-West German declaration signed in Bonn in June of that year, the United States and Canada were described as full members of the common European house. A few weeks later in Strasbourg, Gorbachev spelled it out again.

> The Soviet Union, it is alleged, is too big for coexistence, others would feel ill at ease with it. Present day realities, prospects for the foreseeable future are obvious. The Soviet Union and the United States constitute a natural part of the European international political structure.[22]

Such statements, of course, should not be interpreted crudely as indicating that Gorbachev and his collegues had settled in 1989 on a conception of the common European house as something which in all its dimensions was coterminous with the CSCE system. It was already evolving in Soviet discussions into something much more complex and open-ended. This process was enormously accelerated by the disintegration of the Soviet control over Eastern Europe.

TRANSITION II: ACCEPTING A SINGLE EUROPE

The Dismantling of the Old Order

It is likely that argument will go on for a long time over when the Brezhnev doctrine, which legitimized Soviet intervention to 'defend socialism' in Eastern Europe, finally died. There is evidence of discussions in Moscow as early as 1987 of the feasibility of loosening control in the region, and withdrawing troops.[23] Nevertheless, it is clear, as we have seen, that the new Soviet leadership continued to envisage a two-bloc Europe in the security and political dimension stretching into the future, albeit accompanied by a loosening of communications and by economic rapprochement. No doubt it was hoped that if the East European communist parties had a keener sense of their responsibility for their own fate, they would undertake the kind of reforms which it was believed in Moscow at the time could create a rejuvenated socialism, one which would compete on more even terms with the West for popular support. In the event, reform as a rule failed to come about, and where it did it failed to produce the desired results. As the economic gap between Eastern and Western Europe widened, support was lent to the arguments of reformist elements in the Soviet foreign affairs establishment and, one may conjecture, in the leadership, for the case that the other countries of the 'socialist community' had long since ceased to be an asset to the Soviet Union. They imposed a drain on military and raw material/ energy resources; they made a sorry showcase for the achievements of socialism; and they reinforced the Soviet Union's image as an occupying power in Europe. It would surely be

far better, such individuals argued, if these states were allowed
to follow a 'Finnish' path of development, which would allow
them to become prosperous trading partners, friendly neutrals
rather than resentful and unstable 'allies'.

This trend in the internal Soviet debate must have been
strengthened by the unfolding of domestic political reform.
From this point of view, the 19th Conference of the CPSU in
June 1988, which endorsed the idea of free electoral choice,
was an important milestone. As Gorbachev declared to participants, the principle of freedom applied abroad as well as at
home: 'In this situation the imposition of a social system, way
of life or policies from outside by any means, let alone
military, are dangerous trappings of past epochs.'[24] Kremlino-
logists already detected a distinct change of tone from the
pious declarations about the 'independence' of their allies
which Soviet leaders had issued over the decades. They also
noted important personnel changes in the parts of the CPSU
apparatus responsible for relations with ruling communist
parties. Gorbachev restated his position in Strasbourg in July
1989: 'Any attempts to restrict sovereignty of states, friends,
allies, or any others are inadmissible.'[25]

And this position was being carried through into
practice. At the United Nations General Assembly in December 1988, the Soviet leader announced the withdrawal of large
quantities of forces from Eastern Europe. Even more telling
was the Soviet-sanctioned agreement of the Polish government,
faced with yet another outbreak of unrest among the shipyard
workers in Gdansk in August 1988, to open roundtable talks
with opposition groups including Solidarity, and the Polish
decision in April 1989 to imitate the Soviet example by
organizing partially democratic elections, which fatally destroyed the credibility of Poland's United Workers' Party as a
ruling party.

This outcome, and the slide away from communism in
Hungary which gathered pace in 1989, suggested that the new
permissiveness in fraternal relations was likely to lead not just
to new kinds of 'socialist choice' but to radical political
realignments across the entire region. As the year passed,
however, it became clear that the Soviet leaders were indeed
ready to accept this kind of upheaval in the European house.

On a visit to Helsinki Gorbachev described Soviet-Finnish relations as a model for those between countries with different social systems, and between large and small states.[26] More momentously, he signed a declaration in West Germany in June 1989, which not only affirmed in familiar terms the right of all peoples and states 'freely to determine their own destiny', but also finally enshrined the language which the Bonn government had always insisted on using with reference to the GDR, about 'the right of peoples to self-determination'.[27] Subsequently, the Soviet government sat on its hands as Hungary opened up its borders to East German emigrants and completed the undermining of the Honecker regime. When the Berlin Wall fell on 9 November 1989, Pravda welcomed the event as a 'step towards the common European house'.

Thus Moscow managed not just to accept the East European revolutions with good grace, but even to take a large part of the credit for them, something which went some way towards mitigating the inevitable chill in relations with the post-communist governments in 1990. It would have been surprising, however, if all those in the Soviet Union who had some responsibility for an interest in national security matters had moved as one man to embrace the new 'Sinatra doctrine'. Even those who had made the decision must have been concerned about how to keep the process of change in Eastern Europe under control, as the cogs linking the various European 'clocks' began to jump and grind, and as shifts of public sentiment in East German provincial cities began to upset the calculations of general staffs and arms control experts. In October 1989 in Helsinki the Soviet Foreign Ministry spokesman Gennadi Gerasimov had added his own gloss to Gorbachev's remarks praising the Finnish model, saying that Moscow ruled out any possibility of what he called 'Finlandization in reverse': the countries of Eastern Europe had 'certain international obligations', for example, to CMEA and the WTO. These obligations, he was confident, they would uphold.[28]

In the light of what we know about the liberal and non-Stalinist colouring of the then Soviet leadership's world view, about the nature of its policy in 1988 and the first part of 1989, and about its relative astuteness in international affairs,

Shevardnadze and his collegues must get some credit as the authors, as well as the victims, of the events which followed. Credence must be given to the Foreign Minister's comment in July 1990 that he had 'in principle predicted the changes and felt that they were inevitable'.[29] Although the speed of de-communization in Poland, Hungary and Czechoslovakia surprised most observers, it was allowed to proceed with Moscow's blessing. After a touch on the brakes at the Malta summit in December 1989, when Gorbachev declared 'the actualities of life are such that in Europe there are two German states',[30] the Soviet position was again dramatically softened during Helmut Kohl's visit to Moscow on 10 February 1990: 'The question of the unity of the German nation should be settled by the Germans.'[31] There followed a phase of even more determined-looking foot-dragging on the question of a united Germany's membership of NATO ('absolutely excluded', said Gorbachev on 6 March 1990), followed by sudden acceptance of a package incorporating such membership at the Soviet-German talks in the Caucasus on 16 July.[32] During both these negotiating 'pauses' a bewildering mixture of signals emerged from both official and academic sources in Moscow, some indicating a position far more forthcoming than the current government line, others expressing opposition even to what had been conceded so far.[33] At the same time, a hotch-potch of alternative proposals was tried out by the Soviet side - German neutralization, German membership of both alliances, Germany in NATO on the French model, i.e., not participating in the military structure, and so on.

Behind the scenes, intensive diplomatic activity was kept up, not least in the specialized Helsinki process sessions which succeeded each other during the period. This all seems to fit well with the explanation of the Soviet position subsequently offered by the President's foreign policy adviser, Vadim Zagladin.

> We proceeded from the premise that Germany's unity was inevitable, that we should not interfere with it and that it is impossible to prevent it joining NATO if it itself wishes to do so. This means that the practical task before our policy was

limited to one thing: to ensure the creation of such conditions and bring about such changes on the European political scene that would meet as far as possible the interest of our country's security.[34]

Yet, it was not simply a question of ensuring security in the narrow sense, it was a question of following through to a conclusion the strategy for reconstructing the European house which the abandonment of the Brezhnev doctrine implied. After all, if all that happened as a result of loosening control over Eastern Europe and if the states concerned drifted into the West European sphere of influence, while existing patterns of political, economic and cultural relations between Western Europe and the Soviet Union remained fundamentally the same, it would be difficult to conceive of the whole exercise as a step forward. It would be even more difficult to justify the new policy to those powerful groups in Soviet society and in the leadership who warned against giving away the 'gains of 1945'. The two blocs would have remained but one would have become much weaker than the other.

As Gorbachev and his collegues repeated again and again, the solution to the German problem was inseparable from a new settlement in Europe as a whole.[35] In May 1989, George Bush had called for the dismantling of the iron curtain, self-determination, 'a Europe whole and free'. Only on such conditions could the Soviet Union be welcomed into the community of nations. During the months which followed, it became plain, as we have seen, that the Soviet Union was indeed prepared to give up its wasting military and political assets in Eastern Europe. It was prepared to shelve its current plan for the common European house as a partnership between two less and less separate but still identifiable political-military-economic blocs, in favour of a genuinely single European 'integral political, legal, economic and cultural space'. In the summer of 1990, it was engaged in bartering away its biggest bargaining chip of all, its control of the eastern part of Germany and its military presence there. This concession had to be seen to elicit hard evidence of building a new, safer relationship between the Soviet Union and the rest of Europe. The essential features of the new pattern of relations were to be i) a new relationship between the Soviet Union and Germany itself; ii) a new relationship between the Soviet Union and NATO; and iii) a strengthening of the CSCE and other international bonds. We shall examine briefly each of these areas in turn.

A New Relationship with Germany

Seen from Moscow, it was Germany which posed the greatest threat and at the same time possessed the greatest creative potential in the reconstruction of Europe. The very act of unification created, in Shevardnadze's words, 'a load-bearing structure of the common European house'.[36] In Soviet accounts of the agreements which brought the Two Plus Four talks on the external aspects of German unification to a successful conclusion, great emphasis was put on firm undertakings from the Germans to recognize existing borders in the east and to reduce overall troop numbers. The large transfers of hard currency promised to meet the costs of maintaining Soviet troops in eastern Germany and resettling them in the Soviet Union were seen as an earnest guarantee of solid German support for the Soviet economy in the years to come. Gorbachev and his collegues undoubtedly intended the high-profile reconciliation with Germany to dramatize for the Soviet public a switch from enmity to cooperation on the continent. From the German point of view, the 1980s had brought into sharp focus common interests with Moscow in lowering the level of military confrontation, in breaking down barriers in central Europe, and in using Western capital and know-how for economic recovery in Eastern Europe and the Soviet Union. Indeed, it is not entirely clear whether by 1990 the common European house was better described as a Soviet or as a German project.[37] West Germany's economic weight in Europe and its key geopolitical situation had made it particularly persuasive advocate for the new vision among the Western allies. Soviet commentators have repeatedly emphasized Germany's central role. As Valentin Falin, the head of the International Department of the CPSU, said in an interview with *Pravda* on 20 August 1990:

Germany is returning to world politics at a new qualitative level. If everything happens as the Germans assure us, and the entire potential of a powerful state is used for the benefit of people, and if only peace, not war, originates from German soil, Europe will enter the most constructive phase of its existence.[38]

The idea is occasionally put forward by Soviet writers that a special (political, military, economic) relationship between Germany and the Soviet Union can play the same kind of role in holding together a new pan-European system as the Franco-German partnership did for the European Community in the postwar decades.[39]

A New Relationship with NATO

Yet, as Shevardnadze stated on 20 September 1990, the agreement with Germany on conditions for unification had only been possible because of a 'stable progressive improvement' in relations with the United States and the Soviet Union.[40] In the first half of 1990, the great concern about developments in Germany was that they might disrupt the delicate process of running down the East-West strategic confrontation which had been under way for half a decade, and which was now facing the crucial test of settling a conventional arms agreement which would transform the balance of forces in Europe to the Soviet Union's disadvantage. The Soviet Union had already committed itself to accelerating the process of improvement in East-West political-military relations by embarking on its new strategy in Eastern Europe: in August 1989 Gorbachev was informing the Supreme Soviet about the decision of the Warsaw Pact Political Colsultative Committee to transform the alliance into a political-military institution: this would be the first step on the path to eventual dissolution of NATO and the Warsaw Pact, in the framework of the CSCE. In the meanwhile, he continued, relations between the blocs would be constructed on an increasingly non-confrontational basis.[41] The process was to be encouraged by such steps as the launching of inter-alliance discussions on military doctrine in Vienna in January 1990.

But it was important to maintain the correct sequence of events. The powerful pressures for German unification threatened, as Soviet spokesmen repeatedly complained, to upset the whole framework within which the intricate arms control calculations were being carried out. In autumn 1989 Soviet officials had whetted Western interest in Finlandization/ Austrianization scenarios by hinting that countries like Hungary and Czechoslovakia would be free, if they insisted, to leave the Warsaw Pact.[42] But this was undoubtedly envisaged as happening in a world in which deep arms reductions and a new European settlement had already been achieved and in which NATO too was melting away. Now the Soviet Union was faced with the prospect not only of losing its own 'allies' but of being forced to withdraw by far the largest part of its garrison in Eastern Europe, namely the element located in the GDR, while confronting a still heavily armed NATO which contained a very large and well-equipped united German army.

Since there was no future in trying to preserve the Warsaw Pact by force, or trying to keep Soviet troops in East German territory against the wishes of the government, Moscow adopted a two-pronged strategy. On the one hand, it tried to slow up the talks on Conventional Forces in Europe (CFE), demanding a higher proportion for itself of 'Warsaw Pact' military equipment totals, and on the other it tried to speed up the pan-European institution-building processes which it saw as necessary prerequisites for concessions on Germany.[43] Talking with the British Foreign Secretary in April 1990, Shevardnadze spoke of the need to 'synchronize' the German reunification with a positive evolution of the all-European process, and the formation of a fundamentally new European security structure which would replace the blocs. This kind of statement was frequently accompanied by critical remarks about NATO, such as the one made by Gorbachev in his *Time* interview in May: 'For us it is a symbol of the past, a dangerous and confrontational past. And we will never agree to entrust it with a leading role in building a new Europe.'[44]

There were indications, however, that the Soviet position in private negotiations was more flexible, and the outlines of a 'Germany in NATO' package began to emerge in the run up to the May-June 1990 Washington summit meeting. The NATO alliance would not fade away or dissolve itself into a new collective security system, but it would establish a new relationship with the Warsaw Pact (or to be more accurate, in prospect, with its individual members and ex-members). Germany would not be demilitarized or neutralized, and American troops would not (unlike Soviet forces) be withdrawn entirely from its territory, but German forces, and other NATO forces in Germany, would be heavily reduced in the aftermath of a CFE-I agreement. The CSCE would be substantially strengthened and would acquire new, permanent agencies.[45]

This markedly asymmetrical outcome, which left the Soviet Union without its toehold in Germany, and indeed facing a relatively much stronger alliance, was rendered palatable by the sense that a process had been put in train during which NATO would inevitably shrink in importance and pan-European security structures would grow in importance. There were also the concrete benefits promised by a new relationship with Germany. Of course, Shevardnadze's statement to the 28th Party Congress in July 1990 that 'major steps had been taken to meet the Soviet Union half way' was arithmetically inexact. As he also hinted, his government had little option but to accept the best offer it could get.[46] On the other hand, the change in position represented by NATO's London Declaration of July 1990 was a very radical one, with its admission that the Soviet Union was no longer an adversary, with its undertaking to reduce and restructure allied forces and nuclear weapons, and with its support for reinforcing the CSCE (a potentially rival institution). The alliance did not offer voluntarily to dissolve itself, but it did set out on a transformation to something much less threatening. As a result, while few expect the CSCE to 'replace' NATO and the Warsaw Pact in the near future, Gorbachev's vision of a unified European security structure on the continent no longer looks quite as utopian and as distant as it did before the end of 1989. In this sense, the demolition of the Berlin Wall has helped to force ahead the construction of a European house in the security field further than anyone might have expected.

A New Relationship with Europe

The Soviet approach to building links with European institutions can best be described as Western-focused institutional eclecticism. When in 1987 he referred, in his book *Perestroika*, to the unique expertise which had been built up in Europe in matters of international cooperation and integration, Gorbachev implied that both parts of the continent had made comparable contributions. By 1989, however, the experience of the CMEA in 'planned economic integration' was being written off in Moscow as a virtually total loss. The only salvation for the organization was seen in a restructuring along Western 'Common Market' lines. The European Community, by contrast, was regarded with the greatest admiration in Soviet reformist circles. It was widely assumed that it would inevitably form the nodal point of European economic integration.[47]

Shevardnadze acknowledged this quite frankly, albeit rather tortuously, in January 1990, a few weeks after signing a comprehensive trade and cooperation agreement in Brussels on behalf of the Soviet Union:

> The new political thinking could not exclude from its field of vision the objective prerequisites for economic integration and the political structures that have arisen on that basis, which have spread across the continent in waves and which in a number of cases exert a pull to rapprochement.

His recent visits to Brussels, the Soviet Foreign Minister said, had made him confident that a united Europe could indeed be built, and he commented that the Soviet-EC relationship would play a central part in the project. Here and elsewhere Shevardnadze tied together the proposals for a European 'confederation' centred on the Community, made by Mitterrand and Eyskens, with Gorbachev's vision of a common European house saying that 'they are in tune with this idea and have obviously originated under its influence'. He also tied it to the CSCE framework, pointing out that 'here the main thing is the firm linkage with Helsinki, which the Soviet Union sees as a stabilizing and unifying factor'.[48]

The Council of Europe had also begun to play an important part in the Soviet plan for an interlocking of institutions on the continent. It was at the Council in Strasbourg on 6 July 1989 that Gorbachev chose to deliver the fullest statement to date of his government's European policy. The Soviet Union had been granted guest status, and, he indicated, would pursue a policy of intensifying collaboration.[49] Subsequently Shevardnadze set out the Soviet policy more explicitly. A common European political space, he argued, cannot be created on the move. It must be developed by stages, utilizing experience and structures already accumulated. The Council of Europe could become a 'Common European Forum', while its parliamentary assembly and its twice-yearly Foreign Ministers' meetings could become pan-European institutions in the framework of the CSCE process. Council-sponsored international cooperation at local authority level could be extended to the whole continent. Another important job for the Council of Europe might be to provide the basis for the formation of a "European legal space" - a legal framework for the common European house. For the Soviet Union's part, continued Shevardnadze, it was already making preparations to adhere to several of the Council's conventions - on conservation, international legal information, trans-frontier television, disaster relief and culture. Indeed, Moscow had set as its goal to join as a full member the European Convention on Human Rights and the Council itself.[50] In the course of 1990 it began to look more and more likely that Soviet ambitions to join formally in this dimension of European institution-building would be fulfilled.

If Moscow was calculating that it would be easier to build an all-European network by avoiding too much concentration on bodies which already enjoyed a large degree of bargaining power in the political and economic market such as the European Community, then the experience with the Council of Europe certainly justified its eclectic strategy. The Soviet Union also successfully aroused West European interests in broader cooperation in the fields of energy exploitation and environmental protection. In the summer of 1990 the Dutch Prime Minister proposed to the European Council the establishment of European energy community, which would focus Western investment in the modernization of Soviet energy extraction facilities and the development of infrastructure, involving both private and government-supplied capital.[51] On 19 January 1990 Gorbachev offered to participate from the start in pan-European environmental protection measures. By June the Soviet Union was collaborating with the EC's new European Environment Agency in compiling a register of pollution problems across the continent.[52]

The penalty of such a pragmatic approach to pan-European construction is that the outcome risks becoming untidy. It rapidly became clear, for example, that among the members of the CSCE the United States would be extremely unlikely to accept the subordination of its laws to higher authority which would be implied by joining the Council of Europe. One solution proposed was that the United States and Canada might join as associate members, which would allow them to participate in the Council's parliamentary activities. Subsequently it appeared that the Assembly of Europe which was to meet under the aegis of the CSCE would use Council of Europe facilities in Strasbourg but would be institutionally distinct from it. The Soviet Union's general strategy seemed to be to use the CSCE structure in three different ways. The first was as an organizational umbrella. In May 1990, for example, the Soviet Foreign Minister gave it the ambitious task of coordinating the work of the Council of Europe, the European Community, the United Nations Economic Commission for Europe, the CMEA, the European Bank for Reconstruction and Development (EBRD), the OECD, EFTA, the Nordic Council, *et al*.[53] And indeed, the constant cycle of meetings on security issues, economic cooperation, civil rights, environmental protection and so on, which occurred under the CSCE banner during 1989 and 1990, must have made a real contribution to the smoother running of European affairs. The second was a specialized forum, and seedbed for new institutions, dealing with security matters. The third was as a political lightning conductor, a means of ensuring that the United States does not feel excluded, or perhaps more importantly, that the West Europeans do not feel that the United States is being excluded. The centrality of the European Community, however, and its distinctness from 'Atlantic' institutions mean that this is a difficult line for the Soviet Union to pursue.

One type of Soviet diplomatic activity in Europe which has a sizeable potential for disrupting the delicate balance between Moscow, Washington and the West European capitals is participation in pan-European foreign policy cooperation. On 26 September 1990, on the Soviet initiative, it launched with the European Community what was described in *Izvestiya* as a 'Euro-Soviet initiative', a joint declaration condemning Iraq's hostage-taking policy.[54] This was innocuous enough, but there was also a pledge from the two sides to cooperate in solving other Middle East conflicts, such as the Arab-Israeli dispute and the war in Lebanon. The Soviet Union publicly promised to lend its support to Italian proposals for a Euro-Arab meeting on the Gulf crisis. In Spain one month later, this démarche provided Gorbachev with the opportunity to restate his ideas about 'Europe's mission in the world process...organic to our concept of a common European house. The common European house, in his conception, should serve as a starting point for the 'construction of similar structures in other parts of the world', most immediately in the Mediterranean and the Pacific regions, and should contribute to the building of a new, more just and more peaceful international order.[55]

It is noticeable that Soviet Foreign Ministry statements about the Gulf initiative were cautiously phrased and accompanied by strong expressions of commitment to cooperation with the United States. There is no doubt, of course, that mistrust of the United States lies not far below the surface in parts of the Soviet foreign policy community. There are those who express the hope that the old world will be able to act more definitely and confidently for itself in international affairs. There are those who register approval of Europeanist as opposed to Atlanticist tendencies in the debate going on about the future of NATO.[56] But the lesson of the first transition of the common European house concept has been learned: the United States may in the past have been a volatile and unreliable partner, the superpower dimension of international affairs may be declining in significance, but good relations with Washington are for the foreseeable future a *sine qua non* if any solid progress is to be made in Soviet-European relations. The Soviet Union is also dependent on American goodwill for achieving disengagement from regional conflicts, reaching a new settlement in the Pacific region, and building closer relations with international institutions such as the IMF and the GATT. During the second transition, moreover, confidence appears to have grown in Moscow that a once-and-for-all shift for the better had occurred in relations with the United States. The dismantling of the Soviet sphere of influence in Eastern Europe, the establishment of which played such a large part in igniting the post-Second World War confrontation, turned out to be the final necessary condition for bringing the Cold War to an end. Thus it can be expected that in due course Americans and West Europeans will be able to accept with less alarm the prospect of a closer Soviet relationship with the kind of European institutions which do not include the United States on a balancing basis. But before this can be brought about the Soviet Union itself must change.

TRANSITION III: ACCEPTANCE OF A EUROPEANIZED SOVIET UNION

The three transitions in Soviet understanding of the common European house described in this chapter are not strictly separated in time. They are each more salient at particular periods, but they overlap and interact with each other. Certainly the idea that the breaking down of barriers in Europe would entail a transformation of Soviet society was present from the start of Gorbachev's administration in 1985. In so far as the word 'Europe' was used almost as a synonym for the West, the turn to Europe sent a powerful positive message to Gorbachev's cosmopolitan supporters among the intelligentsia and a negative one to his dogmatic and nationalistic opponents in the party and state bureaucracies. In policy terms it signified a switch of priorities from the goal of military strength for purposes of global confrontation to the goal of prosperity by means of regional cooperation. But the Europeanization of the Soviet Union was first envisaged as a gradual and partial matter. There would continue to be two systems which would continue to compete with each other even if by peaceful means. The language of East-West relations in Europe was the language of parity and balance. By 1989, as the second transition gathered pace, the notion of balance faded away: the Soviet Union was now pictured as a 'partner' in the European process, especially with Germany, the most powerful nation in the western half of the continent. In the following year it was the language of dependence which began to make itself heard, as Europe was ready to compensate for the Soviet regime its shrinking economic capacity, vanishing confidence and dwindling political authority.

In the summer of 1990 Gorbachev was reported to have made a direct appeal through diplomatic channels to German and European Community leaders for financial help. The West German government immediately guaranteed a five-billion DM loan to Moscow, and in cooperation with the French President began to push for large-scale emergency economic aid to Moscow from the European Community. The same issue was discussed at the Group of Seven in Houston on 11 July 1990. Reports were commissioned by both bodies into the feasibility of the project. In October and November 1990, Gorbachev visited France, Spain and Italy, openly soliciting aid, in order to ensure the success of the 'transition to a market economy' which, he assured his hosts, would soon be under way in the Soviet Union.[57] By the end of November all the major West European states (and even Luxembourg) had made interim offers of financial assistance.

The prospect that the forthcoming IMF-coordinated report on possibilities for aid would set strict conditions requiring financial discipline and other measures of economic stabilization was clearly not at all unwelcome to reformist elements in and around the Soviet government, who were beginning to despair as the political capacity of leadership to take the harsh steps needed to deal with the economic crisis was eroded by the effects of indecision and by the deteriorating economic conditions themselves. The West's consistent support for Soviet authority in the face of separatist tendencies was also widely publicized by the central government and its supporters in the press. In Spain in October 1990, Gorbachev noted that Western leaders wanted the Soviet Union to be stronger and to preserve its integrity. Such solidarity sends a good lesson, he declared, to 'hotheads' at home. How could the inhabitants of the Soviet Union hope to be regarded as serious participants in a wider European integration process, it was asked, if they could not even maintain a single market within the frontiers of their own state?[58]

But the leadership no longer had a monopoly on interpretation. The Europeanization of the Soviet Union had already gone far enough by 1990 to make the future shape of Europe and the country's role in it a matter for fierce debate. 'We wish to live in a common European house', declared a speaker at a Sajudis rally in Vilnius on 10 January 1990, 'not in the basement of an empire under the supervision of the KGB.'[59] Senior military commanders, on the other hand, insisted on drawing attention to the fact that the much-vaunted European house was still bristling with weaponry, much of it pointing at the Soviet Union.[60] 'Patriots' like Aleksandr Prokhanov criticized Gorbachev for 'sentimentally theorising about a Common European House' while the structure of the Soviet influence in Eastern Europe fell apart and Germany grew in power.[61] Throughout the first half of 1990, and especially at the congresses of Russian and Soviet communist parties in June and July, the government faced a barrage of criticism of its European policies, couched in power-political terms, from conservatives who aimed to derail the process of internal and external liberalization. Events, however, seemed to favour the radical reformers. As old certainties crumbled, the urge to look to the West for substitute values, for norms and models became stronger.

Europeanist members of the government such as Shevardnadze made a habit of commenting on how reforms in the Soviet Union, as well as the changes in Eastern Europe, played an essential part in encouraging pan-European rapprochement. In the writings of academic specialists and journalists the case was put more boldly. In spring 1989, two foreign affairs experts argued in the journal *Kommunist* that the Soviet Union and the East European states would have to become much more like the West European ones if they were to cooperate with them and be competitive. They would have to reduce the role of national economic planning, and to increase supranational regulation on the one hand, and micro-economic integration on the other, with firms operating independently on an open market: 'In conditions of healthy economic relations, the illusion of traditionally understood equality gives way to acknowledgement of only one right to preeminence - the right resting on greater efficiency of production.'[62] Towards the end of 1990, even TASS releases were implying the need to accept not just Bush's Europe without walls, but Thatcher's Europe of democracy, the rule of law, and free enterprise. The CSCE November summit would lay the groundwork for the future common European house, it was stated, but this house could not be constructed without another major foundation - 'democracies based on market economy...throughout the continent'.[63]

As the sense of urgency behind the common European house project increased, with accelerating economic decline in the Soviet Union, with continuing progress towards integration in the West, and with special arrangements being planned for the Central-East European states, the debate became sharper. In an article published in the Soviet journal *International Affairs* in June 1990, Sergei Smolnikov wrote: 'The world economic and technological express is hurtling into the third millennium. The doors of one of its carriages - Western Europe - are open for us.'[64] The keys to achieving the European 'compatability' necessary to get on board were identified as rapid progress in marketization, democratization and building law-abiding and legitimate state structures. Violence and repressive measures against those national groups aspiring to separation from the Soviet Union should be avoided at all costs. If their activities led to an expansion of the numbers of participants in the CSCE process, so be it. A disaggregated Soviet Union might even create better circumstances for 'more solid involvement in the fabric of European inter-state relations'.[65]

4. THE FUTURE OF THE COMMON EUROPEAN HOUSE

It is the thesis of this chapter that the Soviet concept of the common European house has changed so much since its first appearance a decade ago that little remains of the original notion. It began as a characteristic instrument of Stalinist and neo-Stalinist foreign policy, a slogan designed to appeal to anti-NATO elements in Western Europe, not something which, barring revolutionary changes, had much prospect of being implemented in the foreseeable future. Gradually it evolved into a set of more modest proposals targeted at West European governments, aimed at strengthening pan-European co-operation inside the existing framework of international relations. Finally, it began to embrace radical adaptations in Eastern Europe and in the Soviet Union itself, intended to ensure compatability with Western standards.

The elevated language in which the campaign for a common European house has been couched is reminiscent of traditional Soviet public diplomacy, but it also reflects, as far as can be ascertained, genuine changes in leadership thinking in Moscow about the nature of international relations, and about the real possibility of building a new peaceful order. It plays a role, too, in easing the ideological transition away from Leninism, by focusing attention on high, ethical 'all-human' values. Finally, it suits the purpose of amplifying the supposed bonds of culture and tradition which make Russia un-equivocally 'European'.

Because of the way it was combined with other instruments of Soviet policy, the common European house campaign was remarkably successful in the second half of the 1980s, especially if measured against realistic expectations rather than against the millenarian goals set by Gorbachev in some of his statements. But obstacles lie ahead. It is easier, for instance, to announce the end of the Cold War than to remove all traces of it in people's thinking, especially when huge numbers of weapons are still deployed, capable of obliterating the notional 'enemy' several times over. It will take many years, even in the best case, to dismantle these forces, and to reorientate the huge military-industrial infrastructure which supports them.

Policy-makers in Western Europe are made particularly cautious by the uncertainty which surrounds the political future of the Soviet Union. As the political authority of the central power continues to wane, nationalist and separatist

movements become more intransigent, and supplies of consumer goods become more and more erratic, there is little
confidence that the Soviet state is capable of pushing through
painful measures required for successful market reforms or of
promoting agreement on a new settlement among national
groups. Yet, both these steps are essential for political stability,
in the long, and increasingly, it seems, in the short term.
Analysts such as Pierre Hassner consider that Russia is most
likely to pass through another 'time of troubles' before it re-
covers its political equilibrium, and becomes able to participate
reliably in any joint European ventures.[66]

It will be difficult for the Soviet Union to achieve the
economic compatability and competitiveness with the rest of
Europe which reformists recognize as such a vital prerequisite
for entry into a single market. This is partly because of special
cultural features. The population has had virtually no experience of anything other than a centralized state-run economy, and is generally considered to be reluctant to accept free
pricing, bigger wage differentials, unemployment, and in
general the uncertainties associated with a market economy.[67]
Suspicions about the intentions of foreign capitalists have by no
means vanished among the people. A significant part of the
Soviet intelligentsia remains hostile to alien 'market' values. In
most sectors levels of labour productivity, management and
quality are very low. The view is expressed by some Soviet
writers that overenthusiastic adoption of Western models is
more likely to lead to 'Latin Americanization' of the Soviet
Union than to rapid incorporation with the 'First World'.[68]
While the states of Central-Eastern Europe will themselves
remain tied to Soviet markets for their exports for some time
for the same reason, it seems likely that several of them will
succeed in the next decade in reorientating their trade
significantly to Western Europe. The Soviet Union would thus
find itself more and more distanced from the European economy rather than becoming more a part of it.

A serious blow would be struck to the chances of
economic and political rapprochement in Europe if inflamed
national feeling were to grow into serious ethnic and border
conflicts in Eastern Europe and in the western parts of the
Soviet Union. Quite apart from the direct effects on business

confidence, such events would alter the overall political climate, slowing or reversing the current trend to détente, trust and cooperation. In the worst case they could even provoke a deterioration in relations among the larger powers in the region, and between the Soviet Union and the United States.

Partly because of the considerations outlined above, and partly simply because the Soviet Union is so large, there is a strong tendency in the West to assign it to the outermost of the European 'concentric circles', to regard it more as an outhouse or as an inconvenient, crumbling adjoining property than as part of the future European house itself. Some envisage a geopolitically determined bipolarity continuing in Europe for the foreseeable future, with its nodes in Brussels and Moscow.[69] Such a view is often associated with what Ole Waever calls a 'French' conception of Europe, which reserves the key role for an increasingly state-like, consolidated European Community.[70]

Waever contrasts with this a Soviet conception (mainly built around participation in pan-European security institutions) and a German conception, centring on a general erosion of political boundaries, and freedom to expand eastwards in an economic and cultural sense. He argues convincingly that in 1990, by carefully allowing France and the Soviet Union a large part of what they wanted, the Germans managed to create a Europe of the kind they wanted, one in which, in particular, the eastern boundary would not be sharply drawn. This points to a powerful factor which will tend to favour Soviet inclusion in Europe, namely German commitment to the idea. Waever might possibly have sketched a rather fuller picture of the Soviet ideal Europe, which indeed overlaps to a large extent with the German one, in so far as a central element is the deepening of economic interaction. The evolving of a Soviet-German special relationship is a vivid political reflection of the two states' shared interests.[71]

Moreover, what is true for Germany is true to a greater or lesser extent for the other West European states. In the first place, the Soviet Union is an immensely rich source of fuel, raw materials and cheap labour, some of it highly educated. It represents a huge potential market, and a 'reserve' in global economic competition. Given the appropriate political conditions, it would be a clear priority target for investment in a number of sectors. In the second place, the arguments about political uncertainty and military danger can be turned on their head: the potential for doing damage embodied in the Soviet Union's size, location, explosive ethnic composition, and high level of armaments can be used to support the idea that a determined effort should be made to take the political and economic steps likely to encourage stability. Such attitudes are likely to strengthen as Western publics become accustomed to perceiving the Soviet Union less as an enemy, and more as a supplicant. This kind of strategy would inevitably involve an agreement in the European Community to accord some special status to the country, similar to the association which is being negotiated for Poland, Hungary and Czechoslovakia.[72]

It would be foolish in such a complicated situation to make confident predictions about the future shape of any common European house. What is clear is that there are a whole range of possible outcomes, which will be determined by events both inside the Soviet Union, or whatever succeeds it, and far outside its borders. It would certainly be quite unrealistic to expect, for instance, that the Soviet concept of the common European house, which has already undergone a series of transitions, and is now the subject of fierce debate between rival political tendencies, will remain unchanged. It seems quite possible, for example, that a sovereign Russian republic, with nationalist elements in its legitimating doctrine, would tend to proclaim a rather less determinedly internationalist approach to European affairs.[73] As the events of January 1991 showed, nationalism is one of the factors most likely to trigger off authoritarian reflexes among the Soviet leadership. In conditions of continuing economic decline and disillusion with democratic institutions, a crackdown feeding on the desire for order, and on feelings of national humiliation on the part of Russians, could meet with widespread public support. Such a turn of events would automatically increase the political weight of the military and internal security forces and their allies in the bureaucracy, all of whom tend to share a mistrustful view of the West.

Be that as it may, the experience of the last five years in

Soviet writing and speaking about European policy reflects an epochal shift in Russia's approach to its neighbours in Europe. Supposedly permanent geopolitical factors and established ways of thought were overridden. Social, cultural and political changes inside the Soviet Union increased the relative size and influentiality of groups predisposed to see 'Europe' as a model, rather than as a threat. Simultaneously, changes in the nature of international relations, of the kind commonly referred to in the West as part of the onset of 'complex interdependence', led to a relative decline in the effectiveness of power-political instruments, particularly in Europe.[74] These two kinds of change crystallized in the transformation of perceptions among a receptive group of Soviet political leaders. Circumstances favoured the success of the new conciliatory policy which they devised, and the process of 'learning' spread rapidly throughout Europe and throughout Soviet society. It would be absurd to look forward to a future of unending harmony in relations between Russia and the rest of Europe, but there are some grounds for hope that the old fears and nightmares which have characterized these relations for so long will never again regain their previous force.

NOTES

1.   Gorbachev in Spain in October 1990 (*Pravda*, 26 October 1990 and *Soviet News*, 31 October 1990).
2.   C. A. Binns, 'From USE to EEC: the Soviet Analysis of European Integration under Capitalism', *Soviet Studies*, vol. 30, no. 2, April 1978, p. 238.
3.   See W. Zimmermann, *Soviet Perspectives on International Relations* (Princeton: Princeton University Press, 1969) and A. Lynch, *The Soviet Study of International Relations* (Cambridge: Cambridge University Press, 1987).
4.   See N. Malcolm, 'Foreign Affairs Specialists and Decision Makers' in D. Lane (ed.), *Elites and Political Power in the USSR* (Aldershot: Edward Elgar, 1988), pp. 205-6.
5.   Timo Vihavainen commented in 1989: 'The mainstream of Soviet high culture is at the moment more genuinely pro-Western than it has been since the revolution.': see T. Vihavainen, 'Russia and Europe: The Historiographic Aspect' in V. Harle and J. Iivonen (eds), *Gorbachev and Europe*. (London: Frances Pinter, 1990), p. 20.

6. T. Hasegawa and A. Pravda (eds), *Perestroika: Soviet Domestic and Foreign Policies* (London: Sage/RIIA, 1990); O. Nørgaard, 'New Political Thinking East and West: a Comparative Perspective' in Harle and Iivonen, op. cit., pp. 63-70; and C. F. Herman *et al.*, *New Directions in the Study of Foreign Policy* (London: Allen & Unwin, 1987).
7. *Pravda*, 8 October 1985.
8. H. Adomeit, 'The Impact of Perestroika on Soviet European Policy' in Hasegawa and Pravda, op. cit., and *Pravda*, 24 November 1981.
9. *Pravda*, 13 November 1985; Gorbachev's comments are cited in C. Schmidt-Häuer, *Gorbachev: The Path to Power* (London: Pan, 1986), p. 144.
10. A. Vtorov and Yu. Karelov, 'The Dynamic European Policy of the USSR', *International Affairs* (Moscow), no. 6, 1986, p. 105.
11. *Politicheskii doklad TsK KPSS XXVII S"ezdu Kommunisticheskoi Partii Sovetskogo Soyuza* (Moscow: Politizdat, 1986), p. 19. See also Gorbachev's speech as reported in *Pravda*, 12 December 1984.
12. *Izvestiya*, 25 September 1985.
13. Yu. Karelov, 'USSR-Western Europe: Guidelines of Cooperation', *International Affairs* (Moscow), no. 11, 1985, p. 25; Vtorov and Karelov, op. cit., p. 100; *Pravda*, 1 August 1986 and Gorbachev in *Pravda*, 8 July 1986.
14. See N. Malcolm, *Soviet Policy Perspectives on Western Europe* (London: Routledge/RIIA, 1989), pp. 35-77.
15. M. Gorbachev, *Perestroika: New Thinking for our Country and the World* (London: Collins, 1987), pp. 208-209; see also pp. 190-207.
16. Pierre Hassner describes the Soviet Union as an 'objective Finlandizer' in Europe. (P. Hassner, 'Europe between the United States and the Soviet Union', *Government and Opposition*, vol. 21, no. 1, p. 23)
17. See the report, for example, in *Pravda*, 8 July 1987; see also the report of Gorbachev's speech in Yugoslavia in *Soviet News*, 23 March 1988.
18. *Soviet News*, 23 March 1988.
19. *Soviet News*, 17 February 1988.
20. *Soviet News*, 23 July 1986.
21. Reprinted in *Soviet News*, 27 May 1987.
22. *Pravda*, 7 June 1989.
23. K. Dawisha, *Eastern Europe, Gorbachev and Reform: The Great Challenge* (Cambridge: Cambridge University Press, 1990), chapter 7 and M. MccGwire, *Perestroika and Soviet National Security* (Washington: Brookings Institution, 1991), pp. 356-63.
24. *Soviet News*, 6 July 1988.
25. *Pravda*, 7 July 1989.
26. W. Roberts, 'A New Status for Eastern Europe', *The World Today*, October 1989, p. 165; *The Independent*, 26 October 1989.
27. *Izvestiya*, 15 June 1989; H. Adomeit, 'Gorbachev and German Unification: Revision of Thinking, Realignment of Power', *Problems of Communism*, vol. XXXIX, no. 4, July-August 1990, p. 5.
28. *The Independent*, 26 October 1989.
29. *Vestnik*, August 1990, p. 22. Adomeit, op. cit., makes a strong case for Soviet foresight.

30. At his news conference with Bush in Malta on 4 December 1989 (*Soviet News*, 6 December 1989).
31. *Soviet News*, 14 February 1990.
32. *The Independent*, 7 March 1990; *Pravda*, 18 July 1990.
33. Compare the comment by Gely Batenin in spring 1990, saying that a united Germany's entry to NATO was the optimal solution (*Guardian*, 5 May 1990), with Ligachev's speech at the Central Committee Plenum in February 1990, where he warned of the 'danger of accelerated unification', and of the threat of 'a new Munich' (*The Times*, 9 February 1990).
34. *Soviet News*, 10 October 1990.
35. See Shevardnadze's characteristic comment in *Izvestiya*, 20 February 1990, about the danger of the changes in Germany running ahead of the process of pan-European integration.
36. *Soviet News*, 4 July 1990. Gorbachev remarked at the Bonn treaty-signing ceremony in November 1990: 'Our concord and cooperation make up parts of the load-sharing structures of the Common European House'. (*Soviet News*, 14 November 1990)
37. See the numerous joint German-Soviet statements about the building of the common European house, for example the one issued by President Gorbachev and Foreign Minister Genscher on 10 February 1990 (*Summary of World Broadcast* [SWB], SU/0687, p. A1/11, 10 February 1990).
38. Valentin Falin in *Pravda*, 20 August 1990. This contrasts strongly with earlier concerns expressed by Falin about German revanchism, in 'Po povodu novykh "istoricheskikh debatov"', *Mirovaya ekonomika i mezhdunardonye otnosheniya* (MEMO), no. 12, 1987, pp. 73-84. See also V. Zhurkin in *Izvestiya*, 26 May 1990; T. Kolesnichenko in *Pravda*, 20 July 1990; M. Maksimova, 'Raskryt potentsial sotrudnichestvo', *MEMO*, no. 10, 1988, pp. 61-6, and N. Portugalov in *Bild am Sonntag*, 16 September 1990, on the future global mission of the German state.
39. S. Smolnikov, 'Novaya logika evropeiskogo razvitiya', *MEMO*, no. 6, 1990, p. 28.
40. *Soviet News*, 26 September 1990.
41. *Soviet News*, 9 August 1989. Compare Shevardnadze in *Soviet News*, 20 December 1989.
42. N. Shishlin in *The Independent*, 30 October 1989; E. Primakov in *Guardian*, 2 November 1989 and General Akhromeev, reported in W. Roberts, 'A New Status for Eastern Europe'. Valentin Falin denied that this was government policy (*The Independent*, 30 October 1989).
43. *International Herald Tribune*, 28 March 1990.
44. Shevardnadze in *Soviet News*, 18 April 1990 and Gorbachev in *Soviet News*, 30 May 1990. See also Gorbachev's remarks to Mitterrand on 26 May 1990 (*Soviet News*, 30 May 1990).
45. See Shevardnadze's article in *Izvestiya*, 30 May 1990 and 'The London Declaration on a Transformed North Atlantic Alliance' (Brussels: NATO Information Service, 1990).
46. *Vestnik*, August 1990, p. 26. See also the part of Shevardnadze's speech, reported on p. 24, where he asks hostile delegates to imagine

the consequences of trying to stop German unification by force.
47. H. Timmermann, 'The Soviet Union and Western Europe: Conceptual Change and Political Reorientation' in Harle and Iivonen, op. cit., pp. 103-29 and N. Malcolm, op. cit., chapter 3.
48. *Izvestiya*, 19 January 1990 and Shevardnadze's interview for *Vecherni Noviny* (Sofia), 30 January 1990, reported in *SWB*, SU/0677, A1/2, 1 February 1990. Shevardnadze was still making proposals around this time for trilateral cooperation to establish a "European Economic Space" between EC, EFTA and the CMEA (*Soviet News*, 20 December 1989; statement of 18 December 1989), but the presence of CMEA viability was becoming more and more difficult to keep up.
49. *Pravda*, 7 July 1989.
50. Shevardnadze in *Moscow News*, 4 March 1990, p. 26.
51. *The Financial Times*, 24 October 1990.
52. See Gorbachev's speech to the Global Forum for Environment and Development in Moscow (*Pravda*, 20 January 1990); see also *Observer*, 17 June 1990.
53. *Izvestiya*, 30 May 1990.
54. R. Weitz, 'The Gulf Conflict and the USSR's Changing International Position', *Radio Liberty Report on the USSR*, vol. 2, no. 41, 1990, p. 5; TASS release, 15 September 1990, reprinted in *FBIS*, 17 September 1990; *Izvestiya*, 17 September 1990.
55. Gorbachev's address to the Spanish Parliament on 27 October 1990 (*Soviet News*, 31 October 1990); Gorbachev's interview with *El Pais*, 26 October 1990, reprinted in *Soviet News*, 31 October 1990.
56. For an example of the former, see N. Pavlov (from the Soviet Diplomatic Academy), 'Germanskii vopros i "obshcheevropeiskij dom"', *MEMO*, no. 6, 1990, p. 6; and of the latter, N. Afanasevsky (Soviet Ambassador to Belgium and NATO), reported in a TASS release on 12 October 1990, reprinted in APN, *Defence and Diplomacy Update*, 17 October 1990.
57. See, for example, Gorbachev's interview in *El Pais*, 31 October 1990.
58. ibid., see, too, the reports of Delors' visit to Moscow in the summer of 1990 (for example in *Soviet News*, 25 July 1990).
59. Radio Vilnius in Lithuanian, 10 January 1990, reported in *SWB* SU/066 B/1, 12 January 1990.
60. General S. G. Kochemasov, chief of the Main Staff of the Strategic Rocket Forces, in *Pravda*, 21 February 1990.
61. *Sunday Correspondent*, 28 January 1990.
62. V. Baranovsky and V. Zuev, 'Put k "obshcheevropeiskomy domu": ekonomicheskie aspekty', *Kommunist*, no. 8, 1989, pp. 113-114.
63. *Soviet News*, 7 November 1990. Cf. Margaret Thatcher's proposal in *The Sunday Times*, 15 April 1990.
64. S. Smolnikov, 'The Soviet Economy's Eurovector', *International Affairs* (Moscow), no. 8, 1990, p. 100. See also his above mentioned article in *MEMO*, no. 6, 1990, pp. 18-29.
65. V. Baranovsky, 'Evropa: formirovanie novoj mezhdunarodno-politicheskoj sistemy', *MEMO*, no. 9, 1990, p. 11.
66. P. Hassner, 'Europe Beyond Partition and Unity: Disintegration or Reconstitution', *International Affairs* (London), vol. 66, no. 3, July

1990, pp. 461-75.
67. A. Åslund, *Gorbachev's Struggle for Economic Reform* (London: Frances Pinter, 1989), pp. 167-73 and J. Rollo *et al.*, *The New Eastern Europe: Western Responses* (London: Frances Pinter, 1990), chapter 5. Public opinion polls in 1990 reflected some increase in preference for a market economy, but this was probably largely in reaction to the failures of the existing modified centralism.
68. See, for example, 'Maidan-90. Gostinii dvor "Mezhdunarodnoi zhizni"', *Mezhdunarodnaya zhizn*, no. 9, 1990, pp. 119-34. This contribution illustrates a counter-tendency (albeit still a weak one) against 'Europeanism' in the Soviet intelligentsia.
69. Hassner, op. cit.
70. O. Waever, 'Three Competing Europes: German, French, Russian', *International Affairs* (London), vol. 66, no. 3, July 1990, pp. 473-94.
71. A hopeful forecast for the future course of German-Soviet relations is given by Adomeit, op. cit., pp. 22-3.
72. P. Ludlow, 'The EC and Europe's Political Architecture', *Paper to the Annual Conference of the Centre for European Political Studies*, Brussels, 14-16 November 1990.
73. See, for example, A. Kortunov, 'Russia Should Take a Lesson from de Gaulle', *Moscow News* (London), no. 15, 1990, 1/13 September 1990.
74. R. Keohane and J. Nye, *Power and Interdependence: World Politics in Transition*, (Boston: Little and Brown, 1986), chapters 2 and 3.

Part II

SECURITY ISSUES

4 BASIC CONCEPTS OF GORBACHEV'S NEW SECURITY THINKING

Gerhard Wettig

1. INCIPIENT CHANGE IN THE SOVIET UNION'S SECURITY RELATIONS

When Gorbachev took power in March 1985, Soviet relations with the outside world were at an impasse. The Kremlin's hypertrophical arms buildup had become ruinous, particularly in view of the fact that the state-administrated economy was malfunctioning anyway. The Soviet attempt to capitalize on the only political asset the country had, i.e., a military advantage vis-a-vis NATO, had failed. Not only had the effort to achieve military superiority and thereby a political breakthrough been frustrated, the missile controversy had also mobilized new political and military energies in the West and forced the Soviet Union into an armaments competition that was not only devoid of any hope for success but economically destructive as well. As Soviet critics of this policy have put it later, the pre-Gorbachev leaders had practically become accomplices of those forces in the United States that allegedly had been striving to bring about an arms race which would cause the Soviet Union to break down.

In this situation, it was but natural that the policy-makers in Moscow should be confronted with pressures to open up new avenues to the country's security. As early as the very climax of the missile controversy, two old-type *apparatchiki* had sensed the emerging new climate and responded to it by laying down a line of 'new political thinking'. This was not, to be sure, more than a propaganda slogan;[1] but it did reflect a psychological need, which was to seek more serious expression later. In any case, the term had been coined. It simply waited to be filled with substantive content. Gorbachev, however, for quite a while showed few signs of being a security policy innovator. As for domestic issues, he also began to follow old patterns, simply seeking to do his job more effectively.

The concept of *uskorenie*, i.e., of improving economic performance in the old mould, was paralleled by an attempt to secure a military advantage over NATO more intelligently. For a long time, the key security concept was 'to liberate mankind from nuclear weapons'. The underlying idea was that NATO's cohesion rested on extended nuclear deterrence. If nuclear weaponry was eliminated from the European theatre, as was the object of the campaign, the political basis of the Western alliance would be eliminated. This would make the Soviet Union's conventional military power prevail in Europe and undercut the West European confidence in its being protected by NATO.[2] In the Soviet perception, the Treaty on Elimination of Intermediary-Range Nuclear Forces (INF) of 7 December 1987 was a crucial first step toward depriving NATO of its nuclear base.[3]

The East-West interaction that resulted in the INF Treaty was innovative in character, however. While the denuclearization campaign had a traditionally 'anti-imperialistic' context, the Soviet thinking on relations with the United States and NATO began to change after the Gorbachev-Reagan meeting in Reykjavik in October 1986. Even cooperative tones emerged on occasion. When, in early 1987, the Soviet leader replaced *uskorenie* by a more fundamental revision of the domestic policy line, which was called *perestroika*, he gradually realized that this would inescapably produce implications for security policies. Two formulas were used to express the idea that a new orientation was required: 'reasonable sufficiency' and 'non-offensive defence'. The change of slogans was not matched, however, by new guidelines for their implementation in the political and military spheres. To be sure, the principle of war prevention (which had always been adhered to) was strongly emphasized. But both politicians and military spokesmen continued for some time to call for a capability 'to deter the [Western] aggressor', one that would enable the Soviet forces to 'smash', that is, to 'destroy' him on his own territory in the event of war. In other words, there were no new guidelines that might have clearly changed the Warsaw Pact's planning for offensive warfare.[4]

2. 'NEW THINKING' AS A BODY OF THEORETICAL IDEAS

When Gorbachev espoused *perestroika* in domestic politics, he simultaneously chose to proclaim 'new thinking' as an imperative of foreign policy and international security. Principles of policy-making radically different from those of the past were claimed to be indispensable if impending disaster were to be averted. According to the new thesis, mankind was confronted with the challenge of 'global problems' that required a common effort to solve them. The prospect of a nuclear holocaust was depicted as the crucial danger that had to be faced and overcome. This argument legitimized the ongoing political struggle against NATO's nuclear deterrence as a requirement of human survival. Therefore, Soviet propaganda stressed that all men, irrespective of their class adherence and political creed, would have to join this struggle. Ultimately, not only the public of the NATO countries but equally the Western leaders would have to follow the anti-nuclear recommendation in their best interest (which, after all, was to preserve their physical existence and to ignore the 'class interest' in political survival, if necessary).

This concept was clearly in the old mould of advancing historical progress towards worldwide transition to socialism by putting Western security into jeopardy. But the idea of new thinking also had the potential of inviting conclusions that deviated from previous security postulates. The imperative that the challenge of global problems had to be met could equally be understood to imply that the Soviet Union give up antagonism against the West in order to allow for joint efforts against common challenges such as modern war and constantly growing environmental destruction. For a long time, official comment tended to stress the anti-NATO, the anti-bourgeois 'class', interpretation variant. In the Soviet public, however, *glasnost* increasingly allowed for advocates of East-West commonality to raise their voices and to influence the political climate.

As a political theory, the new thinking was ambivalent also in another respect. It could be understood as a normative philosophy. In fact, its propagandistic claim to introduce an innovation for the sake of the world's redemption could be justified only on this basis. But there was also another version of new thinking according to which it simply implied a change of political methods. The goals to be sought had to remain the same. Given the change of conditions, however, responsive action also had to be changed. It had to be adapted to the new situation that had arisen following the example given by Lenin that one could not stick to old methods which had been useful only under past conditions.

In retrospect, theorizing about new thinking can be viewed as a characteristic of the period from early 1987 to mid-1989,[5] which preceded the subsequent fundamental change of Soviet relations with the outside world. It was only during this period of upheaval that the different ideas under the label of new thinking were practically tested and that they took a clear direction. The meaning of what had been theoretically thought out was concretely determined in the process. What resulted was not mere implementation. More often than not, emerging realities created a dynamism of their own, forcing the Kremlin to adapt itself to new conditions and to accept results that had not originally been intended.

3. THE POINT OF DEPARTURE FOR NEW THINKING

The first case where the Soviet policy-makers had to abandon old ambitions concerned their political and military involvement in the Third World. When, in the 1970s, the Brezhnev leadership had decided to put its stakes into African, Asian, and Latin American regimes with a 'socialist orientation', it had hoped to foster aligned model countries that would be thriving examples of socialism and invite others to follow suit. Thus the Third World would increasingly move from capitalism to socialism and destabilize the political position of the Western powers.

But this expectation did not materialize. While the Soviet Union poured massive resources into the client countries, the beneficiaries underwent progressive impoverishment. The 'states of socialist orientation' became repulsive examples of an apparently obnoxious alignment with the Soviet Union (the counterproductive character of which actually resulted from the takeover of the socialist model), inducing others to choose the Western path of development instead.

Gorbachev decided that this was not the deserved reward for the huge effort made and began to seek ways of gradually getting rid of the commitments in the Third World. In the case of Afghanistan, there was the complicating consideration that the Soviet Union's power position was directly involved and had to be somehow guarded. For this reason, Gorbachev first increased the military commitment hoping that victory could thus be achieved. When, however, the United States responded by making Stinger missiles available to the Mujahedin, it became clear that the war for Afghanistan could not be won, at least not at any reasonable cost. From then on, Gorbachev sought to withdraw from what had become a hopeless military adventure.

It can be argued that the Third World clientele and even Afghanistan subtracted from Soviet power in the world rather than adding to it and that it was therefore power-politically rational to dispense with these commitments. It is clearly different with Eastern Europe, which, since 1945, had been seen by the Soviet policy-makers as a crucial fundament of their power and influence in the world. In particular, the traditional Soviet concept of seeking military security rested on the forward deployment of troops in East Central Europe and on the Warsaw Pact allies' military services being made available to Moscow. It is only on this basis that the Soviet imperative of preventing NATO aggression through the threat of the Western aggressors' destruction on their own soil could be put into practice. Nonetheless, the Kremlin has acceded to the political developments of 1989 and 1990, which have eliminated the basis for the maintenance of such a concept. It is worth noting that, in the whole process, there was no point where Gorbachev had to make a clear choice between the retention of old patterns and acceptance of new ones. Instead, acquiescence to the change was gradual, with the full consequences becoming visible only in the end.

The prime motive for reappraisal of Soviet relations with the East European allies was economic. As early as 1978, the Soviet leadership had commissioned and received a study on how the country fared in CMEA economic dealings compared with the outcome that would result if world market conditions were to apply. The investigation made clear that the Soviet Union was suffering enormous material losses from the CMEA terms of trade. In fact, the conclusion was that it heavily subsidized the East European economies by delivering overly cheap energy and raw materials and getting low-quality, but fully-priced manufactured goods in return. During the Brezhnev era, the Soviet leadership for political reasons had been reluctant to press for a fundamental change in the terms of trades. The East European economies were already experiencing great difficulties. They might break down altogether if they had to undergo further strain. The Soviet interest in keeping Eastern Europe and its domination by the Kremlin stable counselled against economic revisionism. But after Gorbachev's takeover, the Soviet attitude began to change. The new leader was increasingly impressed by the progressive plight of his country and decided that he could not afford to pay subsidies to foreign countries for long.

In autumn 1987, the first basic decisions seem to have been made. The crucial point was that trade on CMEA conditions would be gradually reduced and eventually terminated in 1991. Exchange would have to conform to the rules of the world market. Taking this stand, the Soviet leaders expressly declined to take political responsibility for the well-being of their allies. The Eastern Europeans would have to take care of themselves. To this end, the Kremlin lifted previous restrictions under the so-called Brezhnev doctrine. The East European countries were given leeway both to devise economic reforms of their own choosing and also to turn to the West for assistance. Thus the political responsibility that was thrown off by the Soviet Union passed to the East Europeans and to the Western nations.

4. THE IDEA OF FREE CHOICE AND A CATARACT OF CHANGES IN EASTERN EUROPE

In the period that followed, Soviet politicians and commentators began to espouse the idea of free choice which every country was allowed to claim in determining the path of its political, economic and cultural development. As a rule, the new principle was seen to imply a choice but within the limits of the socialist system. It was held that the socialist countries had irrevocably chosen their political and social order according to the laws of history. The idea that national self-determination had to be subsumed under the peoples' free choice was implicitly, and on occasion also explicitly rejected. Obviously, the Kremlin was fearful that the problem of German unification might emerge as an international issue, with incalculable consequences.

For some time, the East Europeans were naturally cautious in trying to find out what the Soviet hegemonic power was willing to accept. As it appears in retrospect, Janos Kadar's ouster in mid-1988 was the first step across the Rubicon. From then on, Hungary did not content itself with intra-systemic reforms but embarked upon a course of increasing political and economic Westernization. Since a group of reformists had taken over in the communist party, this did not infringe the Soviet imperative that communists had to be exclusively in charge of socialist countries. The Poles were the first to challenge the party's power monopoly in the summer of 1989, when the formation of the Mazowiecki government was on their agenda. The Kremlin had to respond - and it did so by accepting the non-communist premier with some qualifications.

In autumn 1989, dramatic events followed one after another at a quick pace. The crucial precondition was that in August 1989 the Soviet authorities had made clear their resolve not to allow their forward-deployed forces to be involved in their host countries' internal conflicts.[6] This amounted to revoking the Brezhnev doctrine which had assigned to the Soviet forces the function of the ultimate guarantor of the East European communist regimes. Underlying this was a shift of Soviet perception of its interests. Gorbachev had become convinced that the orthodox communist leaderships, such as the Honecker gerontocracy in particular, had turned into open enemies, who were seeking an active collusion with his domestic opponents in order to bring him down. The Soviet leader was therefore willing to rid himself of these 'allies' with whatever means he possessed short of direct intervention in East European domestic affairs.

The Kremlin's decision to keep its soldiers in their barracks was particularly important for the situation emerging in East Germany. For more than a year, the GDR leadership had made massive preparations for the use of large-scale violence against its people. As had been envisaged under both the Brezhnev doctrine and the Soviet-East German contractual agreements on the stationing of Soviet troops, the respective contingency plans provided for close cooperation with the forces deployed by the Soviet Union in a common effort to fight the 'internal class enemy'. Therefore, the GDR authorities were greatly embarrassed by the change in Soviet attitude. In addition, Gorbachev made it quite plain during his East Berlin visit on the 40th anniversary of the GDR in early October 1989 that he disapproved of the Honecker regime's policies and favoured a reformist alternative.[7] The Soviet stand both encouraged rivals in the SED Politburo and contributed to dissuading the regime from forcefully putting down a crucial Leipzig mass demonstration and similar displays of opposition despite the fact that this had already been prepared for in every detail. The intra-party opponents eventually seized their opportunity to oust Erich Honecker.

His successor, Egon Krenz, was wrong in thinking that some appearance of reform would easily re-establish the old order. He came under increasing pressure from mass demonstrations in the streets as well as from massive protests from within his own party until at last, on 9 November 1989, he chose to open what he saw as a security valve, that is, to allow his citizens unimpeded travel to West Germany. This entailed both unpredictable and unheard-of consequences. Hundreds of thousands rushed at once to the border points, demanding that they be allowed to cross over to the West. The border authorities eventually could not but acquiesce in this, abandoning any claim to control the situation. From that night, East Germany's border was open to West Berlin and West Germany, and the rulings made could not conceivably be revoked. This in turn resulted in destabilizing the GDR to the extent that it could not possibly continue as a viable state. The unification of Germany was soon to become the only possible solution.

Honecker's ouster was followed by the breakdown of old regimes in other countries. Mass demonstrations in Prague and in other parts of Czechoslovakia led to the replacement of General Secretary Milos Jakes by President Vaclav Havel, a renowned dissident, who had been released from political imprisonment only shortly before. Soon afterwards, reformers in the communist party of Bulgaria deposed Todor Zhivkov and opened the road to political developments characterized by mass protests, liberalization measures and, eventually, the holding of elections. In the course of this process, the communists managed to remain the strongest political force in the country. Owing to their internal cleavages, however, they had to accept as president the leader of the united non-communist front. In Romania, Nicolae Ceausescu's dogmatic regime was replaced after some bloodshed by a group of new men who were communists of the internationalist variety but sought to legitimize themselves as non-communists.[8]

5. INCIPIENT RESERVATIONS ABOUT FREE CHOICE IN THE INTERESTS OF THE WARSAW PACT

With regard to both East Germany and the above-mentioned other three countries, the Kremlin publicly displayed satisfaction with the political change that was taking place. As was publicly explained, the East European people were exercising their right of free choice. In the beginning, the hope was expressed that the changes would result in new, better forms of socialism. When this expectation met with disappointment in some of the countries in the face of a clear trend towards adoption of the Western model, Soviet politicians and spokesmen nonetheless continued to state their agreement with what was going on. There was, however, one reservation, which was raised when the GDR began to move towards German unification. Self-determination in domestic affairs was declared to be legitimate, but the elimination of existing borders and abandonment of obligations under the Warsaw Pact could not be tolerated. For this reason, the GDR was not allowed to merge with the Federal Republic. It was on this basis that the Ten Points of Chancellor Helmut Kohl, announced on 28 November 1989, which envisaged a gradual rapprochement and eventual unification of the two Germanys, met with Moscow's disapproval.[9] Three weeks earlier, the Soviet side had gone so far as privately to express its displeasure to the East German leadership over the precipitate opening of the border, which was felt to be most unfortunate.

The step East Berlin had taken added to the Kremlin's dislike of Krenz. Honecker's successor had never been a Soviet favourite and was now seen to have proven his inability to govern the GDR. The leadership in Moscow used its influence to bring an old confidant, Hans Modrow, to the top. The new man was expected to cope with the situation. In mid-January, however, Modrow went before the *Volkskammer* saying that the country had been plunged into a full-fledged crisis. Modrow sought reconsolidation by revitalizing the state security organization under a new label. The attempt, however, aroused another upsurge of protest in the country and was then abandoned.

Given the GDR's untenable situation, Soviet rejection of German unification was difficult to maintain from the very beginning. As early as autumn 1989, the Kremlin had realized that there was no way of coping with the GDR's difficulties but to turn matters over to the Federal Republic. The Soviet Union was definitely unwilling and unable to provide the material means needed to stabilize East Germany once the border had been opened. On the basis of the free choice principle, Gorbachev had earlier publicly made known that he could not interfere in the border opening. But he was unwilling to accept the implication: German unification.

Gorbachev took this negative attitude despite the fact that he had been alerted by some Soviet experts several times - at least in July 1987 and in April 1989[10] - that the German problem would inevitably soon be back on the international agenda. But the Kremlin leader felt it would be intolerable if East Germany ceased to be a separate state and an ally of the Soviet Union. On this basis, the Warsaw Pact might break down altogether. So he ruled that German unification must not be allowed to become an international issue. As late as December 1989, Gorbachev insisted in internal discussions that this course of action had to be taken. The feasibility of such a policy rested on the dual assumption that the East Germans would be content to live in a state of their own and that the West Germans would be willing to provide any necessary amount of help unconditionally. That is, the Federal Republic was expected to enter a contractual relationship with the GDR and pay the exorbitant costs of reestablishing East German viability for the sake of reconsolidation of German partition.

Gorbachev's calculation had been made without taking into account the political actors concerned. In East Germany, the people increasingly saw their hope of sharing in West German affluence in unification, and within a short period of time at that. Hence came a rising wave of mass demonstrations in favour of 'one united fatherland'. Also, an ever larger part of the population decided to consummate their own private unification - on West German territory. As a result, the destablization of the GDR rose to unprecedented proportions. All efforts to stop the trend failed. In the second half of

January 1990, Gorbachev concluded that there was no way out of the crisis but to allow the Federal Republic to take care of East Germany at its own discretion and to initiate unification along the lines of Kohl's Ten Points.[11]

The Kremlin's concession, however, fell short of what Bonn had then come to feel was adequate under the new conditions of crisis. Chancellor Kohl was no longer willing to enter a process of slow rapprochement and unification. The challenge was most acute and required speedy, decisive action. Otherwise, East German destabilization would continue indefinitely. When Kohl visited Moscow on 10 February 1990, Gorbachev eventually agreed with his guest that more urgent action was required.[12] During the following months, the Chancellor again and again revised previous unification schedules to respond to what he felt was a compelling urge to quicken the process. The Soviet leadership for a while opposed Bonn's increased haste. The available evidence indicates that Gorbachev and his collegues felt that in the coming elections the East Germans would vote at least for a slow, gradual unification process. This was a gross miscalculation. On 18 March 1990, the parties that had committed themselves to Chancellor Kohl's concept of fast unification won a clear victory. From then on, Moscow's previous public commitment to the Germans' free choice concerning their national destiny left little room for argument against the course advocated by Bonn.

6. THE STRUGGLE OVER THE SECURITY ROLE OF UNITED GERMANY

After Soviet acceptance of German unification, a controversy developed over what role the future Germany was to play in the context of European security. At this point, the Kremlin had to pay the price of having ignored the German problem until recently. It had no clear-cut position on what function it assigned to a united Germany in the context of European security. The Soviet policy-makers took an exclusively negative stand. The future Germany was not to be a member of NATO. What this was to mean in practical terms remained vague. The ideas of neutralization, adherence to some new system of collective security, or dual membership in both NATO and the Warsaw Pact were suggested one after another. It was easy for the Western countries, including the Federal Republic, to demonstrate the inconsistency of all these proposals. None of them offered a prospect for a viable European security order in the future.

A neutral Germany was likely to repeat the experience of the Weimar Republic of the interwar period. All imposed military restrictions notwithstanding, Germany had then become capable of challenging the established order with not only political but also military means and eventually moved towards the Second World War. So it appeared imperative to assign a status to Germany that would prevent it from taking unilateral action. According to some arguments initially advanced by Soviet spokesmen, the requirement had to be met by Germany's inclusion in a European system of collective security, preferably in institutions created in the CSCE context. But the poor performance of the interwar League of Nations did not instil much trust in the feasibility of collective security, as both other Warsaw Pact countries and an increasing number of Soviet security experts pointed out.

Since the Eastern alliance was in a state of progressive decay, there was no choice but to have the Germans integrated in NATO. But the Soviet leadership was hesitant to buy this argument. It rather decided to advocate that the future united Germany become a member of both the Atlantic alliance and the Warsaw Pact and thus form an inter-bloc link, instrumental in overcoming the confrontation of the two sides.[13] This was, however, not accepted by the Western powers. They felt that Germany would be put into a contradictory position, which would provoke rather than eliminate conflict.

The West, including the Federal Republic, insisted that the future greater Germany would have to be integrated in NATO. Europe needed a functioning security network, which could be provided only by the Atlantic alliance. Germany was needed as a cornerstone. If the Federal Republic were to withdraw from NATO, its strength and cohesion could not be maintained. Bonn and the Western governments were also in agreement on the point that the German problem could not be solved in a context other than NATO. Both Germany's strength and its position in the middle of Europe implied that the country had a crucial role to play in European security. There was no other durable solution than Germany's firm integration in an international security organization that allowed all the members to be equal partners and to share the costs and benefits. Otherwise, Germany's neighbours would seek to impose their security conditions on the Germans and the Germans could not but try to make their security needs prevail at the expense of other countries - two possibilities, both of which had been attempted in the past to negative effect. NATO continued to be needed to provide a way out of the dilemma.

The Soviet leadership could not devise an alternative to this security concept. That is why Foreign Minister Eduard Shevardnadze was left alone by his allies when he spoke out against Germany's NATO membership at the Warsaw Pact meeting of April 1990. His collegues from Poland, Hungary and Czechoslovakia even expressly took the view that the future united Germany would have to be in the Atlantic alliance in order to be durably embedded in an international consensus. The Kremlin's position vis-a-vis the West was thus considerably weakened.

The development taking place in the Warsaw Pact added to the embarrassment Moscow was already experiencing on other grounds. After it had become clear that the GDR would not remain in the Eastern alliance, the Soviet leaders decided that their military presence in East Central Europe had become untenable and had to be liquidated. Negotiations on troop withdrawals were therefore initiated with Czechoslovakia and Hungary; Poland was offered a similar arrangement. In the beginning, the policy-makers in the Kremlin retained some confidence that acceptance of the allies' unlimited freedom of action would produce increased voluntary military and political cooperation, which would eventually compensate for most of the losses suffered. This expectation, however, soon ended in disappointment. The smaller countries of the alliance demonstrated their willingness to eliminate their armies' Soviet-enforced structures and to pursue military policies at their own discretion. Thus common action was made not less but more difficult.

Gorbachev realized during the late spring and the early summer of 1990 that he had no means to prevent German membership of NATO. He also began to take seriously what quite a few of his experts had been advocating for some time - that such a solution would foster not only East Central European but also Soviet security. At the same time, his country came under an ever more compelling need for a consensus with the West, particularly with the Federal Republic, which was seen as an indispensable source of economic and other assistance, for conditions within the Soviet Union were changing from bad to worse. The leadership was confronted with all kinds of threatening domestic challenge. It not only lacked the means to carry on protracted conflict with the West but also perceived an increasing dependence on outside help. It was only through West German support that the Soviet Union was able to avert an acute payments crisis in mid-1989.

Given these conditions, Gorbachev felt that the best thing he could do was to sell his concessions as long as he could still hope to get a price for them. His prime objective was to put the Germans under an obligation to the Soviet Union and to initiate a new relationship of broad cooperation with them. It is in this context that, during his talks with Chancellor Kohl on 15 and 16 July 1990, the Soviet leader agreed that the future united Germany would be free to choose the alliance it wanted.[14] This agreement, which amounted in fact to Soviet acquiescence in German NATO membership, had been eased by the Western alliance's earlier decision to abandon any intention of confrontation with the Soviet Union and to extend to it an offer of cooperation.[15]

Gorbachev's acceptance of Germany's continuing role in NATO has been crucial to the shaping of Europe's future security structure. NATO was allowed to persist and to take over East Germany indirectly. The confirmed status given to the Western alliance provided a strong contrast to the progressive disintegration of the Warsaw Pact, which could not even manage to continue as a loose commonwealth, as the Soviet Union had suggested to its allies early in July 1990. The East European countries were keen to emancipate themselves completely from anything that reminded them of previous

Soviet tutelage. The Kremlin's Defence Minister Dmitri Yazov concluded some time later that the Pact would not be effective beyond 1991.

As a result, NATO was bound to be the dominating European security structure in the future. Soviet hardliners who opposed Gorbachev's policies had warned of such a 'defeat' ever since the winter of 1989/1990. There was indeed a possibility that NATO would take over in Europe and leave the Soviet Union out. Under the new cooperative East-West relationship, however, the Western leaders wanted to avoid such an outcome. To this end, the CSCE framework (which includes the countries both of NATO and the Warsaw Pact plus the neutrals and the non-aligned) was activated. Pan-European institutions were designed both for confidence-building in the military field and as an organizational link with the Soviet Union and the East European countries so as to connect them to Europe.

Other links were envisaged as well. It is clear that the European Community will have to play a crucial role in bringing Europe together. The Council of Europe, which may take the function of a CSCE Parliament in the future, will also be important.

7. EVALUATION OF GORBACHEV'S POLICY INNOVATION IN THE FIELD OF SECURITY

Gorbachev's approach had been pragmatic. For both economic benefit and political expediency, he had abandoned the Brezhnev doctrine. He had cared little whether the allied countries would have to undergo major adjustments, which, to be sure, he had not anticipated to be so fundamental as they turned out to be. He had also stuck to the principle of non-intervention in domestic affairs, if with a distinct anti-orthodox bias in the crucial initial period. The change in the Soviet attitude resulted in a process of the satellites' progressive political and military emancipation from the Soviet Union.

There are clearly discernible stages in this process. At

the beginning, the Soviet leadership insisted that the joint communist security structure be left intact. When Tadeusz Mazowiecki formed his government in Poland, he had to reserve the ministries responsible for both the external and domestic aspects of the country's security for communists. When the old government was replaced in Czechoslovakia two months later, only the defence minister continued to be a communist. Subsequently, all the respective restrictions were lifted. The Kremlin simply could not afford to impose conditions any longer.

The breakdown of the joint security structures in the Warsaw Pact extended to a wider sphere when, starting in late autumn 1989, the special party troops, the domestic security forces and the party structures were disbanded in most of the East European armies. At the same time, the new governments decreed changes in military doctrine and military strategy, which made a common orientation in the Eastern alliance illusory. The decomposition was completed by uncoordinated national decisions on military reductions. From then on, the Warsaw Pact became practically non-existent both in its traditional role as an instrument which provided military obedience to the Soviet Union and in its newly assigned function as a body that would allow for mutual coordination on a voluntary basis. Even the requirement that the Pact members had to come forward with joint positions in the negotiations on reductions in Conventional Force in Europe (CFE) did little to ease the problem. Also, the Soviet attempt to revive the ailing Pact by prescribing dual alliance membership to a united Germany failed to produce results. Among the motives that made the Western governments reject the scheme was their unwillingness to put the East Europeans under any pressure to accept a pact they did not want.

The breakdown of the Soviet Union's position particularly in East Central Europe had far-reaching implications beyond alliance politics. Among other things, it entailed the consequence of reifying the revision of Soviet military doctrine and strategy, which had been inaugurated only verbally in 1987. The proclaimed principle of 'non-offensive defence' was practically imposed on the Soviet military by the loss of the offensive glacis west of the Soviet border. By the upheaval in Eastern Europe and particularly in the GDR, the Soviet forces had been put into an awkward forward position that called for correction through withdrawal to the homeland. This implied that the Soviet generals had lost their previous capability to maintain an offensive posture against NATO. The General Staff in Moscow could not but draw conclusions from the altered geostrategic conditions and had to start working out defensive plans in order to cope with the new situation.

The slogan of military sufficiency was also substantiated by unintended developments which in this case were intra-Soviet in character. Not only the increasing economic difficulties, but also growing pressure from the Soviet public, activated by *glasnost*, were making the maintenance of military forces at previous numbers less and less expedient. A vehement discussion in the media set in with strong anti-military over-tones. In particular, the intelligentsia strongly resented military service and military matters in general. This is understandable given the incredible brutality to which conscripts are exposed in the armed forces. One of the principal demands raised was therefore that the draft be abandoned. The army was to be a professional one. This implied that it would also be smaller.

Another point of discussion was that the republics, the ethnic parts of the Soviet Union, should be taken into account. One of the more modest demands was that military service should be confined only to one's own region. The most radical idea posited that the armed forces must be separated along republican or ethnic lines. At the same time, the communist party's control structure in the army was questioned. While it is far from certain what will result from these discussions, it appears clear that a new military structure will emerge, that the troops will be reduced in numbers, and that the military establishment may even be split up.[16]

8. THE NEW SECURITY SITUATION SEEN FROM MOSCOW

The changes in the security situation resulted from spontaneous rather than controlled developments. That is, Gorbachev was often confronted with what he had not intended. How did he, his collegues and his advisers respond to this? It should be noted in this context that no official or semi-official documents are available in which coming events were predicted or anticipated. It is only in retrospect that Soviet leaders and spokesmen have expressed their views which therefore tend to reflect adjustment to events rather than free choice.

After the communist regimes in Eastern Europe had broken down, the CPSU journal offered a rationale to justify Soviet acceptance of developments. As stated, it had been fundamentally ill-advised to base the Eastern alliance on the principle of ideological unity. Thus the illusion of class solidarity between the Soviet Union and its allies had been created. It had blinded Soviet eyes to really existing interests. As the self-appointed guardian of ideology, the Kremlin had dominated and turned its allies into satellites. Under the other countries' seeming support of the common cause, both the total lack of commitment to the alliance and resentment against the Soviet Union had remained hidden. It had been necessary to put an end to this. As was tactically assumed, the allies' unwillingness would be overcome once they were allowed to voice their true interests, which required at least some degree of commonality with the Soviet Union.[17]

The statement cited was made in December 1989 with an optimistic tone. It turned out, however, that Soviet-East European relations worsened rather than improved. In the summer of 1990, spokesmen for the Kremlin had to defend Gorbachev against the charge that the unfavourable turn in intra-alliance relations had been caused by his policy. They argued that it was an illusion to believe that mutual relations had been satisfactory before.[18] In fact, there had never been a genuine 'socialist community'. In contrast to Finland, Eastern Europe had been put under a foreign totalitarian yoke, which it resented. This negative heritage would require time before it could be eventually overcome.[19] Gorbachev himself added that it was inescapable that the previously hidden conflicts and resentments would come out into the open one day.[20] In the course of time, the argument shifted. The political benefit from the East European upheaval was increasingly seen not in the improvement of relations with the East Europeans but with the West. Both the emancipation of the satellites and the Soviet Union's decision to introduce democracy would allow the previous confrontation with NATO to be replaced by cooperation.[21]

A weighty argument with which the Kremlin had to cope was the assertion that change in Eastern Europe greatly affected the correlation of forces to Soviet disadvantage. To disprove this, 'reunification of forced tutelage over Eastern Europe' was portrayed as a 'victory for common sense'. The old concept of a 'sanitary zone' to protect the homeland against aggression had not been useful. Besides, it could not be maintained much longer, one of the reasons being the enormous material cost to Moscow. Furthermore, it had entailed the antagonism of the united Western powers, which had become an intolerable burden, particularly since the West was greatly superior economically.[22]

In the early phase, official comment described the change of regimes in Eastern Europe simply as a systemic modification, which need not imply departure from socialism. Since capitalism had been economically successful, it was wise to adopt some of its elements, such as the market mechanism, and to graft them on to the socialist order. The communist parties thus would have a chance to re-establish their competitive power.[23] This optimism was not to last. It was soon recognized that the East Europeans were moving away from socialism altogether. From then on, Soviet tolerance of this process was justified by saying that any attempt to stop it would not contribute to the Soviet Union's security but jeopardize it. Any Soviet attempt to restrict East European freedom of action, it was held, entailed the prospect of conflict with NATO. As was tacitly hinted, the Soviet Union would then be confronted with an alliance of both NATO and the East European countries.[24]

By mid-1990, it could no longer be doubted in Moscow that the Warsaw Pact was in disarray beyond repair. Gorbachev argued that there was compensation for this. NATO's military doctrine was in a 'process of revision', which would lead to the 'formation of a new security structure on the European continent' replacing the old bloc structures. This would strengthen Soviet security in the long run.[25] At a less official level, the evaluation was more negative. The Warsaw Pact underwent 'fundamental transformation' into a consultative organ and into a rump organization from which at least East Germany and Hungary would be missing. On the other hand, NATO's corresponding transformation had thus far hardly become visible. This created a disequilibrium in case one chose to apply old ways of thinking. Sure, there was no cause for concern even though 'destabilizing consequences' could not be excluded. The Western military threat had not been substantially reduced as yet.[26] While disagreement with official views was not openly acknowledged, the estimate was clearly at variance with Gorbachev's and Shevardnadze's assertions on the elimination of the Western threat.

Quite a few among the Soviet military and *apparatchiki* were particularly concerned over the worsened correlation of forces, which they felt resulted from German unification. Gorbachev conceded that the Federal Republic was a 'great military power' in Europe and that a united Germany would be 'one of the economically most powerful and politically most influential states of the world'. He indicated that the Soviet 'concept of security' had delivered lessons from the Second World War, and hinted at 'positive changes' in Germany that had positively affected the Soviet attitude. He also stressed the need to take real conditions into account.[27] An official spokesman explained that the process of German unification would go on irrespective of whether the Soviet Union wanted it or not. It was therefore necessary to make the best of it and use the opportunity to establish a good new relationship with the Germans.[28] It was also argued that German unification provided a chance to 'overcome bloc psychology' and to promote the idea of a single pan-European security system, which could be developed from the two pillars of NATO and the Warsaw Pact.[29]

It was Foreign Minister Shevardnadze who made the strongest effort to elaborate details of a new thinking on international security. He took issue with the old 'imperial philosophy', which had not taken into account the Soviet Union's real interests or those of others and had resulted in a domestically destructive 'confrontation with the rest of the world'. To avoid previous mistakes, one had to accord priority to 'all-human values in foreign policy'. It was on this basis that the Soviet Union had won a positive image abroad and had been able at last to establish fruitful relations with other countries. Democratic pluralism, respect for human rights and renunciation of ideology in the Soviet Union, the Foreign Minister went on, had greatly contributed to this development. The enemy images that had been cultivated before had proved highly counterproductive. They had 'subverted the stability of whole civilizations and led them into decline'.

Shevardnadze exclaimed emphatically that 'God may prevent us from ever seeking enemies again, be they enemies of the people, of peace, of socialism or of anything else.' Taking issue with the critics of official policy towards Eastern Europe, the Foreign Minister said that, before the turnover of the fall of 1989, the region had been a security risk not only for *perestroika* but also for the Soviet Union in general. There had been a rising wave of destabilization which could not be ignored any longer. In particular, the deployment of Soviet forces in East Central Europe was prone to make a negative impact on the Soviet Union. The Soviet leadership had to put an end to 'pseudo-socialism' in the GDR and similar countries on condition that Soviet security would be maintained. It was not free people, including the unifying Germans, but the unresolved problems of the past that were the challenge to be feared. In the interests of *perestroika*, the new forces in Europe had to be supported. Shevardnadze also made it clear that the present policies vis-a-vis the outside world were sound in that they were 'the [materially] most profitable branch' of the country's activities.[30]

The prospect that the Soviet armed forces would have to undergo restructuring and reduction raised the question of future military strategy. One point of departure seemed clear. There would be no conventional capabilities to deter a potential aggressor by threatening to meet and to beat him on a glacis in front of the Soviet homeland. In the future, Soviet troops would be deployed only at home, and they were likely to lack overpowering strength. Under these conditions, a military option suggested itself, one that the United States and NATO had chosen when they had to protect their security in similar circumstances. Poor conventional warfare capabilities had to be compensated by war-preventing nuclear capabilities, which were comparatively cheap and avoided the risk that the capabilities of waging war would be tested. Accordingly, a Soviet spokesman indicated acceptance of nuclear deterrence as a means to prevent war in international relations. He added the qualification that this would be but an interim strategy to preserve peace as long as the prospective political, economic, humanitarian and ecological links between the CSCE countries were not yet strong enough to guarantee a stable relationship. This argument served the purpose of demonstrating that the previous denuclearization philosophy would be adhered to 'ultimately'.[31]

9. CONCLUSIONS

It is useful to bear in mind the 'anti-imperialistic' philosophy expounded by Gorbachev at the 27th CPSU Congress in order to see the enormous distance between his beginnings and his present attitude towards international security.[32] The motive for this change in policy clearly lies in domestic problems. The Soviet Union was threatened by increasing underdevelopment. To prevent this prospect from coming true, the Soviet leader had to take decisive action, which inescapably implied fundamental change in relations with other countries. Given the fact that Soviet resources are traditionally absorbed to a very large extent by troops and armaments, the relationship with the United States and the other NATO countries obviously required reappraisal. When the issue of restructuring the European security system moved to the foreground, Germany became the natural focus. During the period of confrontation, its two parts had stabilized their respective alliances. When an alternative security system became a practical possibility, Germany's attitude was bound largely to predetermine the future order in Europe.

Gorbachev's new thinking on security reflects primarily the dynamics of a development set in motion when the Soviet president chose to move away from the old mould. The political situation in the Soviet Union - and subsequently also in Eastern Europe - proved much less stable and controllable than he had expected. As a result, all kinds of self-propelling process have started. Gorbachev cannot but try to be sufficiently responsive to them to maintain himself and his team as the makers of Soviet foreign policy and to create an international climate favourable to the solution of the pressing domestic problems. It is characteristic of this situation that the 1987-88 theoretical explanations of new thinking have not been very relevant to the policies subsequently pursued. If one wants to gain an idea of the motives underlying the Kremlin's foreign and security policies of 1989-90, one must look not back at the past but at both the actual political developments and subsequent statements on the matter. It is only *ex post facto* that the Soviet leader, his collegues and his advisers are able to explain what they have been doing.

NOTES

1. Anatoli Gromyko and Vladimir Lomeiko, *Novoe myshlenie v yadernyi vek* (Moscow: Mezhdunarodnye otnosheniya, 1984).
2. The denuclearization concept was publicly announced by Gorbachev on 16 January 1986 (*Pravda*, 17 January 1986) and subsequently explained at the 27th CPSU Congress (see the relevant remarks in the speeches given by Gorbachev and Shevardnadze) (*Pravda*, 26 February 1986 and 2 March 1986, respectively).
3. Cf. the official Soviet explanation 'Pervyi realnyi rezultat perestroiki', *Mezhdunarodnaya zhizn*, no. 2, 1988, pp. 3-6. Significantly, the relevant text has been changed in the English translation (*International Affairs*, no. 2,1988, pp. 3-6), intended for Western consumption.
4. This was revealed by the Czechoslovak military representative at the East-West Strategy Seminar held in Vienna in January-February 1990.
5. For a detailed analysis, see Gerhard Wettig, ''New Thinking' in Soviet Foreign Policy', *Nordic Journal of Soviet and East European Studies*, no. 1, 1990 (forthcoming).
6. See, in particular, an interview with the Soviet Ambassador in the GDR, Vyacheslav Kochemasov, in *Tribuene*, 8 May 1990, p. 1.
7. See Gorbachev's public statements during his East Berlin visit, *Pravda*, 7 and 8 October 1989.
8. Cf. Anneli Ute Gabanyi, *Die unvollendete Revolution: Rumänien zwischen Diktatur und Demokratie* (Munich: Piper, 1990).
9. See, for example, Gorbachev's statements during his joint press conference with French President François Mitterrand in Kiev on 6 December 1989 (*Pravda*, 8 December 1989) and Shevardnadze's address to the Political Commission of the European Parliament in

Brussels on 19 Decmber 1989 (*Pravda*, 20 December 1989). Direct reference to the Ten Points is contained in 'Vostochnaya Evropa na puti k obnovleniyu', *Mezhdunarodnaya zhizn*, no. 1, 1990, pp. 117-18.
10. An abridged translated version of Vyacheslav Dashichev's respective April 1989 memorandum has been published in *Der Spiegel*, 5 February 1990, pp. 144-58.
11. Cf. Gorbachev's suggestion of German unity to the GDR's communist premier Hans Modrow on 30 January 1990 (*Pravda*, 31 January 1990) and Soviet comment on the stand subsequently taken by the East German government (*Pravda*, 3 February 1990).
12. *Izvestiya*, 11 February 1990.
13. See, *inter alia*, interview with Foreign Minister Shevardnadze (*Irish Times*, 28 April 1990), Shevardnadze's address to his colleagues at the Bonn Two Plus Four meeting on 5 May 1990 (*Ost-Information*, 7 May 1990) and Eduard Shevardnadze, 'Towards a Greater Europe: The Warsaw Treaty Organization and NATO in a Renewing Europe', *NATO's Sixteen Nations*, vol. 35, no. 3, June 1990, pp. 18-22.
14. Cf. the joint press conference of Gorbachev and Kohl at Zheleznovodsk on 16 July 1990 (*Pravda*, 18 July 1990).
15. 'London Declaration on a Transformed North Atlantic Alliance', issued by the Heads of State and Governments participating in the meeting of the North Atlantic Council in London on 5-6 July 1990 (*NATO Information Service*, Brussels, July 1990).
16. For the problems related to military reform in the Soviet Union, see Frank Richter and Jobst Echterling, 'Ansätze zu einer Militärreform in der Sowjetunion', *Aussenpolitik*, vol. 42, no. 1, 1991, pp. 49-58.
17. A. Bogatyrov, M. Nosov and K. Pleshakov, 'Kto zhe oni, nashi soyuzniki?', *Kommunist*, no. 1, 1990, pp. 105-13. Criticism of the 'phantom of ideological unity', which previously had taken the place of state interest, is also a principal point in Gorbachev's address to military units in Odessa (*Pravda*, 19 August 1990).
18. Interview with Valentin Falin, *Pravda*, 20 August 1990.
19. Evgenii Shashkov, 'Vostochnaya Evropa: Vospominaniya i novye realii', *Kommunist*, no. 10, 1990, pp. 115-17.
20. *Pravda*, 19 August 1990.
21. ibid.; Shashkov, op. cit., p. 113.
22. Shashkov, op. cit., p. 114.
23. 'Vostochnaya Evropa na puti k obnovleniyu', *Mezhdunarodnaya zhizn*, no. 1, 1990, pp. 115-17.
24. *Pravda*, 19 August 1990.
25. ibid.
26. Konstantin Sorokin, 'Bezopasnost strany na poroge novogo veka', *Kommunist*, no. 14, 1990, pp. 121-2.
27. *Pravda*, 19 August 1990.
28. Shashkov, op. cit., pp. 117-18.
29. A. Vladimirov, S. Posokhov, 'Obshcheevropeiskij soyuz bezopasnosti', *Mezhdunarodnaya zhizn*, no. 9, 1990, pp. 78-80.
30. Interview with Shevardnadze, *Ogonek*, no. 11, 1990, pp. 2-6.
31. Shashkov, op. cit., pp. 118-19.
32. *Pravda*, 26 February 1986.

5 SOVIET MILITARY DOCTRINE AND EUROPEAN SECURITY: END OF COALITIONAL WARFARE PLANNING AND THE GROWTH OF REPUBLICAN ARMIES

Roy Allison

1. INTRODUCTION[1]

Since 1987, Soviet military doctrine has been changing in certain fundamental ways that have helped to transform Soviet policy towards European states. For the Soviet Party leadership, the new content of military doctrine and policy contributes to a broad political strategy aimed at the more effective management of Soviet foreign relations at a reduced cost in the 1990s. At the same time, we should be careful not to attribute too much of the recent change in the structure of East-West relations in Europe simply to modifications in Soviet military doctrine.

The transformation of the European strategic landscape at the end of the 1980s and the beginning of the 1990s occurred at such speed that it probably has not yet been fully accommodated in the framework of Soviet military doctrine. The Soviet leadership could maintain that its new policy in

Eastern Europe is an expression of the rather abstract formulas of war prevention or 'reasonable sufficiency', but the strategic and military operational implications of military disengagement from Eastern Europe for Soviet defence policy were far from clear. Soviet military policy and thinking have necessarily been fluid and reactive during this transitional period in the absence of a consensus in Moscow on the nature of the principal threats to the security of the Soviet Union.

This applies, for example, to Soviet conventional arms reductions. Soviet military doctrine has traditionally had a crucial role in determining force requirements and therefore the latitude of Soviet arms control negotiators. But since the late 1980s, Soviet conventional arms reductions have been driven increasingly by factors besides military doctrine. The military-technical aspect of military doctrine has had a declining role in determining Soviet policy in this field. Nevertheless, significant military doctrinal change could reinforce and make more durable the Soviet force reduction and restructuring programme. The same responsive causation would appear to apply to Soviet military doctrine and the unification of Germany.

The durability of the radical reform which has occurred in Soviet military doctrine and military policy in Europe depends to a significant extent on the internal power constellation and process of democratization and economic reform in the Soviet Union. Under Gorbachev Soviet defence policy has tended to subordinate traditional military-technical concerns to the political priorities of the civilian leadership and Foreign Ministry élite. However, as a result of the changing power constellation in Moscow since autumn 1990, Soviet military perspectives may no longer be so easily subordinated in the formulation of future Soviet policy towards Europe.

In the second place, the interaction between different aspects of Gorbachev's reform agenda means that it is always possible that the innovations in Soviet military doctrine that have helped transform the Soviet defence agenda (under prompting from Soviet politicians and civilian specialists) could fall victim to the eventual collapse of Gorbachev's political-economic programme in other areas.

Western officials should also take note that in Soviet

thinking a given military doctrine, regardless of its characteristics at any given time (for example, whether offence- or defence-oriented), only defines the near- to medium-term Soviet outlook and may be modified or supplanted if the strategic context in which this doctrine was originally formulated changes.

Notwithstanding these considerations, and the possibility of regressive tendencies in Soviet defence thinking or military policy later in the 1990s, key elements of the seminal change in Soviet policy in Europe, such as Soviet accession to German unification and agreement to a military withdrawal from Eastern Europe by the mid-1990s, cannot realistically be reversed. A section in this chapter on the ending of Soviet and Warsaw Pact coalitional warfare planning confirms the irreversibility of Soviet military disengagement from Eastern Europe. This section also considers the military doctrinal implications of this military pull-back to the frontiers of the Soviet Union.

Beyond this military transformation in Eastern Europe, the critical determinants of Soviet military planning in the near term appear to be the changing nature of Soviet threat perceptions and the extent to which Soviet republics assume greater responsibility for their own defence. Much of this chapter is devoted, therefore, to analysis of these significant topics. If the republics acquired more independent control over their defence planning or military forces this would require a fundamental reappraisal of the current military doctrinal assumptions and military organizational framework of the Soviet authorities. This would shape Soviet military thinking and strategy for Europe, both within and beyond the current Soviet frontiers, for many years to come.

2. THE DEFENSIVE SHIFT IN SOVIET CONVENTIONAL MILITARY PLANNING

A Warsaw Pact summit in May 1987 effectively endorsed the idea of non-offensive defence - the need to eliminate the capabilities for surprise attack and large-scale offensive operations. But by autumn 1988, the Soviet General Staff had not yet achieved a clear definition of non-offensive defence for its own purposes. One senior political official revealed that the General Staff and the Ministry of Defence were currently working on 'the problem of defining what non-offensive defence is, what the criteria are for the structure of the armed forces, for the deployment of the armed forces and for the character of the armed forces'.[2] This coincided with an extensive closed discussion in Moscow on the level by which the Soviet armed forces could be unilaterally cut. Research and exercises were carried out by the General Staff and scientists to study the implications of cuts of 300,000, 500,000 and 700,000 men.[3]

The 500,000-man unilateral force reduction agreed on and announced by Gorbachev at the United Nations in December 1987 signified a substantial shift in Soviet military thinking. The cuts were designed to reduce heavily Soviet tank forces deployed forward, withdraw specific forces designed to facilitate offensive operations, and restructure the remaining Soviet armoured divisions in Eastern Europe to enhance their defensive content. Offensive operational concepts such as that of operational manoeuvre groups would also be discarded.

It could be predicted that the implementation of this initiative would have the effect at least of undercutting the Soviet capacity to carry out a standing-start attack in the absence of a reinforcement of the forces remaining in place.[4] The withdrawal of offensive forces, Soviet military spokesmen maintained, would require any attempt at an offensive thrust to be preceded by a regrouping and concentration of forces that would be detected by the other side; and surprise attack would thereby be eliminated.[5]

The unilateral Soviet force reductions scheduled during 1989-91 provided initial evidence of a belief within the Soviet General Staff that a conflict might now be contained on the Soviet periphery and need not escalate to world war, with the lesser force requirements generated by that assumption.

Early in 1989, the Soviet official Viktor Karpov claimed that the May 1987 Warsaw Pact doctrinal declaration envisaged exclusively defensive operations during which political and diplomatic means would be used to resolve a conflict and prevent its expansion to a widescale war.[6] Marshal Sergei Akhromeyev confirmed later in 1989 that, at the outset of an East-West conflict, strategic defensive operations could last several weeks and 'during that time the political leaders of the Warsaw Pact will, as we think, take measures to confine the ongoing conflict and to prevent the extension of war'.[7]

A change in Soviet military planning assumptions on these lines to emphasize the need and possibility of localizing and terminating an East-West conflict had in itself significant implications for the forward deployment of Soviet forces and therefore for Soviet military strategy in Europe.

3. THE END OF SOVIET MILITARY PLANNING FOR COALITIONAL WARFARE

The December 1988 programme to reduce Soviet standing forces in Eastern Europe and reconfigure them along more defensive principles may initially have reflected Soviet military plans to create 'fortified regions' in Eastern Europe. Soviet forces would have had a significant role in this defence concept but such plans would also have enhanced the military profile of the non-Soviet Warsaw Pact (NSWP) forces in designs for integrated coalitional defence and warfare.[8]

The prolongation of this concept of coalitional warfare, which is premised on the integration of the military assets of the Warsaw Pact states, is evident in an article written in autumn 1989 by the commander-in-chief of the Warsaw Pact joint armed forces, Army General Piotr Lushev. He described the efforts of the 'fraternal' countries in the defence field as 'closely interdependent', in a 'dialectical unity...determined by the very nature of our society' and formed on a 'stable military-strategic basis'.[9]

The revolutions in Eastern Europe in 1989, which swept communist rulers from power, undercut any designs that may have been prepared for 'fortified regions'. As a result, the Soviet military command may reluctantly have accepted the need to establish a strategic fall-back position - a true defensive buffer zone in the East - that would be accompanied by further

Soviet military withdrawals. This plan would enable the NSWP allies to implement a more nationally-oriented defence policy in conformity with the growing popular aspirations of these states.

However, by that stage, the Soviet strategic planning requirements were rapidly being overtaken by contrary strategic realities. Soviet military leaders could only respond on an *ad hoc* basis to a transformation of the strategic constellation that exceeded all their expectations. Soviet military doctrine could no longer offer effective guidance or act as a principal determinant of Soviet policy on military withdrawals from Eastern Europe, or the unification of Germany, except at the most abstract level. These profound developments could not readily be reconciled with existing Soviet military plans. Indeed, all Soviet planning on conventional warfare was thrown into disarray as the parameters and the very actors involved in scenarios of future conflict became ever more uncertain.

Early in 1990, the Soviet military leaders may still have sought to retain some forces in Eastern Europe to enable the Soviet Union to re-establish a forward posture should the likelihood of a major conflict arise. Such forces would provide an insurance during a period of strategic uncertainty, though they could later be integrated into new strategic calculations. But this possibility depended on Soviet forces retaining rights of presence in a united Germany that would permit a forward salient. The Soviet leadership was apparently ready to accept a substantial continued American strategic presence in Western Europe if this could help avoid a complete and hasty Soviet disengagement from Eastern Europe. In the event, however, internal pressures in Eastern Europe did not permit such strategic 'parallelism'.

By early 1990, Soviet positions in Eastern Europe were collapsing. The prospect of a substantial if not complete Soviet military withdrawal from this region appeared increasingly credible. The system of operationally subordinating East European armed forces to the Soviet Supreme High Command in crisis or war (as described in the 1980 'Statute of the Joint Armed Forces [of the Warsaw Pact] and Organs of Their Command in Wartime' and other secret bilateral and multilateral treaties within the Warsaw Pact) appeared likely to be revoked by the NSWP states. This and their growing insistence on national decision-making authority on defence issues indicated that traditional plans for the Pact engaging in coalitional warfare under a unified command in theatres of military operation in Europe were no longer realistic.

The commander-in-chief of the Soviet Air Defence Forces, Army General Ivan Tretyak, observed in May 1990 that 'the Central and Southern Groups of Forces [Soviet troops in Czechoslovakia and Hungary] performed certain functions within the common defensive system', so that 'the plans for and the structure of collective defence now need to be rethought and reworked'.[10] But the agreement on German unification, which spelled the end of the Group of Forces in [East] Germany, dealt a mortal blow to the concept of integrated coalitional defence between the Soviet Union and the East European states.

One expression of the collapse of this concept is the apparent removal of the Soviet Western Theatre of Military Operations (*Teatr Voennykh Deistvii,* or TVD) headquarters (established in 1984) from Legnica in Polish Silesia back to Soviet territory. The rationale for maintaining this key war headquarters on East European soil has gone. In addition, the four Soviet front field commands (the Groups of Forces), located in East Germany, Poland, Hungary and Czechoslovakia, need to be dissolved in the early 1990s as these forces are withdrawn back to the Soviet Union. Soviet plans for the wartime integration of the armies of those four WTO allies into the Groups of Forces had already to be abandoned by 1990.[11] These changes render invalid the series of 'status-of-forces' agreements that the Soviet Union negotiated with occupied Poland (December 1956), East Germany (March 1957), Hungary (May 1957) and Czechoslovakia (October 1968).

As an adjunct to and extension of the Warsaw Pact defence obligations, some 21 bilateral treaties of friendship, cooperation and mutual assistance bind the Soviet Union and the states of Eastern Europe. These have created an important layer of Soviet-East European mutual defence obligations. The new East European regimes may have little respect for these treaties, and such agreements cannot effectively replace for the

Warsaw Treaty structure on matters such as military coordination and joint training. But at the beginning of the 1990s, there remained the possibility for Soviet leaders to attempt to develop new bilateral security relationships with East European states in a form that would be consistent with the sovereignty of the smaller countries and yet preserve some kind of security buffer for the Soviet Union in Eastern Europe.

In this context, a group of Soviet specialists has argued that within the Warsaw Pact the interests of the Soviet Union would be better met by adopting a model of relations with the East European countries on the lines of the postwar Soviet-Finnish relationship, whereby the smaller state maintains full political independence but takes account of the security interests of the Soviet Union. They emphasize that, although Finland has been a capitalist, neutral country, its borders have been reliable and its relations with the Soviet Union less problematic than those of Poland, Hungary and Czechoslovakia.[12]

Clearly Soviet and East European leaders could define the basic, legitimate Soviet security interests in Eastern Europe differently. But if it is assumed that a primary Soviet interest is to keep NATO troops out of Eastern Europe, then it is not inconceivable that East European countries such as Hungary (which as noted below is preparing for a withdrawal from the Warsaw Pact) could offer appropriate national security guarantees to Moscow. These could take the form of bilateral accords with the Soviet Union or NATO, whereby the former could be assured that no foreign troops or reconnaissance flights would be allowed in the East European country concerned. This would be somewhat analogous to Finland's neutral position (which is, however, complemented by the military provisions of the 1948 Treaty of Friendship, Cooperation and Mutual Assistance with the Soviet Union).[13] Or to take another parallel, such accords would be similar to the agreement over the unification of Germany, whereby the former East German territory is permanently denied to 'stationed' non-German NATO forces after the Soviet forces have been withdrawn from it (though limited exercises including other NATO countries' forces are permissible).

Under the new conditions, it is undeniable, as one Soviet specialist affirms, that 'the territory of the East European countries remains a buffer which any invading army would have to cross'. But the new element is that the transformations in Eastern Europe now 'provide the West with a definite 'margin of safety".[14] Implicitly this reverses the situation prevailing since the late 1940s by turning Eastern Europe into a security buffer for the Soviet Union rather than for Western Europe.

Such a developing western-orientation in Eastern Europe is expressed in the progressive reduction of contractual security policy ties with the Soviet Union. For example, in early 1990, President Vaclav Havel declared that the Soviet-Czechoslovak Treaty of Friendship, Cooperation and Mutual Security, due to expire that year, should be neither extended nor concluded in a new form.[15] Hungary in turn apparently intends to terminate its May 1955 Treaty of Friendship, Cooperation and Mutual Assistance with the Soviet Union, towithdraw from the Warsaw Pact, and in due course to proclaim itself fully neutral or even develop a rapprochement with NATO.[16]

The loss of strategic depth represented by Soviet force withdrawals from Eastern Europe and the breakdown of the military structure of the Warsaw Pact clearly weighs heavily on Soviet military minds. In March 1990, Lieutenant-General Ivan Sergeyev, deputy chief of the Strategic Rocket Forces, was blunt: 'If we lose space, we shall come closer to danger... The coming changes in the Warsaw Treaty Organization certainly spell a loss for us militarily.' He emphasized the vulnerability of Soviet targets to long-range, high precision American missiles with conventional warheads, and that 'it is very important for our strategic nuclear missiles to be as far as possible from the line of combat contact.'[17] Army General Tretyak viewed such Western weapons as particularly dangerous for Soviet forces and systems in the immediate vicinity of the Soviet borders, since in a conflict 'our air defence systems, especially our surveillance systems, or radar complexes, will be put out of action in the very first hours.'[18]

These views highlight the Soviet interest, on defensive grounds, to retain some coordination with its former allies in

Eastern Europe, especially with Poland, at least in the field of air defence. Hitherto the East European air defence forces (besides those of Romania) have had a double operational subordination, even in peacetime, to national defence ministers and to the headquarters of the WTO Integrated Air Defence Command (IADC) in Moscow. In addition, according to a secret Soviet-Polish agreement of 1980, the IADC head-quarters was authorized in an emergency to give orders directly to the central command of the Polish air forces.[19] While this agreement is likely to be abandoned, the Soviet General Staff would certainly wish if possible to keep open lines of communication with Poland to maintain a forward air defence capability, perhaps through new bilateral arrange-ments. The readiness of the Poles to accede of their own will to such arrangements diminished, however, as Soviet-Polish relations soured in January 1991 over the schedule for the withdrawal of Soviet forces deployed in Poland.

By spring 1990, it was clear that the new East European regimes in Hungary, Czechoslovakia and Poland would be unlikely to agree to their forces taking part in future offensive action into NATO territory. But they could at least be expected to carry out national territorial defence roles and resist aggression.[20] This revision in functions was implicit, for example, in the new national defence doctrine announced by Poland on 26 February.[21] It cannot provide a full substitute for the former military roles of the NSWP states in integrated WTO planning. Nor can the forces of these states any longer be expected to fight alongside Soviet forces (though Soviet reliance on the NSWP forces has long been open to doubt) except perhaps in response to a putative attack by NATO.

At the Vienna East-West military doctrine seminar in January-February 1990, Hungary and Czechoslovakia clarified their intention to develop their own nationally-oriented de-fence doctrines, adapted to their own needs and circumstances. The Hungarian chief of staff, Lieutenant-General Laszlo Borsits, stated that the Hungarians would base their 'defence concept on the principle of territorial defence'. The chief of the Czechoslovak General Staff, Major-General Anton Slimak, stated that 'in case of being attacked we do not envisage shifting combat action on to the territory of another state'.[22] In

June 1990, after a summit meeting of the Warsaw Pact, the Czechoslovak Minister of National Defence, Army-General Miroslav Vacek, emphasized President Havel's view that 'each of the Warsaw Treaty member states should fulfil tasks within the framework of the coalition, above all, by defending its own territory'.[23]

The Soviet military leadership only reluctantly and belatedly came to terms with such intentions. The Soviet commander-in-chief of the joint Warsaw Pact forces, Army General Lushev, in an article signed to press at the end of 1990, still claimed that the Warsaw Treaty defines a group of mutual obligations 'directed at ensuring the reliable security of all the member states of the coalition'. He defined one item on the agenda of the Joint Command as 'scientifically elaborating the theory of coalition operations'. Nevertheless, he admitted that now 'each WTO member state conducts a quite independent policy from the others, conforming to the degree of real external danger, and itself defines measures for its own defence'.[24]

This recognition of reality confirmed the end of the single Warsaw Pact Unified Military Doctrine, although the Soviet General Staff still hoped for some coordination between Soviet and East European defence preparations. In June 1990, Defence Minister Yazov took issue with Havel by stating that he could not agree with the idea that 'each country should defend itself' and pointing to the integrated military strength of NATO.[25]

Soviet military attempts to retain some joint co-ordination in WTO military planning are likely to prove unavailing. Following the Warsaw Treaty summit in 1990, the GDR Minister for Defence and Disarmament, Rainer Eppelman, claimed that the entire military structures of the Warsaw Treaty as well as the joint high command would be abolished by the end of the year.[26] Hungary anticipated this outcome by declaring that it would not take part in the 1990 WTO military exercises and would remove its forces from under the command of the Joint Armed Forces.[27] At the end of September, the Polish, Hungarian and Czechoslovak foreign and defence ministries for the first time held a meeting to discuss the role of their armed forces in the new conditions without inviting a Soviet delegation. By late 1990, the Soviet leadership was resigned to the need to dissolve the military wing of the Pact, although Gorbachev still hoped to transform the WTO into a political consultative body which could maintain the fiction of a Moscow-led group capable of negotiating with NATO. Finally, at a meeting of foreign and defence ministers from the Soviet Union and five East European countries in Budapest on 25 February 1991, a declaration was signed that the military organs and structures of the Warsaw Treaty would be dismantled by 31 March of that year.[28]

These developments have inevitably forced the Soviet military command to review wholesale their planning assumptions. As noted earlier, the idea of adopting the wartime objective of simply restoring borders may have been under review in Moscow during 1989. By early 1990, as the military cohesion of the Warsaw Pact crumbled and Moscow conceded that its forces would be withdrawn from at least Hungary and Czechoslovakia, Soviet military leaders claimed that Soviet operational plans no longer envisaged 'conducting an offensive with the aim of carrying military operations beyond the borders of the Soviet Union's own territory or beyond the border of its Warsaw Treaty allies'.[29] The central question became whether the first or the second of these limited goals governed military planning.

There is growing evidence that by 1990 the basic strategic line of defence in Soviet military planning had reverted to the borders of the Soviet Union. Soviet military spokesmen indicated that the Soviet conventional military structure should be such that it could not launch huge operations outside its state borders, that the objective in conflict should be to restore the *status quo* of the borders.[30] More authoritatively, in his speech to the CPSU Congress in July 1990, Chief of Staff Mikhail Moiseyev conceded that

> the fact that individual responsibility on the part of the Warsaw Treaty states for the defence of their national borders is now coming to the fore compels us to take a new approach to our country's strategic defence planning, now only within the Soviet Union's state borders.

As a result, Moiseyev noted, 'our border military districts are acquiring particular significance'. He maintained that the groupings of Soviet troops are being clarified and given a defensive structure, that the whole structure of operational and combat training, instruction and education for troops and naval forces is being restructured.[31] In January 1991, Defence Minister Yazov confirmed the new approach in stating that 'operational and mobilization plans will have to be reworked, the formation of strategic defence groupings will have to be continued on the territory of frontier military districts and places where fleets are based'.[32]

If such a 'reversion to Soviet frontiers' now indeed underlies Soviet military planning, it reinforces the likelihood that Soviet official promises concerning the withdrawal of all Soviet foreign-based military personnel back to the Soviet Union will indeed be fulfilled in the 1990s. Soviet forces in Eastern Europe are already scheduled to return in the first half of this decade.

At the same time, such a change focuses Soviet strategic concerns and military restructuring requirements on border regions, especially those within the Soviet western military districts. This is a problematic development because it is in just these areas that restive Soviet republics are now demanding greater autonomy in determining their own defence requirements and force postures.

4. NEW MILITARY CONTINGENCIES AND THE ISSUE OF REPUBLICAN DEFENCE

Soviet military doctrine is certainly in a period of rapid flux, but this does not release Soviet military and political leaders from the need to determine the direction and nature of the main future threats to Soviet security and to develop the military means to deal with appropriate contingencies.

Soviet uncertainty over the threat was expressed in the proceedings of a panel of experts which convened early in 1990 with the task of discussing threats to the national security of the Soviet Union. This panel included senior associates of the CPSU Central Committee, representatives of the ministries of defence, internal affairs and foreign affairs as well as scholars and professors of military institutions. In the words of one of the participants, Sergei Karaganov, the group studied 'the level and types of today's and tomorrow's threats' and developed 'a proposal on contours of an optimal model of the armed forces of the future'. The panel sought to define the precise goal of the restructuring and reform of the armed forces of the Soviet Union.[33]

Despite such brainstorming exercises, at the beginning of the 1990s, most Soviet military strategists continued to focus principally on scenarios of East-West conflict and appeared to fix defence levels and structures with this conception of warfare uppermost in their minds.[34] The traditional fixation on NATO was retained. Marshal Akhromeyev was explicit: 'The leaders of the NATO military bloc...all call the Soviet Union their enemy. For that reason, we do not have to select a possible adversary.'[35]

Some more creative Soviet thinking on alternative threat scenarios was expressed in an interview with the Soviet defence analyst Andrei Kokoshin and set out more fully in the preamble to the Ministry of Defence draft military reform plan published in November 1990. These sources accepted that a widescale military conflict between East and West is very unlikely at this stage, but considered that 'an overall military threat will exist as long as major nuclear arsenals and powerful groupings of armed forces exist in those states with which acute political conflicts are potentially possible'. The Ministry of Defence (MOD) noted that the shift in the centre of international tension towards Third World regions, specifically the displacement of this centre from Europe to the Near East area, presented 'a real threat that leading world powers will be drawn into a war through regional conflicts'. This was linked to the intensive efforts of Third World countries to create their own nuclear missile and chemical potentials. The authors of the MOD draft argued that 'lasting tension, especially in the Persian Gulf zone, extremist aspirations in the foreign policy of some leaders...can lead to the employment of nuclear or chemical weapons in this strategically important area'. In conclusion, they maintained that the unresolved nature of problems and conflicts in zones of heightened tension 'predetermines the extreme instability of the situation and the danger that large-scale conflicts and local wars will be unleashed'.[36] In the same vein, Soviet officials have highlighted the dangers of the spread of ballistic missile and advanced conventional weapons technologies.

Soviet civilian specialists have also expressed a growing preoccupation with the probability of local conflicts on the volatile Soviet periphery. The proximity of Gulf War combat zones to the Soviet Transcaucasus region and generalized political instability in the Middle East aggravated by this war can only reinforce such Soviet concerns.

But Soviet civilian analysts also fear prospective dangerous local conflicts in Eastern Europe (an issue perhaps too delicate for the Soviet military to discuss publicly). From this perspective, Third World military dangers have not fully eclipsed those arising in Europe. Some analysts have criticized Soviet treaty arrangements with the East European states which could automatically draw the Soviet Union into a conflict contrary to Soviet interests. They describe the Soviet interests during such a local conflict as minimizing the participation of the Soviet Union in the conflict, and undertaking efforts to localize it, freeze it, and rapidly resolve it on the basis of a compromise.[37]

The two broad kinds of conflict impinging on the Soviet Union (large-scale East-West and local) impose differing demands on Soviet military capabilities and readiness levels. The notion of all-out East-West conflict has traditionally been presented in the Soviet Union as a justification for the need to maintain a military organization on extensive (as opposed to intensive) principles, which would enable the rapid mass mobilization of reserves. By contrast, Soviet analysts who believe that the principal future threat to Soviet security interests will most probably arise from instability in South-South relations argue now that Soviet 'military forces (and military activity in general) should be reoriented from the habitual course of their preparations for a large war with the West...to resolve tasks of a new character and scale'.[38] This raises the prospect of smaller, highly mobile, multi-purpose forces capable of responding to a range of contingencies.

However, the Soviet force structure required by the East-West conflict scenario need not necessarily be at odds with that appropriate for lesser conflicts on the Soviet periphery. Given the new political conditions that prevail in Eastern Europe, both scenarios are consistent with forward-deployed forces in the western military districts of the Soviet Union adopting relatively stabilizing, defensive postures, which would be supported by technologically well-equipped and highly mobile forces further in the Soviet interior. The uncertainties here are again attached to the role of independent-minded Soviet republics in this military organizational structure.

Initially, the challenge to coordinated Soviet defence planning arose in the Baltic republics. The assertion of Lithuanian independence in 1989-90 raised delicate military problems. In July 1990, Soviet Chief of Staff Moiseyev emphasized the need to determine whether Lithuania could provide 'a guarantee for the Soviet Union on the security of its north-west frontiers'. He insisted that the Lithuanian SSR holds an important position within the common system of defence of the Soviet Union. If Lithuania were to leave the Soviet Union,

> the country's defence capability in the region would be significantly impaired, a breach would be formed within the integrated group of troops of the Baltic Military district and the Baltic Fleet forces and the transport, control and communications system would be breached.[39]

By implication, the Soviet Union might need to adopt compensatory military measures in the Baltic and Leningrad military districts. Moiseyev had promised earlier that by the beginning of 1991 the Soviet grouping of troops in these districts would be reduced as a whole by approximately one third (including some 40,000 personnel and 1,200 tanks).[40] However, the renewed Soviet emphasis on border defence, coupled with the Baltic drive for independence, could result in Moscow's reappraising its military restructuring programme in its north-west regions.

The current delicacy of defence issues in this area was underlined by a highly critical Soviet response to an Estonian article that argued that the 1948 Finnish-Soviet Treaty of Friendship, Cooperation and Mutual Assistance represents expansionist policies, imperilling the independence of Finland. The Estonian author, Jaan Kahk, had maintained that the military consultations provisions in the treaty 'signify a possible demand by the Soviet Union to station its troops on Finnish territory'.[41]

This view was evidently related to a declaration by the Estonian Supreme Soviet that the presence of Soviet armed forces on Estonian territory infringes the republic's sovereignty. A decree on 30 March 1990 pronounced as illegal the service of residents of the Estonian SSR in the Soviet armed forces and this was reinforced the following month by a law on such service in the 'transitional period'.[42] In September, the Soviet media even reported that Estonia was intending to establish its own armed forces, initially composed of two divisions (as yet this is only an aspiration).[43] At a meeting between Estonian and Soviet officials the following month, the Estonian delegation stated further that it wished to be a neutral state.[44]

Lithuanian statements similarly began to refer to Soviet 'occupation forces'. As early as September 1989, the Lithuanian SSR proposed negotiations with the All-Union Supreme Soviet aimed at creating 'national military combined units' on Lithuanian territory in which Lithuanian citizens could perform their military service.[45] Latvia for its part has urged Moscow to withdraw its troops from the republic under the observation of the United Nations or CSCE representatives. At the end of July 1990, the chairmen of the Lithuanian, Latvian and Estonian Supreme Soviets spoke unanimously against the continued presence of Soviet forces in the Baltic republics.

The pronouncements of the Baltic republics had a catalytic effect. In mid-July, the Ukrainian Supreme Soviet resolved to establish its own independent national armed forces and internal troops. The Ukrainian SSR even proclaimed its intention to become in the future 'a permanently neutral state which is not a member of military blocs'. This was a medium-term aspiration, advocated strongly by the Rukh organization. In the shorter term, the Ukraine strove to ensure that

Ukrainian citizens perform their military service on the territory of the republic. Towards this end, the Permanent Commission of Youth Affairs of the Ukraine proposed the creation of a committee of deputies responsible for relations with the Soviet Ministry of Defence, together with a centralized republican military committee.[46]

Whatever transitional steps are agreed upon for the Ukraine, however, the head of Rukh, Ivan Drach, is quite committed to the gradual emergence of a Ukrainian army headed by a civilian Ukrainian minister of defence. In September 1990, Drach envisaged two sections to this force: professionals for the real army, and service units of a parade or decorative character.[47] Although the Ukraine is strategically vital to the current Soviet military organizational structure, the Ukrainian position was strengthened by the decision of the Byelorussian SSR to seek control over military activities in this key neighbouring republic.

The drive for autonomous decision-making over military matters spread also to the Transcaucasus. In August 1990, the Armenian Supreme Soviet adopted a declaration on Armenia's independent statehood, which announced the intention of Armenia to set up its own armed forces and internal troops. It prohibited the stationing of military units of 'other countries', military bases and facilities on republican territory without its Supreme Soviet's agreement. Armenia's armed forces could not be used without the agreement of the supreme body of power.[48] Armenian 'self-defence' detachments began to be formed.

The next month, the Moldavian parliament ruled to suspend provisions on obligatory military service contained in Soviet Union laws. The Moldavian government was expected to work out a programme for a national Moldavian army. A new military sub-unit was formed from a detachment of volunteers - the *Tiras-Tigina* battalion - and the prime minister of Moldova (Moldavia) expressed his hope that this would grow into a division and eventually enter forever into the history of the republic.[49]

In Soviet Georgia, nationalist spokesmen called for the creation of a national Georgian army as early as June 1989 to restore and defend the sovereignty of the republic, on economic grounds, and to escape ethnic harassment in the Soviet forces.[50] By the following autumn, reports began to appear that a Georgian national army was unofficially being organized.[51] In December 1990, Dzhaba Ioseliani, the leader of an organization styled as the 'Georgian Army' (*Sakartvelos Mkhedrioni*), claimed that this underground force (one not sponsored by the new republican leadership) had five thousand men. He warned that it could be increased to 60,000 and that if the authorities sought to use force to eliminate it he would launch combat operations.[52]

Partly to outflank such bodies, the Georgian parliament finally voted in January 1991 to create its own army. This would be partly composed of a Georgian national guard of some 12,000 men under the Georgian Ministry of Interior, and would join the republic's 20,000 troops and policemen to create a larger force.[53]

Perhaps the key issue for Soviet strategic planning is the position the Russian Federation (RFSFR) itself will take on defence decision-making. On 19 September 1990, the chairman of the RFSFR Council of Ministers, Ivan Silayev, met with representatives of the armed forces in Moscow. At the meeting it was emphasized that Russia did not seek to set up its own military formations, that the republican Supreme Soviet and the government were interested in general, mutually beneficial cooperation with all military bodies and military formations stationed on the territory of the republic.[54] At the same time, RFSFR defence officials expressed concern that 'in the near future we could find ourselves facing the fact that Russia alone will be forced to bear the entire burden of the Union's defence'. He affirmed that 'if we divide the army according to republics, it would mean in effect the collapse of our Union and the collapse of our state'.[55]

This conciliatory line changed rapidly, however, in autumn 1990 and the new RFSFR constitution proclaimed the unambiguous intention of the republic to control the armed forces located on its territory.[56] This aspiration was also implicit in a resolution adopted by the RFSFR Council of Ministers on the 'solution of issues connected with reduction of the Soviet armed forces on the territory of the RFSFR', to which Defence Minister Yazov reacted with indignation.[57] The

RFSFR proceeded to establish a State Committee on Public Security and Coordination with the Soviet Ministry of Defence and the State Committee on Security (KGB). The post of acting first deputy chairman of this new body was given to the vocal military reformist, People's Deputy Major Vladimir Lopatin, who in 1990 helped to develop an alternative military reform programme to that sponsored by the Ministry of Defence (see pp. 130-1).

At the fourth session of the Congress of People's Deputies of the Soviet Union in December 1990, the radical mayor of Moscow, Gavriil Popov, proposed the creation of territorial troops in the republics alongside a strong federal professional army. Furthermore, at the beginning of 1991, Boris Yeltsin, the RFSFR president, lent his weight in principle to the idea of creating RFSFR armed forces. Clearly, this contentious issue divides Soviet and Russian military opinion. Colonel-General Dmitri Volkogonov, a generally reformist official, claimed that the formation of a Russian army 'would be a great mistake, a step towards civil war'. But certain officers favour at least more elected RFSFR representation in Soviet defence decision-making.[58]

The official Soviet response to the spate of republican declarations on military policy over 1990 appeared uncompromising. Gorbachev insisted in October that the organization of defence should be the exclusive preserve of the Soviet Union, that the system of managing Soviet defence forms 'an intricate complex in which everything is inter-related and which can only perform its tasks if it operates as a single whole'.[59] The Soviet Deputy Chief of General Staff, Colonel-General Grigory Krivosheyev, declared similarly that 'we deploy missiles, aircraft, air defences, the army in accordance with strategic and tactical considerations, rather than demographic or...egotistical sentiments in this or that region'.[60] Defence Minister Yazov insisted that the army should defend all society, the state as a whole, so 'proposals that the army should be distributed among the republics or organized on a two-level basis (one part of the army federal and one part republic) are not serious'.[61]

In public, therefore, the Soviet leadership reacted dismissively to proposals for any substantial dilution of the central military authority of the Union. But Soviet leaders could not fail to recognize that the astonishing developments outlined above challenge in an unprecedented way the organizational framework and therefore strategic capabilities and planning of the postwar Soviet military apparatus. Union-level planning on military policy was thrown into confusion since the General Staff could no longer calculate the demo-graphic base of the military forces available, or rely on the contribution of the republics to the common defence effort.

Much here will depend on the conceptual basis of a re-defined Union-republican defence relationship. In anticipation of this change, the 'initiative group' of people's deputies of the Soviet Union held hearings in the summer of 1990 involving representatives of the Union and republican academies of sciences. These hearings were intended to help accommodate security plans under development in the republics to a com-prehensive security concept for a nation-state entity to replace the Soviet Union after the conclusion of a new Union treaty.[62]

Plans for a Union-wide defence reform, which were examined by the Defence Council in September 1990, depend on the agreement over a new republic-Union relationship. But Marshal Akhromeyev stressed at the end of the year that 'the concept of the Union treaty envisages that the function of the defence of the country, protection of Union sovereignty and territorial integrity and the leadership of the armed forces belong to the powers of the Union bodies'. He argued that this corresponded to international legal standards and pointed to arrangements in 'federative countries like Switzerland, Belgium, Yugoslavia, India and others'.[63]

This line was echoed in the Ministry of Defence draft military reform plan published in November 1990, which set out the need for 'Armed Forces common to the entire Union that are multi-ethnic, regular and manned on a mixed volunteer-compulsory basis'.[64] The influential Russian civilian defence analyst Andrei Kokoshin similarly accepted the need for armed forces common the whole Union but stipulated that they should be 'under the dependable control of democratic institutions'.[65]

The alternative draft reform plan, developed by a group of people's deputies of the Soviet Union and signed by

Vladimir Lopatin, reached, however, different recommen-
dations. It envisaged a 'community of sovereign states' developing in the Soviet Union, which would have the right 'to
have their own armed formations and reserves, with the centre
granted the possibility of their use to ensure the community's
security against an external military threat'. The draft
anticipated the creation of 'a military-political alliance of
sovereign states' and the establishment of 'coalition command
and control entities'. The legislative bodies of the new states
would acquire rights and powers to determine the size of their
armed forces and reserve, and the makeup of their military
equipment and arms, and to appoint their own civilian
ministers of defence. The sphere of joint competence and joint
activity of the centre and the new states would include 'determining possible military threats and appropriate levels of
defence sufficiency; developing military policy, doctrine and
the military reform concept and programme'.[66]

These competing military reform drafts are far apart
and leave open various scenarios for the future organization of
Union-republican defence relations. First, there is the Ministry
of Defence proposal, which has powerful institutional support
but which is essentially *status quo* oriented. Second, a revised
version of this plan could result in a two-tier system of
territorial militias, or reserve forces, located in the peripheral
republics, supported by strategic professional forces. Before
his replacement, the reform-minded Minister of Interior,
Vadim Bakatin, is reported to have suggested that Gorbachev
should examine the possibility of permitting the republics
limited republican armies for local use. This scheme envisages
the central government's retaining control over most of the
armed forces, especially their strategic units.[67]

Third, there is the alternative draft defence reform
concept, which appears to envisage a strategic army composed
of national units, like the former Warsaw Pact forces, with its
organization decided by independent republics. This would be
favoured by many republican officials and leaders. For
example, the Armenian president, Levon Ter-Petrosyan, has
advocated a two-stage process: 1) republic citizens serving on
the territory of their republic; and 2) a year or so later, 'these
parts will automatically become national armies'. It would 'not

be a single army but a real Union army...like the armies of the Warsaw Treaty and the NATO armies', and could express common interests through suitable arrangements.[68]

Fourth, certain republics seek fully autonomous armed forces. An early outline of the process envisaged was given by a Latvian nationalist leader in July 1990. He advocated initially a transitional period involving the withdrawal of Soviet nuclear and chemical weapons and offensive forces, which would leave a limited contingent of Soviet troops at bases and garrisons. Efforts would be made to transfer internal troops, civil defence units, and naval and ground border troops to the republic's jurisdiction. Next, a demilitarization and gradual withdrawal of the remaining Soviet troops in Latvia would occur. According to this scheme, Latvia would only need its own border troops and those for protection of its air space.[69]

In reality, the balance of political forces in the Soviet Union in 1991 did not offer much hope for options two and three in the near term. This was signalled by an uncompromising presidential decree signed by Gorbachev on 1 December 1990, which declared all acts by bodies of state authority of the Union republics on defence issues which conflict with the Soviet legislation as juridically invalid.[70] In an apparent attempt to offset the intransigent image of the Union authorities, however, Marshal Akhromeyev accepted directly after this decree that the republics should be granted wider rights in issues of defence. But he conceded only that the draft Union law permitted the republics to take part in implementing the powers of the Union by jointly forming Union bodies. Issues of the military call-up and troop deployment on republican territory could be 'tackled jointly with the republics and in accordance with new laws'.[71]

As the Soviet military consolidated its political position towards the end of 1990 and into 1991, it sought to reinforce Gorbachev's December 1990 decree on the authority of the Union over military policy through combining consultations with intimidation. For example, consultations on military issues were held between the Latvian leadership and the Soviet Chief of Staff Moiseyev as tensions heightened in Latvia. Moiseyev was adamant that troops performing 'strategic defence tasks - strategic rocket troops, the missile-attack warning troops, space tracking and the Baltic fleet bases' would remain in the republic. The Latvian representatives in fact retracted their earlier demands and conceded that Latvia does not intend to create its own armed forces. They sought instead special talks on the status of the Soviet armed forces on the republic's territory.[72]

Similar consultations between Soviet military leaders and envoys of Lithuania, Moldova, Uzbekistan, the Ukraine and Azerbaidzhan had been held by January 1991. At this time, Moiseyev announced that a special department for permanent ties with the supreme soviets of the Soviet republics on the solution of defence questions would be created at the General Staff.[73] But there is no certainty that other republics will adopt the pragmatic line that Latvia did in its discussions. Indeed, in January 1991, Georgia defiantly announced that it would establish its own armed forces. This indicated that the issue would continue to bedevil Union-republic relations further in the 1990s.

Evidently, Soviet military doctrine, and its military-technical subcomponents strategy, operational art and tactics, are faced with an acute dilemma in accommodating republican demands for greater control over defence matters. The fixed points of central Soviet General Staff planning for conventional forces have been swept away as uncertainty over the role of republican defence efforts in future Union-wide military plans increases monthly. The outcome of this centre-periphery controversy, especially in the Ukraine, in Byelo-russia and crucially in the RSFSR, will be significant for Soviet internal military stability and its Union-level military capabilities. This in turn will influence Soviet military policy in Europe and the security perceptions of West European countries in the 1990s.

5. DOCTRINAL EVOLUTION AND NUCLEAR DETERRENCE IN EUROPE

Official Soviet policy in the late 1980s favoured the complete and universal elimination of nuclear weapons. But Soviet specialists focused their analyses on the conditions under which strategic stability might be secured following nuclear arms reductions that fell short of this ideal long-term goal. Many such analysts may in fact have perceived the idea of complete denuclearization as unrealistic; the purpose of their studies appeared rather to identify the optimal conditions for the maintenance of a relationship of minimum strategic deterrence.

Such views reflected a pragmatic strain in Soviet thinking, based on the assumption that Soviet security requirements would be framed within a strategic environment in which nuclear deterrence would remain for the foreseeable future the dominant means of constraining conflict between East and West. This pragmatism was officially endorsed in a proposal by Foreign Minister Shevardnadze in December 1989 for East-West negotiations over theatre nuclear weapons on the basis of minimum deterrence.[74]

The theme of minimum deterrence has become more established in Moscow at the beginning of the 1990s as the conventional imbalance favouring the Soviet Union in Europe shows every prospect of shifting against the Soviet Union as a result of the withdrawal of forces from Eastern Europe, the collapse of the Warsaw Pact and the terms of the 1990 CFE Treaty.

In these conditions, Soviet military planners may accord a renewed significance to Soviet nuclear deterrent capabilities in Europe (west of the Urals). Andrei Kokoshin notes that 'in averting a whole number of types of aggression we will have to rely to a greater extent on the deterrent effect of nuclear weapons'. Nuclear systems, he implies, may provide a military-political reinsurance at a time of considerable overall strategic uncertainty. Sergei Karaganov agrees that the Soviet Union needs temporarily to increase its psychological reliance on the nuclear factor for its security, that the Soviet nuclear capability makes any threat from the West improbable even if a serious Western superiority in conventional forces were to arise.[75]

This shift in perpective has two implications. First, as Kokoshin argues, the Soviet Union now requires its 'own theory, developed in depth, of nuclear deterrence with its corresponding realization in military doctrine'.[76] Second,

Soviet military representatives have begun to argue that it would be unwise to abandon such weapons altogether, since they can stabilize a potential enemy.

This leads to a contradiction. Soviet analysts argued in 1990 that retaining theatre nuclear weapons (TNWs) might reassure Soviet circles concerned about the effects of drastic asymmetrical conventional arms cuts at a time of German unification. Yet, it has also been understood that the reduction of TNWs and their removal from the territories of the East European states 'would help defuse anti-Soviet sentiments... and make less credible the arguments of those who favour withdrawal from the Warsaw Treaty'. These specialists have favoured the eventual full elimination of TNWs but believe that this may have to wait until the European system of security has been substantially reinforced and restructured.[77]

For the transitional phase, it is argued that

> precise parity in tactical nuclear forces ... i.e., equality in the number of delivery vehicles and warheads or even equality in combat capabilities, is even less necessary to ensure stability and security in Europe than similar parity at the strategic level.[78]

For the reasons cited, however, unreciprocated unilateral Soviet cuts in TNWs are not advocated. Instead, in spring 1990, Soviet specialists raised the possibility of parallel unilateral reductions in Eastern and Western TNWs down to specified interim or even final levels as an alternative to negotiations in a traditional fashion on TNW arsenals. Yet, formal negotiations - as promised by the July 1990 NATO summit - remain the preferred Soviet route to minimum deterrent levels.[79]

The NATO decision in July 1990 to reexamine the concept of flexible response in the context of reducing the role of nuclear weapons won the praise of Foreign Minister Shevardnadze. He also pointed to the potential significance of the terminology of the NATO communique, which spoke of substrategic nuclear systems of the shortest range rather than of tactical nuclear weapons.[80] To the extent that NATO policy shifts from the flexible response doctrine and Soviet leaders rediscover a peacetime function for deterrence in Europe, the nuclear thinking of West and East shows signs of convergence.

At the same time, unfolding political processes complicate the role of nuclear deterrence for the Soviet Union in Europe. Since 1990, the Soviet leadership has come under pressure for the rapid, full withdrawal of its nuclear systems from Eastern Europe. These necessarily need to be withdrawn along with other Soviet military assets in the early 1990s, whether or not an agreement is reached with the West on TNWs. Negotiations on Soviet TNW capabilities would then concern the systems within Soviet frontiers.

Furthermore, the political transformation of Eastern Europe and the breakdown of WTO military integrity may effectively have led the Soviet military command to withdraw its extended nuclear guarantee to the NSWP countries. While the United States maintains its extended deterrence posture for European NATO states (notwithstanding any modifications in the doctrine of flexible response), the Soviet Union would appear now to limit its nuclear commitment to the Soviet homeland.[81] This is implicit in Chief of Staff Moiseyev's assertion at the 28th Party Congress that the Soviet Union is compelled 'to take a new approach to our country's strategic defence planning, now only within the Soviet state borders'.[82]

In the second place, the Soviet Ministry of Defence has been discreetly pulling back to the RSFSR tactical nuclear weapons and other nuclear devices from restive republics, in particular the Baltic states and the Transcaucasian republics.[83] The demands of Soviet republics to determine their own defence postures raises the prospect of the RSFSR eventually becoming the only repository of nuclear weapons in the Soviet Union. In the near term, the only Soviet nuclear systems remaining outside this heartland may be immobile ICBMs.[84] But RSFSR officials have implied that nuclear systems on their republican territory should come under their control. This claim creates the worrying prospect of a political struggle with the Union for responsibility over at least certain aspects of the Soviet nuclear force posture and deployment.

Certain other republics have remained uncertain whether to seek their own nuclear potential, although the republican leaderships in the Ukraine and Byelorussia have conceded their readiness to shed the nuclear weapons on their soil. The head of the Ukrainian Rukh has countered fears over the scattering of nuclear weapons in 'national quarters' by promoting the idea of a nuclear-free Ukraine. His preferred option may be, however, to pass these weapons on to the RSFSR under Yeltsin rather than to the Union authorities under Gorbachev.[85]

Soviet military commanders are adamant that a division of nuclear weapons among the republics is inadmissible, not least since it would breach the nuclear non-proliferation treaty and have international repercussions.[86] Marshal Akhromeyev has insisted that TNWs 'should be supervised only by the centre' and that 'if we talk about strategic offensive weapons, then this centralization reaches its peak'.[87]

The unforeseen need to concentrate nuclear deterrent capabilities in Russia must disorganize Soviet nuclear planning. But Soviet nuclear guarantees are likely to continue to extend to all current Soviet republics regardless of the character of the new law on the federation or the outcome of negotiations to permit republics more autonomy in the military field.

6. CONCLUSION

The analysis in this chapter has concentrated on the processes and perceptions shaping the reformulation of Soviet military doctrine and planning assumptions at the beginning of the 1990s. It reveals that Soviet military thinking is in a crucial transitional phase which makes the identification of its specific content inherently uncertain. It also raises a number of specific unresolved issues, which will preoccupy analysts and officials and be reflected in Soviet military policy towards Europe.

First, we should consider whether military doctrine is still an effective category or framework for analysis of Soviet military thought except at a very abstract level. To a considerable extent, Soviet military policy since 1989 has been reacting to rapidly changing external developments, and strategic planning assumptions appear to have changed only subsequently and often belatedly. Moreover, the institutions defining such doctrine and higher level defence planning, and the overall relationship between the Soviet civilian political and military authorities have appeared in constant flux, whereas military doctrine should have a stable basis. For example, uncertainty attaches to the role and makeup of a possible Soviet National Security Council.

Second, despite these ambiguities, it is worth considering whether the preconditions exist to elaborate elements of a common East-West military doctrine. The evidence of greater convergence or parallelism between the military thinking of the sides, in relation to concepts of both non-offensive defence and minimum nuclear deterrence, offer encouragement to such attempts. The opportunities should be explored at the second Vienna doctrine seminar.

The November 1990 CSCE summit in Paris formally sought to set the Cold War at rest and proclaimed that East and West are no longer adversaries. But is this more than a rhetorical diplomatic gesture? So far it appears that neither the Soviet Union nor the Western alliance has abandoned its traditional premise that an East-West conflict is the principal threat scenario influencing military planning, even if the likelihood of such large-scale conflict is now accepted as remote in the near future. At the same time, the Soviet high command is clearly shifting its attention away from this European scenario towards military dangers on the southern perimeter of the Soviet Union and in the Near East, especially in association with the Gulf War. Eastern Europe is also understood to harbour dangerous instabilities, and Soviet military commanders cannot realistically expect to restore their military pre-eminence in this region in the foreseeable future. This raises the question of how the Soviet Union and Western states should respond in the future to shared threats and instabilities in Eastern Europe and the Gulf.

This leads to the third issue: the continued key role occupied by Eastern Europe in Soviet military thinking, despite the shift in the Soviet strategic line of defence back to the Soviet frontier. Soviet military interests in this region would appear to be in maintaining stability and preventing the expansion of Western military arrangements further east following the shift in allegiance of East Germany. To prevent in the future possible dangerous friction between the West and the Soviet Union, which could restore old animosities, NATO could consider the idea of East-West guarantees on the non-intervention of forces in Eastern Europe (following the Soviet military departure) and possibly on the non-extension of the NATO structure further into Eastern Europe. The Soviet Union in turn could perhaps forgo any attempts to press Poland into a special military relationship with it - once the Warsaw Pact is finally laid to rest - and permit the Baltic republics a large degree of autonomy on military issues.

Fourth, there remains a potential contradiction between the military planning requirements of the Soviet emphasis on strategic defence from behind the Soviet borders - which focus attention on force structures and deployments in the Soviet border zones, especially in the western military districts - and the insistent demands of the republics for partial or full autonomy on military issues concerning their territories.

Much here depends on whether a division of labour can be reached, perhaps through forward defence in republics on the western borders of the Soviet Union principally being exercised by reserve or even national territorial formations. In this scheme, certain strategic defence forces (for example, air defence elements) would still be required in the peripheral regions, but Union-level strategic army units could be held in the rear and central reserve area of the RSFSR.

One major uncertainty here, however, is how far the RSFSR leadership may be able to influence coordinated Soviet military planning through promoting its own views on military doctrine, force restructuring and so on. Efforts in this direction would be a natural outgrowth of any serious attempt by the RSFSR leadership to create its own armed forces, an attempt which Gorbachev described in January 1991 as being fraught with particularly serious dangers.[88] RSFSR officials are sympathetic to the drive for greater autonomy by the smaller republics and appear to support the idea of a substantially new confederation which threatens the role of the All-Union Soviet General Staff.

This leads to the possibility that influential political elements in the Ukraine, Byelorussia, the Baltic republics and other strategically significant republics could seek to obstruct future joint military planning between their republics and the

Soviet General Staff, in a manner analogous to the determination of the non-Soviet Warsaw Pact states to shed the integrated military structure of the WTO.

It is likely that Soviet military commanders regard the possibility of the current union republics adopting a neutral or even adversarial defence posture towards the 'centre' in the future, as some of them sought to do during the Second World War, as a scenario to be prevented at all costs. Indeed, the provisions in the draft Union Treaty seek to prevent its arising. This is a principal concern underlying the hostility of the Soviet military leadership to the idea of republican or territorial armies. One officer described the dilemma bluntly: 'In creating your army, you have to plan on the basis of against whom this army is going to defend you. Against whom ...will the Ukraine, Byelorussia, Georgia, Estonia, Latvia and Lithuania be defending themselves?'[89]

Uncertainty over the future military role of the Soviet republics will continue even if strong measures are taken in the short term to maintain the integrity of the Soviet Union. This creates new pressures for Soviet (All-Union) military doctrine, which anyway is in a process of reformulation; and it helps shape the debate on military organizational reform, which has intensified in the Soviet Union since autumn 1990.[90] Soviet military policy is therefore in a crucial transitional period, which may last through the early 1990s, complicating attempts to forecast Soviet defence interests in the new Europe.

NOTES

1. This chapter is supported by a grant from the Ford Foundation and written within the framework of the project *'Soviet Defence and Conventional Arms Control Policies, 1985-2000'*, based at the Centre for Russian and East European Studies, University of Birmingham. I would like to acknowledge the support of the Finnish Institute of International Affairs in arranging the conference where an initial draft of this paper was presented; the Kennan Institute of the Woodrow Wilson Centre for grant aid enabling further research and for the opportunity to present a more advanced version of this paper; and the Brookings Institution for essential research facilities. The chapter was concluded on 12 February 1991.

2. Vadim Zagladin, Secretary of the Foreign Affairs Commission of the Supreme Soviet, on Soviet television, 30 October 1988 in *Foreign Broadcast Information Service* (hereafter *FBIS*), SU/0304 A1/3.
3. Disclosed by Marshal Akhromeyev during a discussion on Soviet television, 9 March 1990; in *FBIS* SU/0717 A1/3.
4. See the assessment of the Soviet initiative by Sam Nunn, *Washington Post*, 18 December 1988.
5. For example, Major-General R. Simonyan, 'From Realistic Positions', *Soviet Military Review*, no. 1, 1988, p. 53 and Lt-General, ret., M. Milshteyn, *New Times*, no. 7, 1987, cited in *FBIS*, SU/8621 A1/7.
6. *Vestnik Ministerstva inostrannykh del SSSR*, no. 4, 1989, p. 42.
7. Interview in *Agitator armii i flota*, no. 24, 1989, pp. 2-4, as translated in *Joint Publications Research Service* (hereafter *JPRS*) -UMA-90-009, 13 April 1990.
8. For earlier Soviet thinking on coalitional warfare, see M. Sadykiewicz, 'Organising for Coalition Warfare: The Role of East European Warsaw Pact Forces in Soviet Military Planning', *RAND* (Santa Monica), R-3559-RC, September 1988 and J. Yurechko, 'Coalition Warfare: The Soviet Approach', *Berichte des Bundesinstituts für ostwissenschaftliche und internationale Studien*, no. 44, 1986.
9. P. Lushev, 'Edinstvo oboronnykh usilii stran Varshanskogo Dogovora - faktor nadezhnoi zashchity sotsializma', *Voennaya mysl*, no. 1, 1990, p. 13.
10. Interview in *Sovetskaya Rossiya*, 13 May 1990.
11. R. Garthoff, 'The Warsaw Pact Today - and Tomorrow?', *The Brookings Review* (Summer 1990), p. 37.
12. M. Bezrukov and A. Kortunov, 'Nuzhna reforma OVD', *SShA: ekonomika, politika, ideologiya*, no. 3, 1990, p. 31 and S. Blagovolin, 'Voennaya moshch - skolko, kakaya, zachem?', *Mirovaya ekonomika i mezhdunarodnye otnosheniya*, no. 8, 1989, p. 16.
13. This idea has been floated by Laszlo Valki, head of the Faculty of International Law at Budapest's Lorand Eotvos University. See A. Reisch, 'Government Wants Negotiated Withdrawal from the Warsaw Pact', *Radio Free Europe. Report on Eastern Europe*, vol. 1, no. 23, p. 32.
14. S. Karaganov, 'The Problems of the USSR's European Policy', *International Affairs*, no. 7, 1990, p. 78.
15. President Havel after agreement was reached on the withdrawal of Soviet troops from Czechoslovakia with Gorbachev: TASS, 26 February 1990 in *FBIS*, SU/0700 A2/3.
16. On the 1955 treaty, see the views of Foreign Minister Gyula Horn, at the press conference in the USSR Foreign Ministry on 10 March 1990 (*Izvestiya*, 12 March 1990). On Hungarian neutrality, see A. Reisch, 'The Hungarian Dilemma: After the Warsaw Pact, Neutrality or NATO?', *Radio Free Europe Report on Eastern Europe*, vol. 1, no. 15, pp. 16-22; and the interview with the Hungarian Premier after the Warsaw Treaty Summit, Hungarian Television, 8 June 1990 in *FBIS*, SU EE/0787 C1/1-2.
17. *Moscow News*, no. 8-9, 1990, p. 11.
18. Soviet Television, 8 April 1990 in *FBIS*, SU/0742 B/9.

19. See M. Sadykiewicz, 'The Warsaw Pact Command Structure in Peace and War', *RAND* (Santa Monica), September 1988, R-3358-RC, p. 12 and 'Wartime Missions of Polish Internal Front', *RAND* (Santa Monica), July 1986, N-2401-1-OSD, p. 35.
20. Sadykiewicz, 'The Warsaw Pact Command Structure in Peace and War', p. 78. It is likely that the constitutions of these countries will be amended to include the principle of fighting only on their own national territory.
21. See M. Sadykiewicz and D. Clarke, 'The New Polish Defence Doctrine: A Further Step towards Sovereignty', *Radio Free Europe Report on Eastern Europe*, vol. 1, no. 18, pp. 20-3.
22. P. Almquist, 'The Vienna Military Doctrine Seminar: Flexible Response vs. Defensive Sufficiency', *Arms Control Today*, vol. 20, no. 2 (March 1990), p. 22-3. The commitment to national defence doctrines was also made explicit by the East German Chief of Staff, Lieutenant-General Manfred Graetz, *Guardian*, 17 January 1990.
23. Prague radio, 15 June 1990 in *FBIS*, SU EE/0793 C1/3.
24. P. Lushev, 'Varshavskii Dogovor: istoriya i sovremennost', *Voennaya mysl*, no. 5, 1990, pp. 22, 25-6.
25. Interview with Marshal D. Yazov, *Rabochnaya Tribuna*, 26 June 1990, in *FBIS*, SU/0802 A1/1.
26. *ADN*, 9 June 1990 in *FBIS*, SU EE/0787 C1/1.
27. Report on statement by the Hungarian Minister of Defence Lajos Fuer to the Soviet Minister of Defence Dmitri Yazov during talks on Soviet troop withdrawals from Hungary, MTI, 8 June 1990, in *FBIS*, SU EE/0787 C1/3. See also A. Reisch, 'Hungary to Leave Military Arm of Warsaw Pact', *Radio Free Europe Report on Eastern Europe*, vol. 1, no. 26, pp. 20-5.
28. *Washington Post*, 26 February 1991.
29. Report of statement by Lieutenant-General G. Burutin, first deputy head of the directorate of the General Staff of the Soviet Armed Forces, at the Vienna seminar on military doctrines, TASS, 29 January 1990 in *FBIS*, SU/0682 A1/6.
30. Soviet General Staff officer during discussions in Moscow on the Emerging Strategic Future, July 1990.
31. Speech by Army General M. Moiseyev to Congress Section on 'The CPSU's International Activity,' *Krasnaya zvezda*, 7 July 1990.
32. TASS, 2 January 1991 in *FBIS*, SU/0961 B/2.
33. *Krasnaya zvezda*, 23 January 1990.
34. See for example the interview with M. Moiseyev, *Voennii vestnik*, no. 1, 1990, pp. 5-9.
35. Interview in *Agitator armii i flota*, no. 24, 1989, pp. 2-4, as translated in *JPRS*-UMA-90-009, 13 April 1990, p. 14.
36. 'Proekt ministerstva oborony SSSR: Kontseptsiya voennoj reformy', *Pravitelstvennyj vestnik*, no. 48, 1990, p. 6 and the interview with A. Kokoshin, *Trud*, 2 October 1990.
37. A. Bogaturov, M. Nosov and K. Pleshakov, 'Kto oni, nashi soyuzniki?', *Kommunist*, no. 1, 1990, p. 110.
38. S. Blagovolin, 'Geopoliticheskie aspekty oboronitelnoi dostatochnosti', *Kommunist*, no. 4, 1990, p. 118.

39. Interview with M. Moiseyev, TASS, 12 July 1990 in *FBIS*, SU/0818 B/5.
40. TASS, 27 October 1989 in *FBIS*, SU/0603 A1/4.
41. V. Shmyganovskii, in *Izvestiya*, 20 July 1990. The offending article was written by the Estonian scholar Juhan Kahk Jr and published in the Estonian Communist Party Central Committee journal *Aja Puls*. Minister Yazov had stressed before his visit to Finland that there is no need to change the military articles of the 1948 treaty (interview for Helsingin Sanomat, Helsinki Radio, 13 August 1989 in *FBIS*, SU/0535 A2/1-2). Kahk's views were surprising since a nominee for the Latvian premiership, Godmanis, had recently argued before the Latvian Supreme Soviet that the Baltic states should seek to model themselves on Finland's special relations with the Soviet Union in the political, economic and military spheres (Latvian Radio, 7 May 1990 in *FBIS*, SU/0762 B/1).
42. *Molodezh Estonii*, 13 April 1990 as translated in *JPRS*-UMA-90-015, 26 June 1990, p. 64.
43. Moscow Home Service, 10 September 1990 in *FBIS* SU/0866 i.
44. TASS, 30 October 1990 in *Radio Liberty Report on the USSR*, vol. 2, no. 45, 1990, p. 35.
45. Decree of Lithuanian SSR Supreme Soviet, issued on 29 September 1989, 'On Military Service of LiSSR Citizens', *Sovetskaya Litva*, 5 October 1989; as translated in *JPRS*-UMA-89-029, 20 December 1989, pp. 14-15.
46. See Ukrainian SSR Statement, *Pravda Ukrainy*, 5 August 1990, as translated in *JPRS*-UPA-90-051, 5 September 1990, p. 31 and appeal by the head of the Ukrainian SSR Supreme Soviet Permanent Commission on Youth Affairs to implement the Ukrainian SSR's decree on army service, *Molod Ukrainy*, 19 September 1990, as translated in *JPRS*-UPA-90-064, 21 November 1990, pp. 25-6.
47. *Literaturnaya Ukraina*, 13 September 1990, as translated in *JPRS*-UPA-90-064, 21 November 1990, p. 27.
48. Report on declaration of the Armenian Supreme Soviet, Moscow Home Service, 23 August 1990 in *FBIS*, SU/0852 B/7.
49. As reported in the article by P. Rashdov, *Trud*, 1 November 1990.
50. See the article by Z. Kavtaradze, in *Akhalgazrda Komunisti*, as translated in *JPRS*-UMA-89-021, 6 September 1990, p. 2.
51. As in report by A. Sinelnikov, *Zarya Vostoka*, 15 November 1990 in *FBIS*, SU/0941 B/13.
52. Interview, TASS, 9 December 1990; Novosti, *USSR Defence and Diplomacy Update*, 12 December 1990.
53. *Washington Post*, 1 February 1991.
54. Report of meeting on Moscow Home Service, 19 September 1990 in *FBIS*, SU/0875 B/2.
55. Lieutenant-Colonel A. Katenkov, deputy chairman of the joint subcommittee of the RSFSR Supreme Soviet on the defence of the state sovereignty of the republic, Moscow Home Service, 17 September 1990 in *FBIS*, SU/0875 B/2-3.
56. RSFSR Constitution, Part 5.10 (*Argumenty i fakty*, no. 47, 1990, p. 7).

57. Interview with Yazov on Moscow television, 25 November 1990 in *FBIS*, SU/0932 B/3-4.
58. See Captains V. Urban and V. Ermolin, 'Sozdanie rossiiskoi armii bylo by bolshoi oshibkoi', *Krasnaya zvezda*, 25 January 1991.
59. Speech on 17 August in the Odessa military district, *Pravda*, 19 August 1990.
60. *Izvestiya*, 28 July 1990.
61. Interview with Yazov on 19 December 1990; Novosti, *USSR Defence and Diplomacy Update*, 19 December 1990, p. 90.
62. Academician Yuri Ryzhov, chairman of the Soviet parliament committee on science, heads this group, reported by TASS, 6 August 1990 in *FBIS*, SU/0837 B/6.
63. Speech at the USSR Supreme Soviet session on draft union treaty, Moscow Home Service, 3 December 1990 in *FBIS*, SU/0943 C1/1.
64. 'Proekt Ministerstva oboronoi SSSR: konseptsiya voennoi reformy', *Pravitelstvennyi vestnik*, no. 48, 1990, p. 6.
65. *Trud*, 2 October 1990.
66. See 'Proekt, razrabotannyi gruppoi narodnykh deputatov SSSR: O podgotovke i provedenii voennoj reformy', *Pravitelstvennyj vestnik*, no. 48, 1990, pp. 10-11.
67. Press conference, reported in *Radio Liberty Report on the USSR*, vol. 2, no. 44, 1990, p. 36.
68. Soviet television, 30 November 1990 in *FBIS*, SU/0937 b/3-4.
69. Interview of Yanis Baskers, deputy chairman of the Association of Latvian Riflemen, in *Baltiiskoe vremya*, no. 24, 1990, as translated in *JPRS*-UMA-90-017, 19 July 1990, pp. 15-16.
70. Text of the presidential decree on 'Certain Aspects on Defence Matters That have Been Adopted in Union Republics', TASS, 1 December 1990 in *FBIS*, SU/0937 C2/1.
71. Address to the USSR Supreme Soviet on 3 December, Moscow Home Service, 3 December 1990 in *FBIS*, SU/0943 C1/1.
72. Consultations as reported in the interview with M. Moiseyev, *Izvestiya*, 8 January 1991.
73. ibid.
74. A systematic examination of the 'pros' and 'cons' of a posture of minimum deterrence is contained in R. Bogdanov and A. Kortunov, 'On the Balance of Power', *International Affairs* (Moscow), no. 8, 1989, pp. 3-13.
75. Karaganov, op. cit., p. 78; interview with A. Kokoshin, *Trud*, 2 October 1990.
76. Kokoshin, ibid.
77. P. Bayev, V. Zhurkin, S. Karaganov and V. Shein, *Tactical Nuclear Weapons in Europe: The Problem of Reduction and Elimination*, Moscow: Novosti, 1990, pp. 13-14.
78. ibid., p. 38.
79. ibid., p. 42 and P. Bayev, V. Zhurkin, S. Karaganov and V. Shein, 'Is a "Third Zero" Possible?', *International Affairs* (Moscow), no. 4, 1990, p. 10.
80. E. Shevardnadze in *Izvestiya*, 7 July 1990.
81. As argued by Stephan Kux, 'The Soviet Debate on Strategic Nuclear

Arms' in R. Allison (ed.), *Radical Reform in Soviet Defence Policy* (London: Macmillan, 1991).

82. *Krasnaya zvezda*, 7 July 1990.
83. Chief of Staff M. Moiseyev first admitted that nuclear warheads had been quietly withdrawn from potential ethnic trouble spots in September (*Washington Post*, 28 September 1990).
84. At the end of 1990, Soviet strategic missiles were deployed only on the territories of the RSFSR, the Ukraine and Kazakhstan.
85. The interview with Ivan Drach (*Literaturnaya Ukraina*, 13 September 1990), as translated in *JPRS*-UPA-90-064, 21 November 1990, p. 27.
86. This is argued, for example, by Col. V. Seleznev, Moscow Home Service, 3 December 1990 in *FBIS*, SU/0939 B/7-8.
87. Speech at the Presidium of the Supreme Soviet, 3 December 1990 in *FBIS*, SU/0943 C1/1.
88. 'Zayavlenie Prezidenta SSSR M. S. Gorbacheva', *Pravda*, 23 January 1991.
89. V. Seleznev, op. cit., B/7.
90. For a recent analysis of the relationship between military doctrine and military reform in the Soviet Union, see Major-General and Professor I. Vorobyev, 'Vse li vzvesheno v nashej doktrine?', *Krasnaya zvezda*, 26 January 1991.

6 SOVIET CONVERSION AND EUROPEAN SECURITY

Ksenya Gonchar

1. INTRODUCTION

The new deeply transformed political landscape of Europe urgently calls for cardinal restructuring of the whole system of European security. The military resistance line between East and West has radically changed (or even disappeared) and major causes of tension have been reduced, though at the same time the necessity for the creation of new guarantees of stability to replace traditional instruments has become very acute. Ideas for alternative approaches to the questions of military resistance, of the prevention and resolution of conflicts have been developed for several years. However, these ideas had been mainly the subject of unrelated practical policy discussions in scientific, liberal and peace movement circles. They were aimed only at a far distant future.

But today it is clear even to conservative politicians that the postwar security order in Europe is outdated. The bipolar system of military blocs, nuclear deterrence and treaties, known and unknown, which regulated potential situations of conflict, appears to be a threat to human survival, to be expensive and not very effective under modern conditions. The system has been effective in detering more or less large-scale war between superpowers, but has proved to be too primitive and inefficient to build peace and security in broader terms. It is worth reminding those who consider nuclear weapons to be the best way to preserve peace that these weapons have not helped the countries which possess them to escape military conflicts in the last 30 years. Unacceptable to any country, the consequences of such a conflict made the resort to nuclear weapons absolutely irrational. But who can guarantee that irrational war will not take place?

New approaches towards ensuring security became measures of practical policy long before the participants in the Parliamentary Assembly of the European Council in Strasbourg (1990) proclaimed the termination of bipolar confrontation and expressed a common interest in developing a new security concept for Europe. In 1987, the so-called new thinking in the field of international security, represented by the Soviet Union, suggested such reasonable ideas as basing security on cooperation and *glasnost* in order to remove suspicion and distrust, to develop greater respect for international laws and to build 'defensive sufficiency' in the military sphere. This meant forming a military structure and fixing the size of armed forces sufficient to repulse possible aggression but not capable of conducting offensive actions.[1] I see no reason to argue about the Soviet motive for implementing these ideas, which have been described as an 'all-embracing system of international security'. Certainly they were influenced by former political leaders, political scientists and public movements - both in Western countries and in the Soviet Union. In any case, it is highly important to stress that these ideas were revived and promoted by Mikhail Gorbachev and strongly supported by a unilateral reduction of conventional forces.

Certainly, many questions remain to be answered before a clear understanding can be reached as to the real aims and interests of Soviet policy in security matters. It must be asked against whom and by what means would the Soviet Union defend itself and its allies (if any), and what level of armed forces and defence production could be considered 'sufficient' in a militarized country that only with great difficulty is able to carry out *glasnost* in the military sphere. Numerous unforeseen difficulties for the new security order may be created by the domestic problems of the Soviet Union. The solution to the 'German problem' placed the 'Soviet issue' at the edge of European policy. Nevertheless, there are some signs that raise the hope that the new security system will not share the fate of détente and dozens of 'peaceful initiatives'. As President Gorbachev said in Paris, 'détente of the 1970s became a victim of a psychological war'.[2] The new security thinking is based on a higher sense of reasonableness, including the recognition of the priority of all-human values in face of the threat of nuclear and ecological catastrophe as well as the growing military threat from the south and the necessity to create a common security system against it. No less important is the new image and posture of the Soviet Union in the international and European community. In his answers to questions from the newspaper *El Pais*, Mikhail Gorbachev, on the eve of his official visit to Spain, defined the place of the Soviet Union in the future geopolitical structure of Europe as 'participation in the solving of all European questions, including the state of the new security structure and the all-continental system of cooperation in economics, ecology, energy supply'.[3]

Conversion of the army and the military economy - in both the Soviet Union and Western countries - will make an important contribution to the new European security system, which promises to be broader and more complicated than in the past.

Conversion in the Soviet Union is strongly influenced by the new quality of international relations and the estimation of threats to national and international security. Only a durable peace and a reliable security system could create the conditions required for a large-scale reduction of defence expenditures, a real transformation of the military production capacities and the taking of measures to lighten the heavy military burden of the Soviet economy. The depth of today's conversion is surely insufficient to carry out a cardinal restructuring of the Soviet economy: it has inherited huge armed forces and defence production, which have created more trouble than security for the country and absorbed an irrationally immense part of its national wealth as well as technical and innovative potential. The discontinuation of military preparations and the release of resources from defence production are considered to be the only means of reforming and saving the economy (if one does not take into account Western assistance and loans). And this potential has not yet been used to the extent needed.[4]

On the other hand, conversion itself contributes significantly to the creation of the political, economic and human instruments of the new security system. I fully share the opinion of Aleksandr Yakovlev, expressed in the United Nations Conference on conversion'Economic Adjustments in an Era of Arms Reductions'.

> Conversion is not an end in itself or a forced payment for former mistakes. The conversion of military production and the defence spheres of activity may and must become part of the creation of a better world - on both the national and the global scale... It represents confirmation of rational forms of thinking and morality, of rational social and individual behaviour.[5]

A new system of international and European security may spring from this rational mentality, based on recognition of real (not ideologically invented) threats to peace and security and on a reasonable reaction to these threats, which takes into account the common security interests of all the countries involved.

2. CONVERSION AND DISARMAMENT: CONTRIBUTION TO THE NEW SECURITY ORDER

The primary connection between conversion and security is taking place through arms limitation and disarmament. Profound changes in international security can be achieved only at the lowest possible levels of armaments and armed forces. Future reductions of strategic nuclear arms and conventional forces in Europe, the prohibition of chemical weapons and unilateral disarmament measures and bilateral agreements between the Soviet Union and the East European countries are strengthening and extending the progress established by the

Treaty on the Elimination of Intermediate Range Missiles and by the disarmament consequences of German unification.

The direct influence of conversion on disarmament has so far been relatively slight. This can be explained by the fact that the scale of conversion is apparently small compared with the armaments and defence production capacities that are still able to provide an obstacle to peace and security. There exists a deep gap between the course of political negotiations on arms control issues and practical conversion measures. The latter are always results of political decisions by governments and cannot be made before negotiations have been completed.

But at the same time, conversion is fairly examined as one of the possible guarantees of the irreversibility of disarmament. It leads to such a deepening of the process of disarmament that the lowest possible level of armaments is to be secured by the real limitation of its production capacity. It is quite likely that deep reductions of armaments on the basis of international agreements would make it necessary to include some clauses to foresee the cancelling of corresponding defence production and establish guarantees for its non-resumption. Accordingly, conversion can be regarded as an economic and social element of the disarmament process.

On the other hand, conversion brings into play some new elements as well. If the talks on disarmament measures are combined with the planning of corresponding conversion measures, the latter might facilitate implementing real arms reductions with lower short-term costs and larger benefits for the economy and social life. It might help to reduce the possible opposition to actual disarmament measures on the national and international levels as well to create a kind of economic foundation for the shift from military to civilian production and thus promote disarmament negotiations. The Soviet 'State Programme of Conversion of the Defence Production' was not adopted in September 1990 for many reasons. One reason, based only on cuts in military purchases and connected with the unilateral reduction of armed forces, defence expenditures and military production, does not take into consideration the current negotiations on armed forces and armaments reductions - primarily the results of the Treaty on Conventional Forces in Europe. The policy programme must therefore be changed and completed in order not to lag behind the real political processes.

It would seem that currently the indirect influence of conversion on disarmament is more important than the direct effects. Conversion may be considered to be the new art of bolstering trust and confidence among nations. In his opening statement to the United Nations conference on conversion, the Under Secretary-General for disarmament affairs, Yasushi Akashi, said,

> Steps toward conversion are more than just a necessary outcome of arms reductions; they are an essential means of safeguarding and expanding emerging stability. Military-industrial production has long been regarded as a barometer of national intentions. It is therefore the special responsibility of countries engaged in the arms reductions process to ensure that their capabilities are clearly consistent with the principles of restraint and self-defence, and do not threaten to undermine mutual stability as force levels decline.[6]

In this sense, Soviet conversion has already played a critical role; it forced Western governments to believe that the Soviet intentions to take part in the new demilitarized security arrangements are serious, honest and consistent. I believe the many complaints of the managers of Soviet military establishments that during the process profits, advantages and skilled manpower were lost as a result of considerably reduced military purchases. This proved to be a more convincing argument for the Western partners than the loud disarmament campaigns and the peace initiatives, which were not followed by practical measures.

Soviet conversion contributed to frustrating the *pre-glasnost* information system, which, I suspect, had nothing to do with ensuring security, but served mostly to protect the Soviet military-industrial complex from public and parliamentary control. The poor information environment often resulted in overestimation of Soviet military power. As a result, many Soviet actions appeared threatening to the West even though they were motivated by purely defensive concerns. The iron curtain prevented free transfer of scientific and technological information, mostly because nearly all the

Soviet Union's high technology civilian goods are produced by defence establishments. In any event, the Soviet Union was expelled from the international community, and this gave further impetus to the arms race.

Now we have a unique opportunity to create an absolutely new security system in Europe, one that will allow us to achieve the lowest possible level for all the components of the military apparatus. Armed forces structure, modernization, readiness and sustainability - all these factors contribute important, if insufficient, information needed to reach the goal of 'defence sufficiency'. One must be sure that one's partner does not have any hidden intentions. Ample information about the course of conversion from defence to civilian production and the ready availability of data on the structure and output of the military industry are bound to lead to a higher level of trust and confidence between the European nations.

According to the German researcher Wolfgang Schwegler-Rohmeis 'the efforts in the field of conversion from military to civilian production as the new kind of confidence measures may stimulate disarmament.'[7] Time has proved the truth of this affirmation. I consider it very important that the new Treaty on Consent and Cooperation between the Soviet Union and France, signed in Paris in 1990, contains an article recognizing mutual industrial conversion as 'specially important' to their future and to the proposed creation of the European space.'[8] Article 14 of the Treaty on Friendship and Cooperation between the Soviet Union and Italy states:

> The sides will actively cooperate in the field of conversion of military industry, being founded on the Joint Inter-Governmental Statement from 30 November 1989. Taking into consideration positive changes in the European situation, they will aspire to conclude separate agreements on conversion, in particular in the fields of energetics, industrial production, consumption and foodstuffs.[9]

It does not seem sufficient nowadays to speak solely of arms reductions and limitations; it seems to be high time to move towards cooperation in the field of security, where conversion may play an important role. Isincerelyly believe in the positive effects of Soviet conversion, which should contribute considerably to disarmament and a new security order. There are two reasons, however, for not being fully optimistic.

One reason is connected with the fact that the decrease in the domestic demand for military goods and services compels many Soviet politicians, defence industry managers and members of the Supreme Soviet as well as lower soviets to campaign for the growth of the arms trade. It is fair to mention that it is not only the Soviet Union that is tempted to sell arms in the course of conversion. The former government of the GDR supplied Ethiopia with the tanks that were to be reduced by the terms of the Vienna Treaty. The United States sold to Egypt tanks from the American reserve in Europe. Finally China increased its arms exports while reducing domestic military consumption.

According to the official view, the military foreign trade of the Soviet Union should be reduced for the sake of reducing global instability. This actually happened in the case of Eastern Europe: since 1989, when the Soviet export of arms amounted to 11.6 billion dollars (according to Western estimates but published by *Pravda*[10]), arms transfers to East European countries have fallen heavily. But much trouble is caused by Soviet arms exports to Third World countries, most of which are linked, in one way or another, to various regional conflicts. Countries like Afghanistan, Iraq, Angola, Syria and India have been important recipients of Soviet arms. Many voices oppose the idea of applying conversion to the additional arms exports to these countries. They argue that weapons are virtually the only competitive high technology product on the world market that is able immediately to bring in hard currency for the purchase of consumer goods and for directly changing 'guns for butter'. Such arguments work well in a country with a very low living standard, gripped by an economic crisis and severe shortages, in a country where conversion proceeds with immense problems and has not yet brought about any improvement in the supply of consumer goods. Moreover, lack of modern facilities, high prices for tanks and smelting make it cheaper for the Soviet Union to sell or even to give away tanks and other equipment that have to be destroyed according to the CFE Treaty.

It is obvious what kind of negative political and security consequences such decisions might have. It is worth calling attention to the words of the Soviet Foreign Minister Eduard Shevardnadze, spoken in Vienna on 6 March 1989:

> In the Middle East and Southwest Asia, that is, in close proximity to Europe, powerful weapons arsenals are being created. It is not enough simply to mention that 25,000 tanks and 4,500 aeroplanes are deployed and ready for combat in the Middle East. There is a real danger of nuclear and chemical weapons appearing there. Missiles have already appeared there with an operational range of 2,500 kilometers... The conclusion is obvious. The processes of disarmament in Europe and the peace settlement in the Middle East must be synchronized.[11]

This conclusion was driven home by the Iraqi invasion of Kuwait, with large quantities of Soviet-made armaments in the invaders' possession.

The economic profits from arms deals are also questionable. This kind of trade differs from normal commercial business and is often carried out with direct governmental subsidies in the form of arms credits. Western investigations have revealed that Soviet arms deliveries to India, North Korea and Syria do not represent a major source of hard currency for the Soviet Union. Even the countries of the Middle East, which settle their accounts in hard currency, may never in fact make their payments. In the case of Syria, Damascus has built up a debt of roughly 12 billion dollars, of which the Soviet Union has written off 4 billion and agreed that the balance be spread over 40 years, with payments beginning in 1991.[12] A big surprise for the Supreme Soviet. The situation is aggravated by the fact that the arms export deals are not controlled by parliament or by the public, and the recent disbanding of the Central Engineering Board makes the reliability of state control doubtful.

The second source of scepticism is connected with the way conversion is organized and managed in the Soviet Union. So far, conversion has been controlled by the so-called Military-Industrial Commission of the Council of Ministers of the Soviet Union and the defence sections of the State Planning Committee. These are the very organizations that are specifically responsible for arms production. In this situation, the transfer from military to civilian production, the whole process of planning and implementing the conversion pro-grammes, will be carried out according to the priorities of special interest groups. They seem to understand conversion as a way to survive by whatever means possible under the 'threat' of the imminent market. Accordingly, as we all aim to reach the goal of constructing a new security system in Europe, con-version will be slow to become reliable and irreversible.

3. CONVERSION AND THE PROBLEMS OF ECONOMIC AND SOCIAL SECURITY

One of the key elements of the new security order consists of the process of demilitarization and the shift of the centre of gravity from military to political, and requiring economic and human measures to keep up with international and national security. Arms limitation and disarmament represent an important but only a single step on the way to lasting peace and security in a broader sense than merely the absence of war. Other steps are connected with the increasing role of common economic interests and interdependence, which integrate the world community in the long term and diminish former aggressive incentives and mitigate hostile relations.

Disputes over the role of economic interdependence as a guarantee of peace and security have gone on for many years. Two points are important in the arguments of those scholars and politicians who advocate a liberal international policy. Modern states with close economic ties would be disinclined to engage in warlike actions since these would prove a threat to the economic advantages resulting from international trade, industrial cooperation and joint investments. Deep economic ties contribute to the creation of common formal institutions, which may be used for political consultations and cooperation in case of possible conflicts. Post-war European history, de-veloping as it has towards ever greater economic interdependence, has proved the correctness of this theory.

There are sceptics who argue that the postwar peace in Europe has not been achieved by expanding economic co-operation but is the result of anti-Soviet policies, and that common political aims have contributed to the development of interdependence and security. They have also predicted that the decreasing responsibilities of the superpowers in Europe will lead to growing competition between European countries - in both political and economic spheres. Some political scientists have even argued that economic interdependence actually makes war more likely. In this spirit, John Mearsheimer believes that economic interdependence creates dangerous vulnerabilities among nations and may breed increased conflicts within and between states.[13] This statement sounds like nostalgia for the times of mutual military threats, in the same way as some Soviet citizens long for the calm Brezhnev era, being frightened by the unpredictable twists and turns of *perestroika*.

Surely, it is not worth simplifying the situation. Economic cooperation, as we have seen several times in Soviet history, is not a sufficient condition to ensure peace. The level of common interests in the political, economic and humanitarian fields is also far from sufficient. The existing and new-born institutions, meanwhile, are weak and ineffective. The whole situation contains all the dangers of a transition period. There exists a serious threat that Europe, after recovering from its military and ideological division, will face a new 'economic curtain' between its western and eastern parts with all the negative consequences to its peace and security, resulting from the tense relations between developed and under-developed countries. But it would seem that today we have no alternative than to extend and develop all the possible spheres of common interests that will supplement the care of mankind's survival under the threat of a nuclear and ecological catastrophe. Non-offensive defence, confidence-building measures and European cooperation in the security field (including the Soviet Union, in one or another form) are to be supported by a comprehensive set of economic, social, diplomatic and legal approaches. In this context, Soviet conversion can play an important role.

This role is, first of all, defined by an interaction between the process of economic disarmament and transition to the market economy. The need to create new security guarantees and structures in Europe comes up against the fact that the economic systems of the Soviet Union and major European countries are out of joint. The economic and political rapprochement in Europe will change this situation and create principally new international relations. The chairman of the Spanish government, Felippe Gonzales, honestly admitted in one of his interviews on the eve of Gorbachev's visit to Spain: 'We shall undertake serious efforts to support *perestroika* provided we receive confidence and trust in the rise of a new economic and social order.'[14] Certainly, the transition from command planning to the market economy is being carried out, not for the sake of receiving Western help but because the demand of the times and the necessity of an effective revival of the Soviet economy make the transition necessary. Market relations and effective conversion, however, will guarantee that Western loans will not, as before, 'remain in the hands of the discredited party and government and end up in the bottomless coffer of the military-industrial complex', as one of the deputies of the Supreme Soviet has written.[15] Only in a time when a common economic system and a stable democratic order will facilitate the achievement of good international relations will reliable material guarantees of European and international security arise. In other words, a shift from 'planning' to the market economy becomes the fundamental determinant of the security policy.

The critical role of Soviet conversion in the growth of this system is based on two factors. The first is that the results of economic reform depend on the effectiveness of conversion. The huge size of the military economy, the way it is administered and organized and the intolerable burden it inflicts on an exhausted society make conversion not only a regular part of the disarmament process but one of the main conditions for the success of the reforms and, on the whole, the requirement of survival. Even according to the official data, military expenditures account for more than 8 per cent of the GNP. About 40 per cent of the machine-building output and two-thirds of research and development are defence-oriented.

But many experts suspect that the real figures are much higher. It is therefore possible to speak of 200 billion roubles and 20 per cent of the GNP.[16]

It is not my intention now to take part in these disputes. One thing is obvious, however: the burden of the massive defence establishment has become too heavy for the bankrupt economy. This sphere swallows up large amounts of the best and the dramatically limited resources, without the reallocation of which the whole process of economic restructuring will fail. This failure - God forbid! - would have terrible consequences for the European and international community, because the Soviet economy is becoming a part - and the most vulnerable part - of its foreign relations and security.

The second point is connected with the model of Soviet conversion. The question is whether it will be conducted in the old directive manner or become the instrument of market reform, whether it will promote commercialization and development of the new market system or apply brakes to it.

The latest events affecting the Soviet economy have proved once more that military expenditures lie at the heart of the command-administrative system. They represent the most centralized sector of the Soviet economy, being dominated by the state monopoly and marked by lack of competition and flexibility. This will be the last sector to be transferred to the market economy. The situation would have been more or less acceptable if we could speak only of arms production, which usually operates in special conditions under strict state control all over the world. But the Soviet military-industrial complex is monopolistically producing nearly all the high technology civilian goods in the country - 100 per cent of all radio and television sets, videotape recorders and sewing machines and more than 70 per cent of the engines and refrigerators. In the course of conversion, the defence establishments receive additional investments and raw materials towards increasing civilian production. If these heavy new investments and previously existing capacities for the production of civilian goods were kept out of the market under the umbrella of the military-industrial complex, only light industry and the food industry would serve the consumer. It is easy to predict the result of this transition. It is impossible to convert the entire economy into market relations without implementing the market model of defence conversion, which would liberalize, decentralize and demonopolize the economy as a whole. Besides, it would be difficult to reverse the market conversion.

Much was done in this field after the military budget was reduced and conversion started. According to the report of Valentin Smyslov, the Vice-Chairman of the State Planning Committee, at the United Nations conference on conversion in Moscow, about half of the enterprises belonging to the defence complex would reduce their output of military equipment in 1990 by more than 20 per cent.[17] No fewer than 34 establishments of non-defence ministries and six defence-complex enterprises, which have been producing military equipment, are being totally converted. In other words, they are completely terminating the production of arms and are going over to the output of civilian products. Especially drastic is the conversion of enterprises producing tanks, ammunition, gunpowder and solid fuel as well as uranium-mining works and related enrichment facilities. In 1990 more than 500,000 people from the defence sector started to work for the civilian market. Large quantities of military equipment intended to satisfy civilian needs are sold by military depots, including items like cars, small ships, radio equipment and fuel. The air force has established a service of civilian freight transportation on military planes. The Ministry of Defence is returning some land for agriculture. A retaining and loan compensation programme has been adopted. A draft of the State Conversion Programme includes a sharp increase in the production of consumer durables, farm machinery, equipment for light industry and food processing, medical technology, electronics, etc.

But these worthy plans may not be fulfilled for many reasons. One is the traditional arbitrary way the conversion is being managed by the government. It seems as if the principal opponents of reform in the army and the military economy have been forcing the government to adopt decisions on conversion that run counter to the main logic and course of the general market reform. It is disturbing to see how, three weeks before the Draft State Programme for the Conversion of the Defence Industry was to be discussed in the Presidential

Council, the Soviet military-industrial complex exerted heavy pressure on the President. Published in *Pravda* was a letter addressed to the Supreme Soviet warning against 'loss' of the military-industrial complex and urging the preservation of the former 'centralized system of management and distribution of material resources'.[18] Earlier, the Council of Ministers had confirmed by special decision the exclusive right of defence enterprises to receive investments and other material requirements. It also promised to indemnify all losses in wages and salaries of workers in the converting enterprises. These anti-market decisions are hindering the country's efforts to take advantage of the great opportunity offered it after ridding itself of the burden of excessive military commitments. It is a pity, because Soviet conversion has a great potential: it promises to promote radical economic reform, including the attainment of a relatively high technological level and employment of a skilled labour force. This would mean the extension of the possibilities exporting high technology civilian goods and improving the situation of the domestic market. The enterprises undergoing conversion are exactly those that could have become organizational pioneers, especially in the case of establishments possessing a complex structure and relatively advanced research and development activities as well as financial and commercial services.

It would seem that joint ventures between Western firms and converting Soviet defence enterprises and direct Western investment could also contribute to both the process of economic conversion and the shift towards a market economy, not solely because mutual responsibility and international cooperation create common interests in a climate of mutual understanding. The Soviet establishments would gain market experience and become involved in long-term scientific, industrial and commercial relations and responsibilities that would stimulate the growth of openness in the Soviet economy and make it difficult to reverse the conversion process. Accordingly, conversion would also contribute to the growth of economic security.

Conversion is also socially beneficial. There are well-founded long-term hopes for a better social environment as a result of reduced military threats and improvement of the welfare services, decreased taxes and additional jobs created by civilian investments. But there also exist numerous sources of short-term apprehension that compel one to view conversion as a course of considerable social tension. It will be especially painful during the transition to the market economy, which can only increase the insecurity of the political system. It is extremely difficult to adjust to the elimination of low-cost housing, assured employment, low quality but free medical care, bankruptcy-safe enterprises, etc.

Many people and regions are threatened by cuts in defence spending. Highly trained workers and engineers have been hit by pay cuts and are seeking better-paid jobs in cooperatives. In labour-surplus regions and in towns where the defence industry dominates, increasing unemployment has already become a problem. This situation is especially painful following the long years of the announced policy of 'full employment' and because of the lack of legal and practical mechanisms for dealing with unemployment. Residence permits are creating an obstacle to moving; housing shortages in regions with a large labour market also limit the migration of manpower inside the country.

No less difficult are the problems connected to the reduction of armed forces. For several decades, military service was considered to be a secure career path with broad fringe benefits, high pensions and relatively stable living conditions. Today, military employment has become rather risky and insecure. The troops returning from Eastern Europe and Mongolia, the officers who have been discharged in the course of reductions in the size of the Soviet Army, in addition to internal refugees, create tremendous pressure on local authorities who have been forced to assign housing for former military employees. But they have neither the money nor other resources needed to resolve the housing crisis, even in the case of the local population. For that reason, the interests of the civilian population and the army were unwisely pushed aside. The German government will make payments for relocating and housing the troops withdrawn from East Germany on the basis of a bilateral agreement (which might today be the best 'joint venture' in the field of conversion), but those who return from other countries are receiving no support whatsoever.

In this way, the unprepared and inefficient conversion becomes an 'extreme situation' and contributes to the growth of domestic tension. It is conceivable that someday the socio-economic discontent of large sectors of the population (especially of the armed forces) will become a detonator of a political explosion, pregnant with unpredictable consequences. The Soviet political scientist Aleksei Kortunov, writing of the new realities of European security, has warned:

> At present, the 'Soviet threat' is assuming a new and unexpected effect: even if we exclude the possibility of a militarist and anti-Western regime coming to power in Moscow, the political instability, ecological disaster, right-wing and left-wing extremism, millions of refugees, etc., could easily spill over the Soviet national borders and become an ever-present headache for Western leaders. [19]

4. CONCLUSION

The fundamental political changes in the Soviet Union have already made Europe more peaceful and secure in the long run. The process of demilitarizing the country is proceeding consistently, all obstacles notwithstanding. The Soviet conversion has contributed to the extension of disarmament measures as well as to the building of a new order of confidence. This is creating a vast potential space for international cooperation. At the same time, it contains some seeds of danger and unpredictability, caused by the country's general critical situation as well as the contradictory governmental conversion policy and the failure of most of the projects in this field. The solution of the problems involved depends primarily on the initiatives taken at the regional level and by enterprises. The Soviet Union's partners in European politics are also able to render help - primarily by supporting all the Soviet steps leading to demilitarization and the implementation of market relations. No less important will be the linking of the Soviet economy with the European market in the form of joint or completely Western enterprises, large international co-operative programmes and close trade relations.

NOTES

1. In the Joint Declaration of 22 states, signed 19 November 1990 in Paris, the formula of 'defence sufficiency' sounds like preserving a military potential 'necessary for the prevention of war and ensuring effective defence' (*Pravda*, 20 November 1990).
2. The Statement of Mikhail Gorbachev in Paris on 19 November 1990 (*Pravda*, 20 November 1990).
3. *Izvestiya*, 26 September 1990.
4. Though the number of enterprises taking part in the conversion exceeds 400, the volume of reduced military contracts is relatively low in comparison with the need for financial, investment and material resources. The sum of 1.6 billion roubles in one year may be involved if military production is reduced by 19.5 per cent. Certainly, this amount of money cannot play a critical role in restructuring.
5. 'Conversion: Creative Challenge to the Science and Society', statement of Alexandr Yakovlev, a member of the Presidential Council, at the UN Conference "Economic Adjustments in an Era of Arms Reductions", Moscow, 13 August 1990.
6. Opening Statement by Yasushi Akashi, United Nations Under Secretary-General for Disarmament Affairs at the UN Conference "Economic Adjustments in an Era of Arms Reductions", Moscow, 13 August 1990.
7. Wolfgang Schwegler-Rohmeis, 'Rüstungskonversion als Sicherheitspolitik' in M. Breitschwert (ed.), *Rüstungskonversion: Facetten einer Strukturfrage*, (Stuttgart: SPD, 1988/1989), p. 52.
8. *Izvestiya*, 30 October 1990.
9. *Izvestiya*, 19 November 1990.
10. *Pravda*, 15 April 1989.
11. Eduard Shevardnadze's address in Vienna, (*TASS Report*, 6 March 1989).
12. Ian Anthony, 'The International Arms Trade.' (*Disarmament*, Vol. XIII, No.2, 1990, p. 237)
13. John J. Mearsheimer, 'Back to the Future: Instability in Europe after the Cold War', *International Security*, vol. 15, no. 1, Summer 1990, pp. 5-56.
14. *Izvestiya*, 25 October 1990.
15. Yuri Ambartsumov, 'Foreign Policy Successes and Disappointment at Home', *Moscow News*, no. 44, 1990, p. 3.
16. *New Times*, no. 10, 1990, p. 27.
17. 'On the Basic Directions of the Draft State Programme for the Conversion of Defence Industry in the Soviet Union', Report by V. I. Smyslov, Vice-Chairman of the USSR State Planning Committee at the UN Conference "Economic Adjustments in an Era of Arms Reductions", Moscow, 13-17 August 1990.
18. *Pravda*, 6 September 1990.
19. *Moscow News*, no. 46, 1990.

Part III

ECONOMIC ISSUES

7 THE SOVIET UNION AND WEST EUROPEAN INTEGRATION

Heinz Timmermann

1. INTEGRATION INTO THE EUROPEAN COMMUNICATION PROCESS

One of the central issues of the new thinking and action undertaken by the Soviet leadership under Gorbachev consists of an endeavour to turn the country towards Western Europe, the European Community (EC) and its member states. The motives for this reorientation are manifold. The following argument could serve as a common denominator: the Moscow leadership's West European policy is aimed at linking the Soviet Union step by step to the processes of European integration and communication. Furthermore, the West Europeans are to be won over as constructive partners supporting the overall modernization of the Soviet Union. The Soviet Union's retreat from its hegemonic position in Eastern Europe should not therefore be read as a sign of the Moscow reformers' intention to leave Europe and go their own way. On the contrary: in their view, to retreat from Eastern Europe sets the precondition for the country's envisaged integration into European civilization.[1]

Against this background, the country's reorientation

towards Europe is certainly reflected in aspects of its domestic affairs. If this reorientation proves successful and is perceived by the population as having brought about a material improvement in their daily life, then the 'Westernizers' around Gorbachev have been strengthened enough to continue their struggle with the conservatives inside the bureaucracy and the military-industrial and military-ideological complex. However, if this experiment of turning towards Europe ends in failure, Russia will become alienated from this increasingly integrated Europe and be pushed back towards Asia. Such a development could only lead to very negative consequences for the West. Conservatives of all colours would feel encouraged, along with those sections of society that have fixed their eyes on an exclusively Russian path and a specific Russian mission. The Moscow reformers are sounding an urgent warning against separating the Soviet Union from Western Europe or forcing it into a new isolation, that is, 'not hindering its integration into Europe'. Such a development would be tragic, indeed, not only for the Soviet Union but also for Western Europe and the envisaged 'common European home'. In such a case, the Soviet Union, or Russia, could easily emerge as a 'power hostile to the rest of Europe'.[2]

Developments in the Soviet Union as of autumn 1990 - a new formation of conservative forces with a growing influence on national policies - can only increase our doubts about the Soviet Union's, or Russia's, ability and readiness to turn towards Europe. The Moscow centre seems unwilling to transform the forcibly built entity called 'The Soviet Union' into a federation of sovereign states. In economic matters, the center falls back on purely administrative methods and, vis-a-vis the republics, on outright repression. All this is symptomatic of a backward orientation which is potentially undermining promising initiatives that aim at including the Soviet Union in the European processes of interdependency and integration.

At the beginning of 1991, there were many indications that the use of force and repression in the Soviet Union would undermine Western confidence, a confidence that took so much effort to build. If this policy line is continued and intensified, the Soviet leadership could find itself forced to revise its policy of turning towards Europe. If this chapter describes and analyses in detail the beginnings of this policy, then not the least reason is that we are witnessing a serious attempt by members of the political and scientific élite in Russia, the Westernizers, to lead their country out of its historic isolation. Whether the Westernizers' vision will, despite setbacks, be successful in the long run or whether most of what is discussed in the following pages already belongs to history, one cannot yet say for certain.

2. PRECONDITIONS FOR TURNING TOWARDS EUROPE

The Soviet leadership's attempt to establish close relations with the European Community and its member states is based on a far-reaching change of mind concerning ideology, the internal situation and the country's relationship with the outside world. This rethinking spreads into many fields. In the meantime, the Soviet leadership has gone so far as to tolerate and sometimes even to instigate a change in the system (instead of simply reforming it) by trying to establish an internal 'civilized' social order oriented towards (West) European values. This gradual surmounting of the systemic contradictions in Europe made the Soviet Union ready to sign documents in the framework of the CSCE process, documents in which traditional values, fundamental standards and basic norms are fixed and formulated in concrete terms (final accords of the Vienna CSCE conference, economic conference in Bonn, human rights conference in Copenhagen and Paris CSCE summit of November 1990).

It is not at all a case of convergent values in East and West, according to a noteworthy article published by the Soviet Foreign Ministry in 1989. Rather, it is described as an asymmetrical process whereby the Eastern societies of the former 'real socialism' have to orientate themselves towards the models developed by the West. These models, the article continues, have followed 'universal laws of development of human society' that have proved their value over many centuries. Furthermore, they are based upon the 'physical and intellectual work of previous generations'.[3] With all this, the

Westernizers around Gorbachev have stressed their intention to transform the written norms and principles of the CSCE process into a living reality secured by the Soviet constitution. They have signed the Paris 'Charter for a new Europe', by which the leaders guarantee to safeguard the human rights and basic liberties of their peoples, while at the same time acknowledging a market economy and private property.

This in turn has encouraged West Europeans to support the comprehensive restructuring of the Soviet Union, to open the European Community to the Soviet economy and to animate the Helsinki process. It is no accident that, as of 1989, all the treaties and agreements concluded between West European states and the Soviet Union explicitly point out the European dimension of bilateral relations. This can be seen most clearly in the German-Soviet treaty signed in November 1990. It is worth noting that Germany commits itself to help the Soviet Union to 'develop cooperation with international and especially European organizations'.[4]

France is even thinking about a new EC agreement with the Soviet Union that goes further than the EC-Soviet trade and cooperation treaty of 1989. It plans for an institutionalization of political relations. In any case, with the conclusion of the Soviet-French treaty of October 1990, Paris commits itself to 'contribute to the deepening of relations and to work for the conclusion of an agreement between the Soviet Union and the EC.'[5]

The European tendency towards unity in a diversity of values does indeed encourage integration. The main problem, however, will be how to make the Soviet Union, or rather the components of the Soviet Union, ready for it, if they want to be integrated at all. Security in the narrow sense of the word does still play an important role and is the framework for comprehensive cooperation. But it is no longer the formative principle: today this principle is determined rather by endeavours to create a Europe with room for viable economic, ecological and democratic institutions, and one that honours human and civil rights.

On the other side, the Soviet leadership has undertaken a basic reassessment of the country's national interests, abandoning confrontative and hegemonic thinking and adopting instead categories like freedom of choice for each as well as voluntary cooperation among all. This change became visible to all when Moscow tolerated the changes in Central and Eastern Europe. In December 1989, Eduard Shevardnadze emphasized the freedom to choose one's own path and methods when building new societies in the region. Certainly not by accident, he said this to the Political Commission of the European Parliament in Brussels:

> Our respect for this choice means respecting the full sovereignty of East European countries, a respect that is not limited by ideology and includes their desire to be independent. Our tolerance does not even exclude possible transformations of social, economic and political institutions.[6]

There are several reasons for this attitude, one being the intention of the Soviet leadership to present its country to West Europeans as a power willing to anchor its basic values in the norms and principles of the European tradition. Decisive here was the realization of the Moscow reformers that the West Europeans, for their part, did not try to take advantage of the internal weakness of the Soviet Union and of its retreat from Eastern Europe in order to enchance their own position. Rather, Western politicians were and are trying to take part in this historical process of transforming repressive social systems into democratic pluralistic ones. They are doing this in a cooperative way beneficial to all sides involved. The West - according to Gorbachev in his speech before the Spanish Parliament in autumn 1990 - is interested in seeing 'the Soviet Union developing into a strong, newly integrated, successful and respected state'.[7]

And lastly, the reassessment of 'capitalism' and 'imperialism' has in turn fundamentally changed in a positive way in the Soviet Union the image of the EC and its integrating mechanisms. Unlike in the past, today the EC is considered a forward-looking model of how to achieve voluntary and successful integration - not the least in view of the disintegration of the Soviet Union as a union of republics and the difficulties of reorganizing the republics in confederative structures. The most important success of the EC is seen to be its capability

> to join together economic and political components of the Community, to integrate spontaneous market processes and regulative measures into a combined mechanism, to find a rational relation between national, international and supranational elements in the system of mutual relations among the states of the region.[8]

Most interesting in this context are Gorbachev's readiness to learn and his changes of mind concerning the EC. We find examples of this in a book written by an Italian Communist Party (CPI) politician, A. Rubbi.[9] The author is a Soviet specialist, who has lived there for several years. He took part in seven summit meetings of the CPSU and CPI leaders between June 1984 and November 1989. In his book, he describes the preliminaries, course and background of these meetings. Quite early, Gorbachev showed himself to be an open sympathizer of the CPI reform programmes and its pro-European attitude. In March 1988, for example, he wanted to know 'from where capitalism drew its dynamics and its ability to profit from the objective process of the internationalization of the economy'.[10]

At the beginning, Rubbi writes, the Soviets were 'not familiar with the Community nor with its order, functional mechanisms and policies'. At each meeting, Gorbachev asked his CPI partners to give him an analysis of the EC and the way it functions. As early as 1986, he made known his wish to see the Community take over more responsibility on the European as well as on the global scene. It is obvious that the influence of the CPI on Gorbachev's thinking and action was not without consequences. In March 1988, the Secretary General claimed to have convinced himself that capitalism had been more successful in 'making use of the objective tendencies towards interdependency and globalization of the economy' than the socialist states so 'terribly backward' in this respect. In addition, he acknowledged that capitalist countries were better aware of the 'needs of modern developments in science, technology and the forces of production'.

Against this background, the EC is today 'a great

economic and trade power and an important factor within the world economic system'. If the EC, Gorbachev says, is also going to develop into a political union, then it would gain in weight regarding world politics. Gorbachev considers this to be a positive development because 'a true convalescence of the world would be impossible without Western Europe's weight and contribution'.[11]

One should certainly not overrate the influence of the CPI on Gorbachev's new thinking. After all, the CPI was only one partner in discussions with the Soviet head of state and the party, even if it was a privileged partner in the sense that the CPI was considered rather close. Still, Rubbi's report seems to show that the CPI did have considerable influence on the process of Gorbachev's political and programmatic rethinking as well as especially on his assessment of European integration. As an integral part of Italian democracy and being an active promoter of European integration, the CPI has obviously helped the Soviet leadership gain a more realistic idea of the West and of how to integrate the Soviet Union into the all-European processes of integration and communication.

It is certainly no coincidence that Gorbachev was greatly impressed by the 'interest, sympathy, enthusiasm and benevolence' shown him during his visits to Western Europe in summer 1989. Instead of previous hostility and aversion, Western Europe has now quickly developed 'an awareness of how necessary understanding and cooperation with us' has become. In particular, Western Europe seems to be ready 'to discuss each problem on the basis of realities and a balance of interests while overcoming confrontational attitudes'.[12]

In consequence, the Westernizers around Gorbachev place great hopes in the EC and its member countries. In their eyes, the West Europeans are the most capable and cooperative partners supporting their country's modernization and Westernization. Moreover, West Europeans are seen as natural crisis-managers helping to avoid 'chaos and disorder' (according to Shevardnadze) in Eastern Europe, able also to assist financially the turning of the region towards Europe. It is in the vital interest of the Soviet Union to see the EC assume its role as 'a coordinator of assistance given to Eastern Europe', states a series of Soviet articles. This would stabilize the situation in the region and encourage the countries there to restructure their economy. According to Westernizers, 'stronger ties between Eastern Europe and the EC will enable Europe to complete the whole system of mutual relations and provide the Soviet Union with the chance to enter Europe' (*voiti v Evropu*).[13]

Seen in this way from the point of view of the Moscow reformers, the EC is economically and politically the main point of reference with regard to future all-European structures. This is all the more true since the Soviet leadership appears to have resigned itself to the dramatic loss of function and the possible complete disappearance of the CMEA and the Warsaw Pact. It is at least aware of the fact that the character and functional structures of the two organizations make them useless as parts of an all-European architecture. Symptomatic of this view is a paper written by Vladimir Baranovskii, a well-known Soviet specialist on Europe. Concluding his analysis, he names the EC, NATO, the Council of Europe and the CSCE as the most viable institutions of European co-operation.[14] This is interesting not only because he fails to mention the CMEA and Warsaw Pact, but also because of a convergence with Western intentions. We see an endeavour to make use of those multilateral institutions and mechanisms that have proven their worth beyond the era of East-West confrontation and can thus serve as instruments of all-European cooperation.

It remains to be seen, however, what sort of an answer the Soviet Union is willing to give to the following question: should the EC dissolve itself in the envisaged all-European community (unacceptable to the EC members)? Or should the EC be seen as the core of an all-European union, which other states may join once they are ready and capable of integrating themselves into it (a thesis of the concentric circles)? Let us recall that Shevardnadze commented positively on the intention of the EC 'not to limit itself to West European integration but to overcome the factual division of Europe by enlarging itself'.[15]

3. THE EUROPEAN COMMUNITY AS A PARTNER IN ECONOMIC MODERNIZATION

Against this background, the Soviet leadership has tried to intensify its relations with the EC and its member states, especially in economic matters. A symptomatic example is the Soviet-EC trade and cooperation treaty of December 1989. Significantly enough, Shevardnadze appreciated it not only as an important bilateral document but also as an agreement 'strengthening the belief of all Europeans in the possibility of a united Europe and adding a new quality to the process of an East-West rapprochement'.[16] The main points are regulations concerning the liberalization of trade; cooperation in the fields of conservation, scientific research, technology, and the peaceful use of nuclear power; and facilitation of joint ventures and EC investments in the Soviet Union.

A similar picture arises from successful Soviet endeavours to participate as a founding member in setting up the European Bank of Reconstruction and Development, in which the EC countries have the majority of capital. It may look as if the Soviet Union could at first get only very little out of participation in the Bank's activities and that for the moment the political-psychological effect is more important. But one should not underrate those positive effects that direct contacts with the international world of finance would have on the Soviet currency and credit relations, which are in the process of being reformed. Josef Attali, president of the Bank, found in Gorbachev a careful listener when he explained to him the readiness of the Bank to set up a system of commercial banks in the Soviet Union after the transition to the market economy and to assist the Soviets in privatizing firms and enterprises.[17]

The considerations of Western orientation centre on two aspects. First, by exposing their country to the magnetic field of West Europe, the Soviets hope to increase internally the pressure to go through with an economic *perestroika* by creating simultaneously appropriate mechanisms and patterns of behaviour. The Soviet leadership is well aware of the fact that Western aid measures can work and turn into effective stimuli only if accompanied by the development of a 'culture of economic management' inside the country. Second, according to Gorbachev, coordination, multilateralization and integration are the typical characteristics of international economic life in which the Soviet Union wants to take an active part.[18] In the view of the Moscow reformers, a close contractual partnership with the EC, which is an economic power active all over the globe, presents them with the best chance to integrate the Soviet Union gradually into the world economic system and to help it join the international trade, currency and credit relations.

It is true, however, that, as early as 1989, Gorbachev acknowledged that there is the danger that his strategy of opening up towards Europe and the West might end up in failure owing to insufficient internal preconditions in the Soviet Union:

> In the past, we expected the largest calamities to happen when we implement our new international policies concerning human rights and disarmament. Now the whole thing looks quite different.The difficulties do not result only from the barriers raised by the West - they exist and continue to exist - but also from our own lethargy, our lagging behind in rethinking our economic development and also, frankly speaking, from our inability to handle the world market, from our incompetence and prejudices and sometimes simply from our laziness.[19]

This gloomy picture is confirmed by developments which began at the end of 1990. Not only does the failure of *perestroika* threaten the internal democratization of the Soviet Union but also the new thinking and the activities of its leading representatives vis-a-vis the West.

4. MORE INTENSE POLITICAL COOPERATION

With regard to the political dimension of the European Community, the Soviet leadership takes into consideration a fact that actually fits well with Marxist thinking, namely that the economic strength of the EC, based on its integration, leads to a growing tendency among its member countries to act in unison also on the political front and to exert a decisive influence on the shaping of the future all-European structures. That the EC is going to shut itself off from the outside world by implementing the unified domestic market in 1992 is a view now being rejected as wrong.[20]

Soviet experts rather support the following line of argument: as the world's strongest trade power, the EC will continue to pursue its vital interests, namely the further development of its foreign relations. In addition, NATO's loss of function is going to increase the importance and weight of the EC as a political entity. This can be seen even now in the manner the EC constructively handles problems such as accepting the EFTA countries, crisis management in Central and Eastern Europe, and German unification. Moscow emphasizes the fact that all this is very significant, not the least because the Community, with its efficient organs and integration mechanisms, possesses the institutional preconditions necessary to help transform the disintegrating international structures of Eastern Europe into new transnational ones.

Symptomatic of this view is a remarkable contribution published by the Institute for World Economy and International Relations (IMEMO) in Moscow. IMEMO has on several occasions anticipated new thinking and action in Moscow's foreign policy:

> In order to build a common regional system in the whole of Europe, one should maybe just follow the path the EC members are already pursuing, but only on an enlarged scale. It is the EC that could serve as the core of a future regional system, as its most highly developed part.[21]

As a consequence, the Soviet leadership has intensified political dialogue with the EC, as can be seen from Gorbachev's meeting with the 12 EC foreign ministers in New York in September 1990. According to Shevardnadze, this dialogue only 'increases in speed' and is proving to be a 'promising channel for contacts between East and West'.[22] This, by the way, does not concern only purely European regional issues but also global ones, such as the Gulf crisis. During their meeting in New York, the foreign ministers agreed upon a common position towards this crisis and issued a joint declaration.

5. THE EUROPEAN COMMUNITY - THE HEART AND ENGINE OF ALL-EUROPEAN STRUCTURES

Since the integration and foreign relations of the EC are seen in such a positive light by Moscow's Westernizers, it is to be expected that they will try very hard to intensify the Soviet Union's relations with the EC and its member states. In contrast to earlier times, the Soviet Union now sees the political and economic union into which the EC is growing as a point of reference and an engine stimulating the building of cooperative all-European structures. Its internal functional mechanisms are regarded as an example. That is to say: Gorbachev and his supporters are most probably not going to resist an enlargement of the EC to include other European states - from EFTA and from the dying CMEA. On the contrary, they may even support such an enlargement and regard it with benevolence.

In this context, let me quote once more Vyacheslav Dashichev, the Soviet expert on Europe:

> The European Community can serve as an example for Europe in the future. It has proved to be a very effective form of cooperation among several states, not only in the economic but also in the political field and concerning the organization of human contacts, etc. After the process of overcoming incompatibilities has been completed in Eastern Europe and the Soviet Union, the question of these countries joining the EC will arise. They will join it first as associate and later as full members. This corresponds to the goals of Soviet policy, to Soviet interests, including its return to the community of European peoples.[23]

Inside this Europe of intended interdependencies with the generally accepted and dynamic 'European Community', the membership of other countries depends therefore on the consent of the EC - and then only on the political intention of each single state - as well as on whether or not they themselves are economically competitive and capable of integrating. However, the Soviet leadership will follow this direction of policy only if the EC and its member states continue to show their willingness to support effectively the modernization of the Soviet Union and to link it to the process of European interdependency. Bilateral treaties and multilateral agreements supplementing each other could bring about such a linkage.

6. GERMANY AS A BRIDGE BETWEEN EAST AND WEST

Against this background, the Moscow reformers believe the unified Germany to be of increasing importance and weight. They remember well the fact that since the conclusion of the German-Soviet treaty of 1970, Bonn has played the vanguard role in promoting East-West dialogue. In addition, the Soviets believe that, compared with other EC members, Germany possesses a more realistic perception of the problems arising from an integrating Russia: Germany's experience in integrating the former GDR into the Federal Republic adds to its sensibility and competence when it comes to doing the same for the East Europeans, or so the Soviets believe. In this way, Germany could become the experimental ground for the integration of Europe's eastern and western parts, which are so different in terms of politics, economy and psychology. The reformers regard Germany, with its strong economic power and its historical relations with Russia, as an ideal economic partner, especially in view of the fact that the economic links between the Soviet Union and Germany are by far stronger and more numerous than those with any other country in the world.

No less important, however, is another aspect. Considering its central influence within the EC, the Westernizers hope to see Germany functioning as a bridge between East and West. Thanks to this influence, Germany is able to assist the Soviet Union to integrate itself more and more into an all-

European process (EC, CSCE, new security structures, etc.). A divided Germany could not have played that role and, even less so, an ideologically orthodox GDR defending itself against changes in the Soviet Union. An influential CPSU consultant has stated that Germany is going to play a 'leading role' when it comes to 'integrating the Soviet Union into the world civilization'.[24] This remarkable vision of Germany's future role shows that the Moscow reformers are not interested in continuing the postwar practice of exploiting the fears of Germany's other neighbours to promote their own goals. Nor are they interested in reviving the special historical relationship between the two countries. On the contrary, they place their hopes in a Germany solidly anchored in the West European structures of integration and bent on achieving this on all-European foundations.

7. RAPPROCHEMENT WITH THE COUNCIL OF EUROPE

In this context, the Soviet leadership has laid great stress on the Strasbourg Council of Europe, which in 1989 conceded a special guest status to the Soviet Union. According to Gorbachev, the Council of Europe could become 'one of the fundamental pillars of the all-European home, a venue for important common initiatives'.[25] Shevardnadze made a similar comment when speaking in front of a high-ranking delegation of the Council of Europe in Moscow. He stated that the Council of Europe should become the 'venue for a meeting between East and West' so that its Parliamentary Assembly could become the parliament of the future 'all-European community'.[26] By working for a rapprochement between the Soviet Union and the Council of Europe to the point of wanting to become a full member, Gorbachev and his followers hope to prepare the ground for their country's acceptance as an integral part of European civilization and treatment accordingly as an equal partner. Gorbachev's speech in Strasbourg in July 1989, at the Parliamentary Assembly of the Council of Europe, offers impressive proof of this fact. Typically enough, on this occasion, he specifically criticized all those who 'place the Soviet Union outside of Europe from the Atlantic to the Urals, wanting to reduce Europe to the space between Brest (in Bretagne) and Brest (on the Polish-Soviet border)'. This view is unacceptable, he said, because historically the Soviet Union is, just like the United States, 'a natural part of Europe's international and political structure'.[27]

Furthermore, the Soviet Union's more active relations with the Council of Europe must be understood as a signal for the EC to take note of the willingness of the Soviet leadership to adopt binding obligations with regard to human and civil rights, ecology, social security, and culture, and to orient its own restructuring at home to the respective conventions of the Council. For the first time, the Soviet Union signed three conventions in November 1990. Moscow does not, however, harbour any illusions that their membership in the Council of Europe could be, so to speak, the first step towards full integration into the EC, as the Hungarians hope. Rather, their expectations seem to focus on this: if the Soviet Union plays a positive role in the Council, this may strengthen the readiness of the EC to include Soviet experts in certain institutions and programmes.

If the generous financial aid to the Soviet Union from the Western democracies is dependent not only on the economic but also on the domestic conditions (e.g., the guarantee of human and civil rights and their protection by the law), it makes sense to align the country more closely to the Council of Europe. This could provide the West with an institutional framework going beyond the CSCE in order to gain the necessary legitimation for interference in the internal affairs of the Soviet Union.[28]

In addition, the Council of Europe, with its basic convention on cooperation reaching across borders, does not provide the Soviet Union with the chance to intensify contacts between regions and local organs, something which is being emphasized by Soviet authors themselves.[29] This creates additional possibilities to influence constructively from the outside the process of decentralization in the Soviet Union.

8. THE UNION REPUBLICS' CHOICE OF THEIR OWN ROAD TO EUROPE

The thoughts and activities of Gorbachev's Westernizers as well as of governments in the West show that most of them still assume that it will be a 'common Soviet home' looking for its place in Europe. The draft of the new Union Treaty of November 1990 especially intends to transfer to the republics the realization of the basic concept of the Union by dividing it into detailed operative categories. Key sectors of the economy (armaments, energy, transportation, research, etc.) as well as competences in areas of important political decisions (credit, currency, prices in key industries, customs, foreign trade, environment) will be left to the authority of the centre.[30] As for foreign relations, Yevgeni Primakov, a member of the former Presidential Council, has already urgently warned the republics not to engage in special relations with the West. Those Soviet politicians calling for special relations between the West and the republics instead of the centre, Primakov said, are 'immature' and 'unprofessional' politicians.[31] But with the disintegration of the Soviet Union as a functioning centralized state, the union republics are acting more and more on their own as political and economic entities.

The republics claim sovereignty for their foreign relations as well. Many - among them the two largest republics, Russia and the Ukraine - are exploring for themselves the road to Europe and trying to establish contacts with West European countries. They not only desire bilateral relations but also hope to be included in European processes and organizations, such as the EC, CSCE and the Council of Europe. The Baltic states, Armenia, the Ukraine and even Russia all want an observer status in the CSCE and the Council of Europe in the hope of later becoming full members. The Moscow centre will certainly not be able to preserve in principle this trend of shifting power and competences for itself and away from the republics even if a new union with confederal structures (without the Baltic states) might one day be set up.

These internal Soviet developments present not only the

centre in Moscow with new problems. The West is equally being challenged by complicated questions, especially, how to react to the aspirations of the union republics, that is, how to accompany effectively this irreversible trend towards self-determined restructuring without snubbing the reformers and pro-Westerners at the centre, which could lead them to break off their policy of openness, cooperation and interdependence?

As a general concept, a differentiated strategy would be advisable, with a flexible adaptation to the real shifts of power within the Soviet Union. The West should not wait for a new Union Treaty to take effect before it concludes far-reaching treaties and agreements with the authorities of the centre and of the republics. Consequently, it should continue to support Gorbachev, while at the same time intensifying relations with individual republics to the extent to which they can succeed in securing *de facto* self-determination and sovereignty. Apart from establishing informal bilateral relations between Western countries and union republics, other measures at the transnational level are possible. These include linking individual republics to the CSCE process, to the Council of Europe and its commissions and to certain EC programmes and committees; granting them an observer status or establishing contact bureaus; providing direct financial aid and supporting the setting up of modern political and economic infrastructures.[32]

Such developments must be in the interests of the West, not least because the chance to gain self-determination and self-realization would fill the people living there with hope and encourage them to take an active part in the rebuilding of their home country. Conversely, the continuing dependence of the republics on the centre can only deepen the desperation of young people striving for an improvement in their lives. Such a bleak outlook would, to a great extent, stimulate what the neighbours of the Soviet Union and the EC countries presently fear most: an uncontrolled stream of economic migrants, a modern East-West mass migration of peoples.[33]

In the West, the struggle of the republics for national self-determination is still often portrayed as a dangerous, isolationist nationalism. This one-sided view overlooks the fact that this struggle is directed against Moscow's centralism and pseudo-internationalism, by which nations were violently suppressed and cut off from developments in Europe. Of course, just as with the countries of Central and Eastern Europe, there is the danger of seeing national self-determination turn into national populism or even national chauvinism, especially in the event that living standards continue to decline.

So far, however, this does not seem to be the main trend. There are many signs pointing to the fact that the new élites of the republics, just like the Westernizers around Gorbachev, are searching for a road to Europe in order to enter the community of states with constitutions based upon democracy and pluralism. In their view, the EC serves as a model for supranational structures, not the least because it combines efficient supranational integration with a conscious cultivation of all variations of national interests, cultures and traditions.

The new reform-oriented Russian élite, with its symbolic figure Boris Yeltsin, is pushing in that direction as well. In a remarkable speech, Alexei Kozyrev, Foreign minister of the Russian Federation since autumn 1990, pleaded for Russia's membership in the European Community and called it 'a matter of principle'. According to him, the West European countries, having lifted the '*Rechtsstaat*' and economic efficiency on to its highest level, are characterized by effectively functioning mechanisms of mutual political and economic relations. The states and nations of the Soviet Union should learn from this experience and make good use of it when restructuring their mutual relations. After that, Kozyrev argued, their path towards Europe would include more fruitful relations among themselves.[34]

9. PROSPECTS

Let us assume that the Soviet Union will be successful in decentralizing the Union and in creating a new federation of sovereign states based upon self-determination and sovereignty for every individual republic. This would help to improve the relations of Russia and other union republics with Moscow's former allies in Eastern Europe, who are all looking to the West. The union republics are less burdened by the heritage of the past of coercion and repression, as one Soviet analyst has argued. The republics are therefore 'more willing to do away with arrogance and conceit'. They would in that way 'become the main force of those doing constructive work for the better future of the whole of the Soviet Union'.[35]

The transformation of the Soviet Union into a federation of sovereign states would be positive from another point of view as well. In such a case, the countries of the region could in the long run expect better opportunities for cooperation with Western Europe. It is, after all, Moscow's repressive centralism that is to be blamed for the sorry state of affairs in politics, economy and society almost everywhere in the Soviet Union. It also explains why the people throughout the country are practically unable to absorb Western aid and to adopt Western-style mechanisms of consensus-reaching and integration.[36]

Soviet specialists, by the way, take a similar view. Vladimir Baranovskii, an expert on Europe as mentioned earlier, believes, for example, that the constructive balance of interests between the Moscow centre and the union republics, especially those in the western parts of the Soviet Union, is to be a very important precondition for the European prospects of the Soviet Union. It is his contention that the necessary preconditions will be fulfilled only after the Soviet Union has satisfied four criteria: 1. to avoid seeking solutions for the problems of the republics through force; 2. to make sure that the restructuring of the relations between various republics does not create new tensions in the relations of the Soviet Union with European countries (mainly immediate neighbours like Romania, Hungary and Poland, to whom separatist forces could appeal); 3. to create and promote constructive if not privileged relations with those republics that leave the Soviet Union; 4. the new Union Treaty should provide all members of the Union (ob"edinenie) with efficient mechanisms, enabling them to pursue a common foreign policy, mechanisms that legitimize this policy course.[37]

Developments that have become visible since winter 1990 give little hope that the Westernizers in the central leadership and in the union republics will be able to reorganize internal relations in the Soviet Union according to the model of West European integration and thus build the foundation for a common turn towards Europe. On the contrary, in the face of the economic chaos and collapse of the empire, the President, now in the possession of far-reaching powers, threatens to use force, supporting those who have promised to enforce discipline and order, namely, the army, KGB, communist party *nomenklatura* and the economic management in the military-industrial complex.

If domestic and foreign policy do indeed form a whole, as protagonists of the new thinking have repeatedly emphasized, then the return to an authoritarian regime or even to a dictatorship - as Eduard Shevardnadze in December 1990 warned - would sooner or later have its impact on the foreign relations of the Soviet Union. The West Europeans would most probably be affected most, simply because it is with them that the Soviets have nurtured the closest partnership. We already see here and there the resurrection of old concepts of the enemy as well as the redrawing of delimitation lines already believed to have been eliminated.[38]

It looks therefore as if in the foreseeable future the situation in the Soviet Union will be less determined by its turning towards Europe than by growing internal tensions and sharp conflicts, which can be influenced from the outside to a very limited degree only. Nevertheless, the West should not fail to avail itself of even these limited possibilities to exert an influence. It is in the West's own interests to continue to offer the reformers in Russia further incentives for linking their own country to Europe.

NOTES

1. Cf. my study 'Die Sowjetunion und der Umbruch in Osteuropa', *Berichte des Bundesinstituts für ostwissenschaftliche und internationale Studien*, no. 51, 1990.
2. As model examples, see the interviews of Vyacheslav Dashichev, 'Es geht um die Rückkehr in die europäische Zivilisation', *Leipziger Volkszeitung*, 30 May 1990 and 'Rückkehr nach Europa: Am Ende zweier Sonderwege', *Blätter für deutsche und internationale Politik*, no. 11, 1990, p. 1350.
3. B. A. Shmelev, 'Obshcheevropeiskii dom - balans interesov', in

Evropa v XXI veke: sotsialisticheskaya kontseptsiya obshche-evropeiskogo doma (Moskva, 1989), p. 18.

4. The German-Soviet 'Treaty on Good-Neighbourliness, Partnership and Cooperation' was published in *Pravda*, 11 November 1990.

5. The Soviet-French 'Treaty on Concord and Cooperation' was published in *Pravda*, 30 October 1990. See also *Le Monde*, 28/29 October 1990 and the spokesman of the Soviet Ministry of Foreign Affairs Vitali Churkin (TASS, 15 December 1990).

6. *Pravda*, 20 December 1990.

7. TASS, 26 October 1990.

8. V. Baranovskii and V. Zuev, 'Put k obshcheevropeiskomu domu: ekonomicheskie aspekty', *Kommunist*, no. 8, 1989, p. 111. See also S. Smolnikov, 'Novaya logika evropeiskogo razvitiya', *Mirovaya ekonomika i mezhdunarodnye otnosheniya (MEMO)*, no. 6, 1990, pp. 18-29. For the whole complex, see Heinz Timmermann, 'The Soviet Union and Western Europe: Conceptual Change and Political Reorientation' in Vilho Harle and Jyrki Iivonen (eds), *Gorbachev and Europe* (London: Frances Pinter, 1990), pp. 103-29 and Neil Malcolm, *Soviet Policy Perspectives on Western Europe* (London: Routledge/RIIA, 1989).

9. A. Rubbi, *Incontri con Gorbaciov: I colloqui di Natta e Occhetto con il leader sovietico giugno 1984 - novembre 1989* (Roma: Editori Riuniti, 1990).

10. ibid., p. 167.

11. ibid., p. 182.

12. Speech in the Supreme Soviet of the USSR on the visits to Great Britain, the Federal Republic of Germany and France (*Pravda*, 2 August 1989).

13. Report on a symposium of the Moscow IMEMO Institute on 'Economic and Legal Aspects of the Construction of the Common European House', *MEMO*, no. 10, 1990, p. 140. See also Sergei Karaganov, 'The Year of Europe: A Soviet View', *Survival*, no. 2, 1990, p. 125.

14. V. Baranovskii, 'Evropa: formirovanie novoi mezhdunarodno-politicheskoi sistemy', *MEMO*, no. 9, 1990, p. 18.

15. *Izvestiya*, 18 January 1990.

16. *Pravda*, 20 December 1989.

17. ADN, 25 September 1990.

18. 'Letter to Mitterrand as the Host of the Paris Economic Summit of July 1989', *Le Monde*, 18 July 1989.

19. Speech in the Supreme Soviet, op. cit.

20. For this, see Baranovskii and Zuev, op. cit., p. 112 and Baranovskii, op. cit.

21. Baranovskii, op. cit., p. 14.

22. *Pravda*, 20 December 1989.

23. Dashichev, op. cit., p. 1350.

24. N. Shishlin, Central Soviet Television, 21 July 1990.

25. 'Speech to the Parliamentary Assembly of the Council of Europe' (*Pravda*, 7 July 1989).

26. 'Put v bolshuyu Evropu', *Moskovskie Novosti*, no. 9, 1990, p. 12.

27. ibid.
28. See R. Weitz, 'The Council of Europe and the East', *Radio Liberty Report on Eastern Europe*, vol. 1, no. 34, 1990, pp. 49-57 and H. W. Maull and A. von Heynitz, 'Osteuropa: Durchbruch in die Postmoderne? Umrisse einer Strategie des Westens', *Europa-Archiv*, no. 15, 1990, p. 448.
29. Cf. V. Kamyshanov, 'Strasburg, Sovet Evropy', *Mezhdunarodnaya zhizn*, no. 10, 1990, pp. 51-3.
30. The draft of the Union Treaty was published in *Pravda*, 24 November 1990.
31. 'SSSR i SShA v novom mire': interview with *Literaturnaya gazeta*, no. 40, 1990, p. 14. See also Olga Alexandrova, 'Präsidialrat-Mitglied Jewgenij Primakow zu aktuellen Fragen der sowjetischen Aussenpolitik' in Bundesinstitut für ostwissenschaftliche und internationale Studien, *Gelesen, kommentiert...*, no. 17, 1990.
32. Cf. Heinrich Vogel, 'Die Sehnsucht nach Europa', *Europäische Zeitung*, no. 11, 1990, p. 17.
33. Cf. B. Knabe, 'Eine neue Völkerwanderung von Ost nach West - Steht die Europäische Gemeinschaft vor einer Massenzuwanderung aus Osteuropa?',Bundesinstitut für ostwissenschaftliche und internationale Studien, *Aktuelle Analysen*, no. 67, 1990.
34. 'Politika zdravogo smysla', *Dialog*, no. 16, 1990, p. 13.
35. M. Besrukow and A. Kortunow, 'Abschied von den Illusionen', *Neue Zeit* (Moscow), no. 51, 1990, p. 17.
36. For a model example, see A. Lebahn, 'Kann der Westen der Perestrojka wirtschaftlich helfen?', *Europa-Archiv*, no. 19, 1990, pp. 581-92.
37. Baranovskii, op. cit., p. 10.
38. Cf. the speeches of the KGB chief Vladimir Kryuchkov on Soviet Central Television (11 December 1990) and in the Congress of People's Deputies (*Pravda*, 23 December 1990).

8 THE RISE AND FALL OF THE COUNCIL OF MUTUAL ECONOMIC ASSISTANCE

Laszlo Csaba

---

1. INTRODUCTION

The revolutionary transformations that took place during the second half of 1989 have fundamentally reshaped Eastern Europe and consequently the entire post-Yalta construction of international relations. Along with this development and at least partly accelerated by the thorny and in many ways unpredictable twists and turns of *perestroika*, state socialism with its regional extensions, the Council of Mutual Economic Assistance (CMEA) and the Warsaw Treaty Organization, lost its *raison d'être* and collapsed. This collapse was brought about by a severe economic crisis, which is simultaneously structural, systemic and politico-social in nature. At the same time, the growth pattern has been changed.[1] In other words, the collapse of the political superstructure resulted from a weak economic foundation and the inability of the old regime to address the causes of the current crisis during at least the past 15-20 years.[2]

All this implies that overcoming the neo-Stalinist institutional and political barriers does not automatically lead to the emergence of a pluralistic political and economic order throughout Eastern Europe. The causes of the economic crisis - the outdated and internationally non-competitive production and sales, exaggerated occupational and social security, and inadequate income-distributory systems - cannot be removed for quite some time. The forces of socio-political regression are therefore strong, and the democratic structures have a long way to go before they can establish themselves firmly in Eastern Europe.[3] Because of that - and also due to the obviously different prospects of the respective countries - it is even more difficult than normal to forecast anything for certain in the longer run. However, it might be just the flux, inherent in the current state of affairs, that may attract some interest in the current development of intra-regional affairs in Eastern Europe.

2. THE FATAL ILLNESS OF THE CMEA

The emergence and history of the Council for Mutual Economic Assistance is a much discussed issue in international economics.[4] What is relevant from our standpoint is that the CMEA was originally set up for political reasons rather than on the basis of conventional considerations of how to integrate the socialist economies. The basic aim was to secure Soviet dominance and 'free' the member states from 'dependencies' inherent in participation in the Marshall Plan and later in the 'capitalist international division of labour'. The CMEA served as an international extension of, as well as a feedback and support for the respective systems of mandatory planning by establishing, in theory at least, foreseeable and governmentally manageable trade flows for the bulk of the international intercourse. The aim - though not the outcome - was to create what some call *Weltplanwirtschaft*, a command economy on an international scale.[5] The CMEA has always served, despite recurring opposite political statements, an inward-looking, import-substituting and growth-oriented strategy of economic development. One of the most traditional and, at least for some Western analysts, the most incomprehensible features of the intra-CMEA division of labour is the pattern of exchange. The exchange of Soviet primary commodities for East European finished products has to do with the predominance over the decades of this partly extra-economic consideration.

Economic calculations, be they based on opportunity costs, factor endowments, domestic input/output ratios or comparative advantages, have always remained secondary, although they have constantly grown in influence with time. Contrary to the general internationalism of the communist ideology, this industrialization pattern factually drew heavily on the economic nationalism of the interwar period and resulted in a two-tier import-substituting strategy, where regional international cooperation basically served the strengthening of the national autarkic strategy.[6] In other words, in deciding on major national priority projects, the requirements of the Soviet market were normally kept in mind. And the other way around: as far as political factors could influence real trade flows, the Soviet Union to a decreasing extent always tried to treat trade with its East European partners as a political priority. This served to strengthen both the communist party rule and the planned economies as well as the traditional Soviet concern for its own strategic 'invulnerability', though for inherent reasons of size and development level, Eastern Europe has always been a rather poor proxy for the 'rest of the world'.

The fundamental problem of integration among planned economies has not been the frequently discussed issue of 'who is a burden on whom', since decisions in major issues have never been made on this basis. True, this as well as their obvious over-trading, compared with the usual international standards, led to mutual losses of efficiency. Still, the most serious problem has been the lack of success in integration, both according to internal standards and in the light of international comparisons.

As far as internal standards are concerned, the fundamental paradox of the CMEA has been the impossibility of integration through supranational planning, owing to the lack of multinational cooperation. In other words, Soviet dominance in the political sphere and mutual intertwining in the economic sphere have never been so overwhelming as to lead to the formation of a mighty international planning agency that could instruct obedient national governmental organs. It is not that 'good intentions' would have been lacking: since 1949, once in every five to six years attempts have been made to 'streamline' the functioning of the CMEA organs according to the logic of mandatory planning. These attempts, however, have remained futile as the strongholds of 'national egoism' have been central planning organs which play the role of national superministries. Obviously, they would have had to be deprived of some of the prerogatives of economic sovereignty, provided supranational planning had actually been supported by everybody. This, however, was a far cry from reality. National planning and political organs were not slow to pinpoint the problems of the incommensurability of costs and benefits across national borders, this being a state of normalcy under currency inconvertibility. We should add, however, that it was a pretext rather than a cause, since the incomparability problem exists also within the respective national economies (also owing to the internal inconvertibility problem).[7] Still, major allocative decisions are regularly made, since there is a single socially uncontrolled centre that can wield its power. This, however, has never been the case at the CMEA level.

Integration via the market proved impossible, too, basically for the same reasons. Market integration presupposes that the markets already function within all the constituent national economies, or at least that each of them is on the way to a full-fledged market system, as was the case with the members of the European Payments Union (EPU) in the 1950s. The economic reforms of the 1960s were thwarted - except in the case of Hungary - while the attempts made in the 1980s either remained on paper or were only half-heartedly and partially implemented. Real conditions for market integration have thus never emerged. To illustrate this point, let me cite an article published in the monthly of the Soviet communist party. It showed that, despite many decrees and some delegation of authority in foreign trade decisions, the measures of 1986-89 as a whole distanced the Soviet management system rather than bringing it closer to the conditions of currency convertibility.[8] Thus, among the non-market economies, no 'unified socialist market' could come about.

If we address the other major dimension, international

competitiveness, the picture obtained is not particularly convincing either. On the one hand, the CMEA countries as a group have been losing ground increasingly vis-a-vis the developing nations. The more we look at the newly in-dustrializing countries and at the more highly processed product groups, the greater is the gap.[9] On the other hand, the CMEA countries are less and less able to meet one another's needs, while the incongruence between their mutual supply and demand structures is growing commensurably. Such much discussed issues as Soviet inability to keep pace with the primary product needs of its East European partners or the East European inability to come up to the quantitative expectations of the Soviet partner, when supplying agricultural commodities or consumer goods, are manifestations of this problem. The bilateral clearing system has simply proved unable to deliver the only thing this arrangement can normally claim among its indisputable merits, namely, balancing bi-lateral trade flows and payments. This situation has been characteristic of the CMEA during the last 15 years. It is a system, based traditionally on the redistribution of increments in the international coordination of macroeconomic plans, that has been faced first with stagnation and then, at the end of the 1980s, even with a quantitative decline.[10] It has therefore proved unfit to cope with this challenge. The entire plan-based mechanism of regional cooperation has become increasingly irrelevant from the viewpoint of real economic processes taking place within and among the constituent economies. Stability, foresight, central manageability and other tradition-ally postulated features of the CMEA simply melted away in the late 1980s. The irrelevance thesis is supported especially by the ever widening gap between policy statements (plans) and reality, in both political and economic terms. The contradiction between the heavily weighted documents, the ritual self-complacent statements and the reality, moulded by, *inter alia,* the escalating customs war among the countries, has become unbearable.[11]

    This brings us to the crucial issue of economic reorientation, emerging as a reaction to the mutual incon-gruency phenomena and aimed at correcting the problems caused by the over-trading. Reorientation in its pure form implies, by definition, a systemic change, doing away with the methods of command planning that have dominated the trade regimes of most of the CMEA countries. It aims primarily to transform all the trading partners by giving up the primacy of ideology in politico-economic decision-making. Therefore it implies a growth in the share of those nations - not only Europeans - that constitute the mainstream of the worldwide technological and economic development. Reorientation in the 1990s is thus not a mere foreign policy act as in the case of Yugoslavia in the late 1940s or of Romania in the 1970s. The aim is to rethink the entire economic strategy of the member states. Moreover, unlike in the 1970s and 1980s, this is not basically a reflection of the different price dynamics in intra- and extra-regional trade, but a conscious and reciprocal policy action of the member states.

3. THE CONCEPT OF REORIENTATION

Reorientation as an overall strategy emerged as a definite concept in both Hungary and the Soviet Union in autumn 1988. By that time, the limits of reforming the CMEA as a multi-lateral organization, the constraints on perestroika as an economic programme as well as the exceedingly limited results of the increased efforts at regional self-reliance - exemplified by the CMEA Long-Term Technological Programme till the year 2000 - had become rather unpalatable. For obvious reasons, the reaction to these new realities was primarily political in the Soviet Union, exemplified by the August meeting at the Ministry of Foreign Affairs and by Shevardnadze's speech there as well as by the wide-ranging discussions among the high-ranking officials concerning the overall foreign economic strategy of the Soviet Union.[12] In Hungary the reaction was basically economic (with strong foreign policy overtones), with the emphasis on the large unplanned and unusable surpluses in the rouble clearing area as well as on the sweeping repercussions of a contracting Soviet market and their effect on the entire Hungarian economy and the economic system.[13] The foregoing sources stem directly from the contemporary Governmental Committee on Economic Reform, headed by Rezsö Nyers. True, Hungary's independent foreign policy line, having advocated expanding East-West ties, became quite pronounced after 1983.[14] Still, it remained an isolated policy move, an act restricted to one particular area without placing its direct imprint on other areas, the economy in particular. Some of the largest import-substituting joint investment projects, the Yamburg-Tengiz pipeline and the equally inward-looking projects of the CMEA Technological Programme in manufacturing, were signed and launched in December 1985 with substantial Hungarian participation.[15] By late autumn 1988 or early 1989, however, reorientation had gained official blessing in Hungary.

Of the other small East European countries, only the GDR pursued comparable policies at that time, while Poland, Czechoslovakia and Bulgaria as well as Ceausescu's Romania tried to intensify their reliance on the CMEA. Of the non-European members, Vietnam had already signalled its interest in turning towards the ASEAN, since its previous economic orientation towards the CMEA did not pay enough.[16] Two other CMEA members, Cuba and Mongolia, however, remained firmly committed. In the meantime, the Soviet Union changed its conventional approach to the CMEA. This was a direct consequence of Soviet domestic developments.

It was during the short Andropov reign that the Soviets started to give up looking at the CMEA primarily in military-political terms. This, of course, implied a tougher stance on the economic performance of the allies and a growing 'economization' or depoliticization of the intra-bloc affairs. The endeavours of the early Gorbachev years to accelerate technological progress basically via self-reliance and discipline proved to be utopian, at both the domestic Soviet and regional CMEA levels. Thus, following the All-Union Party Conference in June 1988, a new strategy was elaborated. It was a radically pro-market approach to domestic economic affairs, coupled with a policy marked by an all-out economic opening. The latter was embodied in the fairly liberal December 1988 decrees aimed at reforming foreign trade.[17] True, much of the substance of these regulations had 'transitorily' been withdrawn already in March 1988, but still the change in the overall strategy seems to be demonstrable.[18] Ever since, nearly every major policy statement made by the principal Soviet leaders has included references to rouble convertibility, economic opening and increasing reliance on external contacts and experience.[19]

The Soviets tried first to stick to the concept of the socialist common market. This idea, adopted by all the member states in the October 1987 Council Session, reflected the earlier state of affairs, a less radical (gradualist, longer-term) approach to introducing a real market and a postulate that, in addition to the European Community (EC), the CMEA would continue to exist for a long time as its parallel, East European equivalent.

All in all, this standpoint has become obsolete rather quickly. The Soviet Union was not slow to recognize that the agreement of most of the other CMEA partners on the unified socialist market was restricted to general issues. This was the only possibility, because all the practical steps promoting this end were continuously sabotaged, especially by the GDR, Romania and the non-European members. It was not very difficult to recognize - and Soviet officials did put it quite bluntly - that they could hardly rely on the East European countries to restructure their economies.[20] This is quite an important finding. Whether one interprets the Soviet foreign trade interest in terms of modernization (as in 1985-87) or in terms of a more traditionalist preference for agricultural and consumer goods (as under Andropov and Chernenko as well as in 1988-90), the economic power of the small CMEA partners can hardly be a substitute for that of the USA, Japan and the EC, the natural counterparts of the huge Soviet federation.

In view of this, it seems rather inappropriate to talk about 'who has lost Eastern Europe' or about 'dismantling socialism in the commonwealth based on the blood spilled in the Second World War', as Egor Ligachev has put it. This is not the issue, even if abstracted from the nature and depth of the Soviet economic and nationality crises or from the fundamental features of the new technological revolution. Since politics, as the art of the possible, must focus on actual issues, irrespective of reminiscences, it remains to be answered what, at the end of the day, these nine - or, following German unification, only eight - crisis-ridden economies could contribute to alleviating the Soviet ills. Credits? Technology? Management skills? Raw materials, intermediate or consumer goods? Anyone familiar with actual figures would find these propositions naive. Therefore, whatever its ideological stance might be, reorientation is a necessity from the Soviet point of view as well.

4. INTRA-BLOC TRADE IN CONVERTIBLE CURRENCIES

If the major priority of the Soviet Union in the 1990s is to join the global trading and financial system, its previous preference for bilaterally cleared trade with the ex-socialist countries has become quite relative. From a major ideological, political, military and economic priority, it has been transformed into one of administrative convenience. In other words, it would certainly be less troublesome for the bureaucrats of the still almighty Gosplan if there were other countries trying to continue to find the products Soviet planners wish to purchase in exchange for oil, gas and other major export items. No matter how noble this consideration may sound, it does not appear to be overwhelming. In other words, the Soviet interest at the level of governmental policy no longer relates to the maintenance of state trading. On the contrary, the appeal that they can spend their foreseeable surpluses vis-a-vis the CMEA partners in other parts of the multilateral international payments system emerges as rather temptating to them and may appear to be a danger for the smaller East European states.[21]

It was the Hungarians who proposed this option during the late March 1989 top level meeting of the leaders of the two countries. The Hungarian motives can be summarized in the following way. Since 1968, one of the major obstacles to the marketization of the Hungarian economy has been the dominant share of the CMEA, i.e., the dominant share of the non-market environment. The CMEA has been a constraint in both policy and systemic terms. All the major projects have adhered to priorities and possibilities of the CMEA partners, primarily those of the Soviet Union. In the indirect management system, the Hungarian government agencies did not instruct companies to follow suit, but made it artificially advantageous for them to do so (by way of investment preferences, access to convertible currency inputs, etc.). Since the mid-1970s, it has thus been the corporate interest in maintaining and securing soft and protected markets that has acted as a major factor in reproducing the one-sided eastward orientation of the Hungarian economy. This is explained by the multiplier effect of large projects, spilling over to many smaller firms as well.

Further, as the CMEA has by necessity remained a system tailored to the needs of the command economy, it was Hungary with its minority position that had to adjust its domestic arrangements to the nature of integrational arrangements rather than vice versa. Therefore, the high share of the CMEA in total Hungarian trade - on the average, three-quarters in the 1960s, two thirds in the 1970s and one half in the 1980s, with 40 per cent in 1989 - explains to a fair degree why the centralized forms of control remained so lasting in Hungary despite repeated attempts to change them.

Thus by 1988, when the Hungarians had realized the unfeasibility of reforming the multilateral arrangements in the CMEA, the idea emerged that perhaps the Soviet Union could be talked into a more progressive bilateral arrangement. Given that two-thirds of the total Hungarian trade with the East was transacted with the Soviets, this option seemed to have solved the systemic problem. From the Hungarian perspective, the basic issue is twofold: to do away with all forms of state trading and to secure the interest of the growing number and variety of Soviet suppliers (whoever they may be) in exporting to Hungary under the conditions of the obvious collapse of the domestic Soviet market. Making payments in actual convertible currencies is the only sensible way to meet this end.

Needless to say, this proposition implies such a radical break with all former approaches and stances on how to improve CMEA cooperation that it fuelled a long and heated debate among economists.[22] It is worth noting that much of the debate was sidetracked by the governmental agencies reinterpreting the problem as if the issue were to improve the accounting system of the basically untouched CMEA and unchanged Hungarian system of intertwining the domestic and integrational markets. As pointed out earlier, this was a fundamental misunderstanding, as the point was not to 'perfect' a dead horse but to find a new horse on which to ride.

What are the most relevant objections to abolishing state trading and clearing arrangements in Hungarian-Soviet trade? First and foremost, the state of the Soviet economic system in general and of the foreign trade regime in particular bears very little resemblance to markets of any sort. Even the prospects for them to evolve are usually seen as poor. The suggestion, therefore, implies an asymmetric system, for on the Soviet side the state will continue to have a decisive role in the foreign trade decisions.

The existence of asymmetry would be a decisive counter-argument if the aim were some kind of a bilateral 'socialist common market'. But the aim is to free the hands of the Hungarian decision-makers from the traditional constraints stemming from the centralized nature of the Soviet economy. If and when anyone wants to do business with the Soviets they must take or leave their system as it is. Still, this implies by no means that, in shaping the new internal Hungarian arrangements, any allowance should be made to conformity with the Soviet partner. Realistically evaluated, the Soviet share in Hungarian trade will be reduced to about 10-15 per cent in the 1990s. This segment should therefore not determine the entire trade regime any longer. The risk of doing business with the Soviet Union has to be delegated to the companies that have decided to enter these peculiar conditions. Consequently, they have the right to harvest the gains therefrom (unlike the traditional practice). But their equal duty is to bear the costs of possible miscalculation of their opportunities, which also constitutes a break with tradition. The second argument warns of the shock caused by an abrupt change in the bilateral trade regime. Preliminary calculations computed by the bureaucracy produced horrendous sums of Hungarian losses (between 1 and 3.5 billion roubles, i.e., 1.6-5.6 billion dollars, according to the official exchange rates).

Let us forget for a moment that these calculations presume the possibility of doing nothing, and extrapolate the 1987-88 conditions to 1995 or 2000 as a feasible option for economic policy. Achieving the *status quo* would not require, among other things, the refinancing of the clearing surpluses from convertible currency capital markets. By mid-1990, it has become clear that what was being feared by the officials actually occurred prior to any reformatory step. The Hungarian transition costs include the terms-of-trade losses resulting from the fallouts of overpriced but soft export items, the budgetary losses from the collapse of an artificially constructed profit revenue previously taxed away and spent by the state, as well as employment and the capacity losses sustained by those companies that prove unable to reorganize their production and reorientate their output to competitive markets.

In 1990, owing to the heavy contraction of the Soviet market (by 20-25 per cent in one year) as well as to the need to run a deficit (to ameliorate previous Hungarian surpluses), practically all the three dangers mentioned turned into reality, adding an extra 2-3 per cent to the recession of the Hungarian economy. This is sad; but at least it is now clear that these costs are not due to systemic change but to indecision and the postponement of action in 1986-90.

The third serious argument runs as follows. Owing to the segmentation of the single Soviet market and to the growing shortages, most deals will become barter agreements of various sorts. This does not sound much like free trade. Freedom of trade must, however, be interpreted in the light of given conditions. The difference between barter and soft clearing agreements remains immense. In the case of company-level barters, the inherent risks in dealing on the chaotic markets are not socialized, unlike under soft clearing arrangements. And this is precisely the point of the entire exercise. Dealing with companies of the increasingly diverse Soviet (con)federation requires special skills, knowledge, contacts and even abilities to evade certain regulations. This kind of knowledge is typically decentrally available and unevenly distributed. No central agency in any form can therefore be an appropiate substitute. Still, as K. Lanyi elaborates in her article, under the conditions of trading in dollars, a large number of factors countervailing the currently evolving collapse of bilateral trade flows will be mobilized.[23] Therefore, no matter how paradoxical it might seem, the bilateral trade mechanism to be introduced in order to foster the reorientation policies of both countries is the only way to save what is economically sensible from the traditional intercourse of these two neighbours.

5. UNRESOLVED QUESTIONS IN TRANSITION AND PROSPECTS

The debate over whether or not to change the bilateral trade and payments system in the CMEA was practically decided by Prime Minister Ryzhkov's statement in the January 1990 Sofia session, where he proposed the starting of trading in convertible currencies from 1991 on.[24] Even so, much of the issue has still remained unsettled. It is not clear at all what the ways and means of attaining this goal are, while even the goal itself is open to interpretation. Since Ryzhkov's statement contained a passage referring to the need to continue to tie together the joint supplies of 'macroeconomically most significant' deliveries (as, for example, Soviet oil to Hungarian agriculture), the door is left open for an inter-state clearing arrangement. Since the 1987-89 expert-level debates on CMEA finances, the Soviet Union has repeatedly rejected the Hungarian proposition to settle the year-end balances of the (rouble) clearing in hard currency. A safety clause is most probably included in the current Soviet approach. This would lead to a soft inter-state clearing, with a major share of inter-governmental bargaining concerning the conditions of larger deals.

There has never been the slightest doubt that it is the probably sizeable and immediate terms-of-trade gain that induces the Soviet Union to go for the hard currency trade. Still, if the foregoing interpretation, having dominated the Soviet approach in expert level talks, were the main line of transformation, it would imply the combination of unfavourable features for Hungary and nothing more; i.e., terms-of-trade losses (resulting from changes in pricing and the pattern of trade) coupled with the maintenance of the antiquated system of state trading in a slightly modified version. In a way, events seem to have supported the somewhat sarcastic observation that the Gosplan people must have learned from the press the figures produced by the Hungarian officials opposing the systemic change, multiplied them by six (the number of European CMEA members) and thought that it might be just as well to gain an extra 10-12 billion dollars merely by changing the unit of account.[25]

This approach would certainly have been congruent with the governmental programme of economic consolidation and postponement of all the substantial reforms of the Ryzhkov government as submitted to the second Congress of People's Deputies in December 1989.[26] However, with the ever-deepening crisis, this project as well as its modernized version - rejected by the people's deputies in June 1990 - have fallen out of touch with the Soviet reality. Recurring statements are being made about the radicalization of reform, about the new market-type system. But, owing to the political turmoil and the open struggle for power, these plans are not being implemented. This has become a problem for the Hungarians, as in June 1990 no agreement could yet be made on the bilateral trade and payments regime. This was due to the fact that the Soviet side was in no position to give any indication even about the cornerstones of the actual arrangements to be implemented from 1 January 1991 in their country (to which the bilateral solutions are to be dovetailed).[27] Still, the June 1990 talks of the two prime ministers resulted in a common view that hard currency trade rather than clearing is the fundamental feature of the new system. It subsumes the Soviet regrouping of Hungary from clearing to hard currency relations, irrespective of how they might finally trade with the West. Hungarian firms, therefore, may or may not adjust to these rules in the same way as their French or Spanish counterparts.

Since the transition to the new system is a complicated and expensive task, small wonder that propositions aimed at circumventing or softening its impact proliferate. For example, the Poles and the Soviets have agreed that, as a first step, 10-15 per cent of their trade will be transacted in hard currency.[28] This, however, is hardly a step in the right direction. Hungary has had this type of 'limited convertible currency accounting' with the Soviet Union for nearly two decades now, without this having influenced the bulk of trade towards extended multilateralism. By a detailed analysis of this experience, it can be shown that the rather disillusioning outcome is inevitable under the predominance of the traditional CMEA arrangements.[29] In that framework, the share of free trade cannot significantly grow, whatever might be the intentions of policy-makers.

Alternatively, the idea has been raised that the small countries in Central Europe could create an Eastern version of the European Payments Union (EPU) of the 1950s.[30] The main motive behind this suggestion is twofold. If it comes from the West, the consideration is how to consolidate the Central European ex-socialist economies in a cheaper way, by drawing on the analogies of the Marshall Plan. If it comes from the countries concerned, the chief motivation is to soften the shock of an instantaneous change to the market on rigid, protected economies that are already in a recession.

It must be added, however, that the conditions in Western Europe after the Second World War have nothing to do with those prevailing in Central Europe after four decades of state socialism. First and foremost, the West European nations constituted the bulk of world trade (the sterling and franc zones included). Accordingly, the multilateralization of their trade was equivalent to liberalizing world trade in general. Simultaneously, these nations took internationally coordinated parallel steps to liberalize and monetize their respective domestic economies.

These two conditions are conspicuously missing from Central Europe. The share of Czechoslovakia and Poland together is less than 5 per cent of the total Hungarian trade.[31] Thus, to declare a free trade zone, a monetary union or whatever would be a confusing signal for most companies, and the concomitant intergovernmental rituals might well sidetrack entrepreneurs from reorientation.

Moreover, the three countries are in very different situations. Since the Balcerowicz plan, Poland has attained the internal convertibility of the zloty and does not need a multilateral clearing for this end. Hungary has basically secured convertibility for non-resident investors and is on the way to gradually introducing to the market economy predominantly private ownership, where the convertibility of the forint is the end-result. Poland follows the Sachs-therapy by not even paying interest to the commercial banks.[32] Hungary, for its part, has always fulfilled all its obligations and can manage its economic consolidation without debt relief. Except for their history and geographical location, there is nothing common to the economic stories of these two countries; they are not in the same boat. Czechoslovakia, for its part, is yet to start abolishing its mandatory planning system, so that its problems are also qualitatively different from those of the two other countries.

All in all, there is not much justification for a common approach. If we add to that the combined market share of the three countries, which is normally in the 1 per cent range in the world economy, it becomes clear why the room for a *viribus unitis* approach remains rather narrow in the future as well. Small wonder that the Czechs did not even want to discuss the idea and the new Hungarian government rejected the Polish proposal to start working on this issue. Consequently, Hungarian-Polish trade, too, has been transacted in hard currency since 1 January 1991.

Last, it should be mentioned that the unification of Germany has deprived the CMEA of its second strongest economic partner. Trade in German marks is an obvious consequence, especially since Czechoslovakia will certainly want to trade in hard currency only. Both bilateral and multi-lateral clearing is becoming a marginal phenomenon in what used to be the intra-bloc trade in the CMEA. Meanwhile, trade with the non-European members has openly become what it has always been, namely, a foreign policy issue of the Soviet Union.

6. CONCLUSION

Finally, one question should yet be addressed: what will remain of the CMEA as a multilateral organization? According to recent Soviet policy statements, maintaining the CMEA in its traditional form and content would be senseless, even harmful.[33] The Soviet Union does not need the CMEA any more than others do. Accepting the reorientation policy, a major Soviet official goes as far as to propose transforming it into a business club, which in the same way as the OECD-secretariat could serve as a forum to discuss policy issues and promote the emergence of a single European economic region.[34] In view of the common history and location, I cannot see why it would even be in the interests of neutral Hungary to leave this economic grouping. What used to be a burden for a small market economy in the old CMEA is already dead - as I have tried to prove in this chapter.

What is the interest of the West in these 'purely internal' affairs of the one-time Eastern bloc? First and foremost, if intra-CMEA trade is becoming a hard currency turnover, the small countries can actually serve as a bridge to the Soviet markets. Expertise, personal and business contacts, experience, knowledge of languages, is available. Second, in a more macroscopic view, it is a basic IMF and GATT target to abandon state trading and bilateralism. It would therefore be logical for the major international financial organizations to contribute to reducing the costs of the transition. Third, the systemic change from dictatorship to pluralism is taking place in Central Europe amidst conditions of a severe recession, which will last for some years to come. This model is closer to the experience of the Weimar republic than to the recent Spanish, Portuguese and South Korean experiences of entering the road to pluralism. The dangers inherent in a protracted crisis in the heart of Europe and its repercussions are obvious. It would be naive to pretend that the Western democracies could be spared the spillover effects. There is thus an element of commonality of interests in Central Europe's success in overcoming the crisis, where an important and influential component is the collapse of the CMEA.

NOTES

This paper was written in October 1990, while the author was Senior Visiting Fellow at the Instituto Universitario Europeo in Florence under the PHARE Programme of the European Communities.

1. It is generally believed that it is not possible to maintain the traditional growth model, that a lasting recession is inevitable unless new factors, patterns and driving forces are being created. See B. Kadar, 'Liberalisation - the Hungarian Way' in A. Köves and P. Marer (eds), *Liberalisation: Hungarian and International Experiences* (Boulder: Westview Press, 1991).

2. Laszlo Csaba, 'Why Just in 1989? Reflections on the Demise of State Socialism', *The Journal of Communist Studies,* 1991 (forthcoming).

3. L. Shvetsova, 'Kuda idet Vostochnaya Evropa?', *Mirovaya ekonomika i mezhdunarodnye otnosheniya,* no. 4, 1990, pp. 99-100.

4. See S. Ausch, *Theory and Practice of CMEA Cooperation* (Budapest: Akadémiai Kiado, 1972); Michael Kaser, *Comecon: Integration Problems of the Planned Economies* (Oxford: Oxford University Press, 1965); J. van Brabant, *Economic Integration in Eastern Europe: A Handbook* (New York: Harvester Press, 1990); and A. Zwass, *The Council for Mutual Economic Assistance* (Armonk: M. E. Sharpe, 1989).

5. P. Welfens, *Internationalisierung von Wirtschaft und Wirtschaftspolitik* (Berlin: Springer Verlag, 1990), pp. 98-102.

6. A. Köves, *The CMEA Countries in the World Economy: Turning Inwards or Turning Outwards?* (Budapest: Akadémiai Kiado, 1965).

7. The segmentation of markets is an inherent consequence of planning in physical terms and the subordination of financial categories to the former. As prices and profits reflect rather than determine plan decisions, it is inevitable that prices and profitabilities of the same activity diverge grossly by companies and products as well as by areas of use. Consequently, no uniform purchasing power of the monetary unit exists or may exist under central planning: see Laszlo Csaba, *Eastern Europe in World Economy* (Cambridge: Cambridge University Press, 1990), chapters I-III.

8. B. Fedorov, 'Ekonomicheskaya politika i konvertiruemost rublya', *Kommunist,* no. 8, 1990, p. 50.

9. A. Inotai, *Industrial Export Performance of Socialist and Developing Countries* (Empirica, 1988).

10. T. Kiss, 'International Coordination of National Economic Plans', *Eastern European Economics,* no. 1/1976.

11. 'Nesostayavshayasya model ekonomicheskikh otnoshenii?', *Mezhdunarodnaya zhizn,* no. 3, 1990, pp. 58-60.

12. *Mezhdunarodnaya zhizn,* nos. 9-10, 1988.

13. See A. Köves, 'Eine neue Situation im Ungarns Handel mit der Sowjetunion: Was ist zu tun', *Europäische Rundschau,* no. 3, 1988; 'How to Bring about a Socialist Market Economy?', *Public Finance in*

Hungary, no. 47, 1988); and 'Opening towards the World Economy', *The Hungarian Economy,* vol. 17, no. 1, 1989.

14. The top of this iceberg are the articles of Matyas Szürös, the first having appeared in February 1983 and the second in January 1984: M. Szürös, 'National Cause - Common Cause', *The New Hungarian Quarterly,* no. 90, 1983 and M. Szürös, 'Active Foreign Policy in the Service of Peace', *The New Hungarian Quarterly,* no. 96, 1984.

15. It is a different story that this wide-ranging import-substitution drive finally has not materialized as it could not objectively materialize. The timing of its launching, however, still proves the dominance of these approaches over the more open foreign policy. For an elaboration and substantiation of the first half of this statement, compare with Laszlo Csaba, 'Das Komplexsprogramm für den wissenschaftlich-technischen Fortschritt der RGW-Länder bis zum Jahr 2000' in H.-E. Gramazki, K. Klinger and H.-G. Nutzinger (eds), *Wissenschaft, Technik und Arbeit: Innovationen in Ost und West* (Kassel: Verlag vwl-inform, 1990), pp. 251-66.

16. V. Khoan, 'Economic Reforms in Asia and Europe and Cooperation with Viet Nam', *Journal of Development Planning,* no. 20, 1990.

17. See 'O dalneishem razvitii vneshneekonomicheskoi deyatelnosti gosudarstvennykh, kooperativnykh i inykh obshchestvennykh predpriyatii, ob"edinenii i organizatsii', *Ekonomicheskaya Gazeta,* no. 51, 1988.

18. This was reinforced by the presidential degree of 2 November 1990, compelling Soviet companies to continue to submit *de facto* over 90 per cent of their currency intake: 40 per cent for serving the All-Union debts and the rest to feed various 'targeted' central funds. See also *Népszabadsag,* 3 November 1990.

19. Aleksander Kapto, 'Prioritet nasikh otnoshenii s sotsialisticheskimi stranami', *Mezhdunarodnaya zhizn,* no. 10, 1988, p. 32.

20. See L. Klepatskii's Contribution to the Round Table Discussion 'Sotsialistcheskoe sodruzhestvo: demokratizatsiya i obnovlenie', *Mezhdunarodnaya zhizn,* no. 12, 1988, p. 135.

21. O. Rybakov, 'Ekonomicheskaya platforma vzaimodeistviya', (*Kommunist,* no. 6, 1990, p. 117.

22. For good summary of these, note 23.

23. A. Köves, 'Transforming Commercial Relations within the CMEA: the Case of Hungary' in Köves and Marer, op. cit.; G. Oblath, 'Unresolved Issues of the Intra-CMEA Trade in Convertible Currencies' in Laszlo Csaba (ed), *Systemic Change and Stabilisation in Eastern Europe* (Aldershot: Dartmouth, 1991); I. Szegvari, 'A jo dollar es a rossz KGST', *Figyelö,* no. 32,1989; and K. Lanyi, 'Veszelyes-e dollarban kereskedni a Szovjetunioval?', *Külgazdasag,* nos 6 and 7, 1990. An English version of Lanyi's article 'Is It Really Dangerous to Trade in Dollars with the Soviet Union?' is forthcoming in *Acta Oeconomica.*

24. *Izvestiya,* 10 January 1990.

25. K. Lanyi, 'Vége a multilateralitas latszatanak?', *Vilaggazdasag,* 9 January 1990.

26. *Izvestiya,* 14 December 1989.

27. I. Tamas, 'Hol itt a piac?', *Magyar Hirlap,* 11 June 1990 and I.

Szegvari, 'Ovintezkedesek a dollarelszamolas startjara', *Vilaggazdasag*, 4 August 1990.
28. *Izvestiya*, 10 January 1990.
29. See Csaba, *Eastern Europe in World Economy*, op. cit.
30. J. van Brabant, 'On Reforming the External Payments Regimes in the CMEA', *Jahrbuch der Wirtschaft Osteuropas*. vol. 14/2. (Munich-Vienna: G. Olzog Verlag), 1990, pp. 7-31 and P. Medgyessy, 'A kis KGST-integracio', *Nepszabadsag*, 8 January 1990. I have abstracted from the politically motivated proposal by the US millionaire G. Soros that would include the Soviet Union as well. Knowing the current and forseeable state of the Soviet foreign trade mechanism, this proposition is out of touch with realities. Arguing for the Central European option discussed above, Zbigniew Brzezinski goes as far as to suggest that Western governments make the implementation of the CEPU an explicit prerequisite for their financial involvement in the reconstruction of the region: Zbigniew Brzezinski, 'Jenseits des Chaos', *Europäische Rund-schau*, no. 3, 1990, p. 58.
31. KOPINT-Datorg, 'Külkereskedelmi statisztikai gyorstajékoztato', 1990, I-IX ho. (Budapest, October 1990).
32. On the Sachs-therapy, see Jeffrey Sachs and David Lipton, 'Poland's Economic Reform', *Foreign Affairs*, vol. 69, no. 3, Summer 1990, pp. 47-66.
33. 'Nesostayavshayasya model...', op. cit.
34. Rybakov, op. cit., p. 120.

Part IV

REGIONAL ISSUES

9 THE SOVIET UNION AND THE PROSPECTS OF BALTIC COOPERATION: AN ESTONIAN VIEW

Priit Järve

1. THE IDEA OF THE BALTIC FEDERATION

The idea of Baltic cooperation was proposed in Estonia on 7 September 1917. *Eesti Maapäev*, the body for Estonian self-determination, elected under a decree of the Russian Provisional Government, discussed for the first time the international standing of Estonia. Jaan Tönisson, a prominent Estonian politician, suggested:

> If the peoples of Lithuania, Latvia, Estonia, Finland and Scandinavia would unite, then, as a union of nations thirty million strong, they could be rather influential at the peace conference. The general interests of Great Britain as well as those of the United States of America more or less coincided with the gains of Baltic-Scandinavia.

He went on to urge:

> Should we not become active now and unite with the other Baltic-Scandinavian peoples, for the destiny of the Baltic states ought to be so decided upon as to prevent them from

211

being subjugated by Germany and enable them to attain political independence with other Baltic-Scandinavian peoples?[1]

One should bear in mind that 73 years ago the idea of an independent Estonia was not yet under discussion. The debate over the Baltic Union may therefore be regarded as an important step towards this idea.

Bronis J. Kaslas has claimed that Lithuania was the first to express the common desire of the Baltic peoples to win freedom. As he has pointed out, the first tentative steps towards developing the idea of a union among the Baltic countries were taken in 1917 by one of the founders of the Lithuanian Renaissance, Jonas Sliupas, who advocated the fusion of the Lithuanians and the Latvians on the basis of the same racial stock and similar languages.[2] Anyhow, the idea of some kind of Baltic Union seems to have been in the air. In November 1918, a large-scale project to form a Baltic League, including Denmark, Sweden, Norway, Finland, Estonia, Latvia, Lithuania and Poland, was proposed by the Estonian delegation in Paris.

The proposed Baltic Union, or Baltic-Scandinavian federation, was never formally established because of the different political interests of the states concerned. Nevertheless, in the 1920s, independent Estonia managed to cultivate good economic and cultural relations with the Scandinavian countries, notably Sweden and Finland. The economic crisis of 1929, however, seriously disrupted this cooperation. The decline in trade between the small countries of the Baltic area was deeper than that undergone by world trade, so that these countries could not restore their trade relations to the level of 1929 before the Second World War. Moreover, during the second half of the 1930s, the cooperation between the Baltic states and the Scandinavian countries was also inhibited by the establishment of authoritarian regimes in Estonia, Latvia and Lithuania, while in Scandinavia democracy was making headway.

The Second World War brought with it a deep and long freeze. By incorporating the Baltic states, the Soviet Union separated them from the Scandinavian countries. However, during the war, Finland, for example, and especially Sweden provided shelter for thousands of refugees from Estonia, who left their homeland to escape subsequent Stalinist repressions. It is worth noting that some Estonian volunteers also took part in Finland's wars against the Soviet Union in 1939-44. But this kind of assistance, whatever importance it may have had to many people, cannot be regarded as normal cooperation, which was practically ended. When it occasionally did occur, it had to be done via and under the censorship of Moscow. There were some exceptions, however. Unauthorized political cooperation took place among the Baltic dissidents, who sent numerous letters and appeals to various international organs in the 1970s and 1980s concerning the continuing occupation of the Baltic states as well as the violations of human rights and the environmental damage done in the area.

As a consequence of the war the earlier Baltic cooperative activities were divided into two separate spheres of cooperation. One involved the Nordic countries, including Finland, which formally joined the Nordic Council in 1955. The other involved the Baltic states, that is, Estonia, Latvia and Lithuania, which were pressed to cooperate more with Moscow and the rest of the Soviet Union rather than with each other, let alone the West.

Here a terminological point has to be made, because different meanings can be given to the word 'Baltic'. As Tonu Parming has pointed out, the concept of the term "Baltic" has historically had four different applications. In linguistics, the 'Baltic languages' refer to Latvian, Lithuanian and old Prussian, but exclude Estonian. In history, the 'Baltic Provinces' stand for three *guberniya* of Tsarist Russia from the beginning of the 18th century, roughly including present-day Estonia and Latvia but excluding Lithuania. 'Baltic' has further been applied to the Baltic-German subpopulation. And finally, the term 'Baltic states' has been used to refer to the independent interwar republics of Estonia, Latvia and Lithuania as well as sometimes also to their successors within the Soviet Union, more often referred to as the 'Baltic republics'.[3]

Recently, at the 'The Baltic Family' conference, held in Kaunas, Lithuania, in October 1990, "Baltic" was used in a broader sense (the concept of "Baltic rim") to designate all the countries and nations bordering on the Baltic Sea. In the aforementioned presentation by Jaan Tönisson, "Baltic" was used in the broader sense as well. Therefore we can, roughly speaking, discriminate between broader and narrower meanings of "Baltic". The present chapter, following the logic of recent history, deals with both the narrower and broader meanings of "Baltic" and of respective cooperation.

Considering a narrower meaning of "Baltic", that is, in reference to the cooperation between Estonia, Latvia and Lithuania, we should point out that there were, and still are, some formally Baltic forms of cooperation, such as the Baltic Railways, the Baltic Military District and many institutions with so-called Baltic sections. However, they have all been imposed and managed by Moscow.[4] In other words, this cooperation has come from above, not from below.

2. SOVIET ATTITUDES TOWARDS BALTIC COOPERATION

The Soviet Union seems to follow (or has followed) at least two different policies with regard to Baltic cooperation. On the one hand, it has held the three republics as a special regional entity, often referred to in Russian as *Sovetskaya Pribaltika*, the Soviet Baltic. Clearly, it was a single entity for the Soviet Union after the agreements concluded with Germany in 1939, when simultaneous 'revolutions' were staged one year later in Estonia, Latvia and Lithuania. Cooperation was therefore promoted chiefly in fields like art, theatre, sports and certain others, with Byelorussia and the Kaliningrad region sometimes also being included as additional participants. Whether there was hidden nationalism or not, Russian, as the most common *lingua franca* of this cooperation, made it at least an exercise in Moscow-style internationalism.

On the other hand, Soviet and party authorities, especially those of the republics themselves, carefully avoided any initiatives in the sphere of political cooperation that might have exposed them to accusations of sectionalism. This was regarded as a very dangerous political imputation because of the alleged undermining of the most jealously guarded value - the unity of the Party.

Besides, officials in the Baltic republics probably remembered how the Soviet Union had reacted to the Baltic cooperation in 1940. At that time, this cooperation was publicly interpreted as something hostile and threatening to the Soviet Union. The level of suspicion (as well as incompetence) in the Soviet view of Baltic cooperation was best demonstrated by the fact that even the publication of the joint cultural and historical journal *Revue Baltique* figured as one of the arguments in Stalin's ultimatum prior to the occupation of the Baltic states in June 1940. Now we know that these accusations were at least partly hypocritical. The Soviet Union had simply decided to enforce the secret protocol of the Molotov-Ribbentrop pact in the Baltic states. Towards that end, any pretext was justified. Notwithstanding the arbitrariness of the official Soviet justifications, the possibility of subsequent Soviet actions had to be taken seriously. The majority of the people in the Baltic republics knew and know that.

The Soviet population at large has also had mixed feelings about the Baltic republics. First of all, they have been perceived as a region with better living conditions. All-union ministries and departments created new jobs on a massive scale in the Baltic area, generating record-breaking rates of migration, especially to Latvia and Estonia. As a result, in Estonia, for example, during one generation, from 1945 to 1989, the share of ethnic Estonians dropped from 95 to 60 per cent, while the number of Estonians living in Estonia today has not even reached the level of 1939, owing to the losses suffered during the war and the Stalinist repressions as well as to unsatisfactory living conditions and the prevailing atmosphere of insecurity.

But the Baltic republics were also viewed as former capitalist countries with all the ensuing ideological and political consequences, resulting in the indigenous population's being branded as fascists by recent migrants in face-to-face emotional exchanges. Perhaps such branding was and still is important psychologically and for reasons of self-justification on the part of the recent migrants in their adaptation process. But simultaneously they affront the Estonians, Latvians and Lithuanians, aggravating their attitudes towards Russian-speakers.

Objectively, however, for the rest of the Soviet Union, the Baltic republics have played an important role as a mediator, helping in transferring technology, know-how and various innovations from the West to the Soviet scene. This role can also explain the relatively generous investments and installation of imported equipment in this area by the central government. Given the economic performance of the Baltic republics, the planners in Moscow had reasons to believe that the investments made there would yield relatively good results. All of that turned the Baltic republics into socio-economic test sites with associated pressures and frictions that were not conducive to internal cooperation. The existing cooperation in the area was organized and supervised by Moscow, proceeding from the broader geopolitical, economic, military and other interests of the Soviet Union as a whole. So, until recently, we have been able to speak of cooperation in the Baltic republics as initiated by Moscow but there was not much genuine Baltic cooperation.

3. TOWARDS NEW BALTIC COOPERATION

The situation has changed since 1988, when *perestroika* and *glasnost* triggered massive amounts of local initiative in the Baltic republics. The simultaneousness of the 'revolutions' of 1940 backfired. All of a sudden, there was much self-organized cooperation between Estonia, Latvia and Lithuania, starting with the popular fronts, because the problems created during the last 50 years were basically the same.

The cooperative activity has been mainly political in nature. The principal aims were to support *perestroika*, introduce democracy and restore the independence of the respective republics. Such cooperation was also evident among the people's deputies from the Baltic republics in the summer of 1989 at the first Congress of the People's Deputies of the Soviet Union, held in Moscow. This teamwork was televised worldwide and attracted much attention.

After the decades of political hibernation, overt manifestations of national and political revival were very prominent, the most spectacular being the famous Baltic chain of 23 August 1989, when hundreds of thousands of people from Estonia, Latvia and Lithuania joined hands and formed a human chain from Tallinn to Vilnius to express in a very explicit way their determination to become free and inpendent. This event needed a great deal of cooperation between the republics and was carried out by their popular fronts. The local ability to cooperate and organize people for such a massive demonstration provoked an irritated reaction from Moscow in the form of an infamous statement by the CPSU Central Committee, including a notorious threat of genocide.

In time, the political cooperation moved to less visible spheres, taking on more sophisticated organizational forms and becoming more exactly targeted. Some prewar forms of cooperation were restored. Among them was the Baltic Council, with the chairmen of the Supreme Soviets and the prime ministers of the three Baltic republics meeting regularly to coordinate their policies for negotiations with the Soviet government and the Russian Federation. In 1990 there were many meetings of the ministers, presidents of the Academies of Sciences, etc.

By February 1991, Estonia and Latvia had signed bilateral agreements with the Russian Federation, while a corresponding agreement between Lithuania and the Russian Federation was in the process of preparation. Shortly after the bloodshed in Vilnius in January 1991, the three Baltic republics and the Russian Federation signed in Tallinn a joint statement, in which they recognized each other's state sovereignty, considered 'inadmissible the use of armed forces to solve domestic problems, unless officially requested by legally elected organs of the state power' and expressed 'their readiness to provide concrete support and aid to each other in the event of a threat to their sovereignty'.[5]

This statement and the bilateral agreements with the Russian Federation may turn out to be of crucial importance for Baltic cooperation, providing the Baltic republics with an indispensable contractual framework for the development of political and economic relations with the East in a changing situation. By now, these agreements constitute a countervailing factor against forces that I should mention at least briefly here, because they can also be considered as a domain of Baltic cooperation. I mean the conservative, interfront-type movements of the Russian-speaking migrants in the Baltic republics. The constellation of these movements is an almost exact mirror image of the respective popular fronts. As a matter of fact, they came into existence as a reaction to the popular fronts.

The popular fronts have been too preoccupied with the respective problems of the Estonians, Latvians and Lithuanians and have paid insufficient attention to those of their local counterpart. Only a small fraction of the local Russians have been integrated into the popular fronts and other new democratically oriented organizations. While the Estonians, Latvians and Lithuanians were marching towards democracy and their much worshipped independence, happily singing formerly prohibited songs, the Russians could read in the newspapers about what their countrymen had done in the Baltic republics shortly before and after the war in executing Stalin's orders. All this created a terrible confusion in their minds. Both their privileged position as the 'big brother' and the corresponding world outlook began to collapse.

To halt that trend and to maintain the political and economic *status quo*, 'international workers' movements' were organized in all the Baltic republics. The supporters of these movements came mostly from large enterprises, mines and factories subordinated to Moscow. People from the party apparatus and directors of the large Russian-speaking enterprises constitute the organizational backbone of these movements. Their overt goals are to protect socialism, to preserve the Soviet Union as a great power and to guarantee equal human rights to everybody. Individual human rights are opposed to the nationality rights accentuated by the popular fronts.

The cooperation between the Baltic 'intermovements' was parallel to that of the popular fronts. But, in addition, the Russian Federation was considered to provide solid political rear support for the intermovements, making them feel extremely confident. After the aforementioned agreements had been reached between the Russian Federation and the Baltic republics, the integrity of this backing was lost. That is why the intermovements became very hostile to the Russian President Boris Yeltsin after he signed the agreements on behalf of the Russian Federation. Some interfront activists even called him a traitor to the interests of the Russian-speaking people in the Baltic republics. It can therefore be said that the logic of political evolution in the Baltic republics seems to lead them towards broader cooperation. And also, if broader cooperation does take place, it would be politically more meaningful and efficient.

4. ECONOMIC CONSIDERATIONS

The cooperation in the economic sphere has proved to be more problematic than in the political field. In this sphere, no Baltic chain has ever been organized. There were attempts to assist Lithuania after the economic blockade was declared by Moscow in 1990, but this assistance was doomed to remain rather modest. The reason is very simple. The three republics lack certain vital resources, notably oil, but also metals and numerous other raw materials. Nearly all the supplies needed come from other parts of the Soviet Union. Almost all their trade takes place also with the Soviet Union. If something were to happen to these ties, Estonia, Latvia and Lithuania could not do much to help each other, even in the event of the closest possible cooperation between them. In general, the political aspirations of the Baltic republics and their internal economic realities correspond poorly. This seems to suggest once more that the solution might be found in the framework of broader cooperation, where good relations with the East will remain of paramount importance for years to come.

Philip Hanson has made a rare academic effort to evaluate the economic and political implications of the secession of Estonia, Latvia and Lithuania from the Soviet Union. He has also pointed out that the Baltic region is a net importer of most products and that at the level of world market prices the Baltic republics would suffer.[6]

In order to illuminate the general prospects for Baltic

economic performance, it should be asked what the position of
these republics is in the world economy. According to
Ferdinand Braudel and many others, the world economy is
divided into successive zones: the heart (which is the region
around the centre), the intermediate zones around this central
region, and, finally, the wide peripheral regions, which in the
division of labour of the world economy are subordinated
rather than true participants. Within these peripheral zones,
Braudel asserts, life often resembles purgatory or even hell.[7]

It goes without saying that Estonia, Latvia and Lithuania
have never been in the centre of the world economy or even
very near to that centre. Consequently, the only question here
is how far from the centre they are or have been. If we confine ourselves to this century and compare the interwar period
with the postwar situation, the common feature is that in both
cases Estonia, Latvia and Lithuania are typical peri-pheral
areas. There is an important difference, however. During the
interwar period, they were the peripheral extensions of
Western Europe, whereas for the last 50 years they have
functioned as peripheral parts of a very peculiar centre -
Moscow. It is Moscow that has progressively demonstrated the
peripheral relationship in most of the basic spheres of society,
except, possibly, that of military power.

With the military buildup becoming obsolete and
counterproductive, the Soviet Union is being unmasked as
existing almost totally on the periphery of the civilized world.
Estonia, Latvia and Lithuania must recognize the sad fact that
while the movement of European civilization was upwards,
these three republics were by comparison moving downwards.
This also means that in case of their becoming a direct
periphery of Western Europe again, they would find themselves, at least for some time, standing nearer to Ferdinand
Braudel's hell than ever before during this century. The only
hope in such a situation would be that some broader regional
integration might give a human touch to the hard imperatives
of the centre-periphery relations.

Right now, during the so-called transition period, the
Baltic republics remain, against their will, still heavily de-
pendent on economic, financial and political decisions made in
Moscow. The problem with the periphery is that it is always

more tightly connected with the centre than with other peripheral parts. My point here is that Estonia, Latvia and Lithuania are all peripherally linked to Moscow in terms of Soviet realities, whether they like it or not. It means that, so long as such realities exist, the macro-sociological logic of the centre-periphery interactions would work against the cooperation between these republics. The available statistics on the trade relations of Estonia with other parts of the Soviet Union seem to support my point. As shown in Table 9.1, the relative share of Latvia and Lithuania in Estonian foreign trade has even decreased in 1977-87.

Table 9.1. Export-import relations of Estonia with other parts of the Soviet Union

Republic	Imports to Estonia		Exports from Estonia	
	1977	*1987*	*1977*	*1987*
Russian SFSR	54.6	58.7	59.9	60.6
Ukraine	12.8	14.4	10.8	13.0
Byelorussia	5.6	6.8	4.0	4.9
Uzbekistan	3.5	1.7	1.8	1.7
Kazakhstan	3.0	1.9	3.2	3.7
Georgia	0.8	1.0	1.0	1.2
Azerbaidzhan	2.4	0.8	1.1	1.0
LITHUANIA	4.4	3.7	2.9	2.5
Moldova	1.8	2.6	1.4	1.6
LATVIA	8.0	6.0	7.4	7.2
Kirgizia	0.4	0.4	0.4	0.5
Tadzhikistan	0.5	0.8	0.4	0.5
Armenia	0.5	0.8	0.9	1.3
Turkmenistan	0.4	0.7	0.5	0.3
Unknown	1.3	0.0	4.1	0.0
Total	100.0	100.0	100.0	100.0

Source: *Aripaev*, 28 May-3 June 1990.

Another significant fact is that 97 per cent of Estonian exports go to the East, that is, to other parts of the Soviet Union, whereas only three per cent go to the West, mainly Finland and Germany. The main reason for such an export structure is that the quality of Estonian goods is far too low for Western markets. This brings us to the problem of Baltic cooperation in a broader sense, which includes the countries around the Baltic Sea. In practical terms it means for Estonia, Latvia and Lithuania a reorientation towards the new centres in Western Europe. What can be harmful for the prospects of future cooperation in this case is probably the very tough competition between the newcomers to an integrated Europe in establishing the best possible relations with these new centres.

5. CONCLUSIONS

The Hungarian journalist and political scientist Laszlo Lengyel has written about the competitive situation in Eastern and Central Europe:

> The collusions of the poor, the stability of the alliances of the have-nots given to daydreaming will be strong until the powerful and the rich make a proposal. Ravaged Poland, industrial Czechoslovakia, with its poisoned environment, or impotent Hungary wallowing in vanity - they all lose mutual attraction as soon as the well-fed shape of the beloved Germany in an elegant car looms on the horizon. They stick together because they all impatiently want to get rid of the Soviets, of Russia. As soon as Germany appears, they scurry towards it, pushing each other and shouting: 'Stay with me, not with the others!'[8]

It is to be hoped that the situation will not be like that, at least in some areas of cooperation, such as culture, science and perhaps a few others. Moreover, there are common concerns in the Baltic area, such as environment and disarmament, which should facilitate the teamwork and mutual assistance between all the countries of the area.

Given the relatively modest economic basis for cooperation between the three Baltic republics, one should not expect that self-sufficient economic integration will develop within this small region. Generally speaking, the economic ties between the north and the south in this region are going to be less important than those with other regions both east and west.

The present state of the ties with the East is, of course, rather different from those with the West. The Baltic republics have been subjected to 'integration under duress'[9] by the Soviet Union since 1940, with a break from 1941 to 1944 because of the Second World War. This has modified the structure of their economies according to the needs of the Soviet Union. These needs were, however, largely political. According to the inner logic of the single party-ruled state, Estonia, Latvia and Lithuania became humble subordinates of the centre, i.e., Moscow. Economy was the main tool in producing the desired political goal. But to do so, economic rationality had to be ignored and replaced by political considerations. As a result, there emerged an economy whose structure and inefficient functioning can best be explained in political terms.

The main features of the economies that were developed in the Baltic republics by following political guidelines include over-industrialization, relatively low quality of manufactured goods, heavy dependence on imported oil and raw materials, and lack of autonomy and coherence of the economy as a whole. This goes hand in hand with the orientations of large industrial enterprises towards labour sources, raw materials and markets outside the Baltic republics. This happens because different enterprises belong to different ministries in Moscow and their conglomeration on the territory of Estonia has a loose correspondence with local needs and resources. So, the republican economy has a political structure. That is why economic progress in the Baltic republics is so dependent on political development in the Soviet Union. The same is true of cooperation in the Baltic area.

NOTES

1. Cited in Kaido Jaanson, 'Pöhjavalgus voi fatamorgaana? Balti-Skandinaavia liidu idee ja koostöö sünd ühest suurest sõjast teiseni' in

Perioodika, no. 9, 1990, p. 1894.
2. See Bronis J. Kaslas, *The Baltic Nations - the Quest for Regional Integration and Political Liberty* (Pittston: Euramerica Press, 1976), pp. 118-9.
3. See Tonu Parming, ''Baltic Studies': The Emergence, Development and Problematics of an Area Studies Specialization' in Dietrich A. Loeber, V. Stanley Vardys and Lawrence P. Kitching (eds), *Regional Identity Under the Soviet Rule: The Case of the Baltic States*, Publications of the Association for the Advancement of Baltic Studies, no. 6, p. 16.
4. See also Dietrich A. Loeber, 'Towards Baltic Regional Identity' in Loeber, Vardys and Kitching, op. cit., pp. xiv-xvii.
5. *The Estonian Independent*, 17 January 1991.
6. See Philip Hanson, 'The Baltic States: The Economic and Political Implications of the Secession of Estonia, Latvia and Lithuania from the USSR', *Special Report*, no. 2033, March 1990.
7. See Ferdinand Braudel, *Afterthoughts on Material Civilization and Capitalism* (Baltimore: Johns Hopkins, 1977).
8. *Moscow News*, no. 36/1990.
9. See Jan Åke Dellenbrant, 'The Integration of the Baltic Republics into the Soviet Union' in Loeber, Vardys and Kitching, op. cit., pp. 101-20.

10 THE SOVIET UNION AND THE GERMAN QUESTION

Pekka Visuri

---

1. INTRODUCTION

Many people may think that the unification of Germany has solved the so-called German question for our time, perhaps forever. The rapid rapprochement between the two former antagonists, the Soviet Union and the Federal Republic of Germany, was one of the most dramatic events in the present European revolutionary process. It also proved the correctness of those arguments according to which the keys to the problem of German unification were in the hands of the Soviet Union.[1]

The agreement reached in Stavropol on 16 July 1990 between President Mikhail Gorbachev and Chancellor Helmut Kohl, which resulted in the basic treaty of cooperation signed in November 1990, signaled, above all, a return towards a traditional Russo-German policy of interest-sharing, though thereby a potential great power rivalry as well. Naturally both the Soviet Union and Germany are now acting in a wider European and global context than in the past. Germany is today an essential participant in the advanced integration of the West and seems to be reluctant to activate its political role in the security sphere.

For a future-oriented study of the Soviet-German

relationship, we must also keep in mind its long tradition as well as the historical concept of the "German question". The recent 50 years of Soviet-German antagonism are already passing into history, and the period has actually been a very short one as such. Both nations, in the same way as several others in Central and Eastern Europe, are searching again for their roots and thus striving for a new start after frustrating experiences.

2. ORIGINS OF THE GERMAN QUESTION

After the Second World War, the concept of the German question referred mainly to the problem of the division of Germany. However, the concept has also a wider historical meaning, which refers to Germany's position in the European system of states. The basic problem boils down to how a power like Germany can exist in the middle of Europe without dominating the whole continent, especially the neighbouring countries, and how the other powers react to the German potential.

The origins of the German problem can be found in the Thirty Years' War and the Peace Treaty of Westphalia concluded in 1648. Most Germans thought that the weakness and dispersion of the Holy Roman Empire (of the German Nation) was a result of interventions by surrounding powers. This created the myth of the 'late-coming nation' (*Verspätete Nation*), which had to free and unite itself violently in the 19th century and then hurry after others in the imperialistic competition.[2]

Both Prussia and Russia had common enemies, Sweden and Poland, and they could quite well share their interests by dividing Poland together with Austria in the late 18th century. They met with some difficulties in the Baltic provinces, however, from where the Swedes had to withdraw because of their failure in the Great Nordic War against Peter the Great's Russia. Even so, Russia and Prussia were allies during the last phases of the Napoleonic Wars and were founding members of the Holy Alliance after the Congress of Vienna in 1815.

German unification and the rebirth of the Reich in 1871,

after the Franco-Prussian War, changed the structure of the European balance of power. The Reich for the first time challenged the old sea power Great Britain as well, and thereby France as the continental power, now ready to seek revenge for its lost provinces. After the resolution of the unification problem on the basis of a 'small Germany', relations with Austria improved and the internal struggles in Central Europe were smoothed down. While the large *Mitteleuropa* became integrated and flourished, nationalistic movements in the East and in the Balkan region surged, demanding loudly more power and sovereignty for the Slavic peoples.

3. RUSSIAN AND GERMAN EMPIRES AS RIVALS

Chancellor Bismarck instigated the successful balance of power policy which had already resulted in the building of the Reich. His special concern was France, while in the east he saw both Austria and Russia as balancing powers. But a serious problem was their striving for influence in the Balkans, emerging especially after the Berlin Congress of 1878.

Bismarck tried to solve this dilemma by concluding a secret neutrality agreement (Reinsurance Treaty) with Russia in 1887, which dealt especially with cases in which either Germany or Russia became an object of aggression. Both parties were obligated to remain neutral, that is, not to support the aggressor. The most relevant possibilities for aggression were France versus Germany and, on the other hand, Austria attacking Russia. Bismarck's démarche has later often been praised as brilliant, but political reality very soon overwhelmed the diplomatic skill. Great power rivalry and the waxing pan-Slavist movement, in addition to Germany's own inherent imperialistic drive, destroyed this delicate structure.[3] A realistic-rationalistic approach in Russo-German relations was in those circumstances impossible. The failure of Bismarck's *Realpolitik* in the east led, among other things, to the First World War, which was to be disastrous for both nations.

4. TWO LOSERS IN COOPERATION

The Treaty of Rapallo in 1922 between the new Bolshevik regime of Soviet Russia and the republican regime of Germany was a surprise for many diplomats, but had considerable logic from a traditional point of view or one of political realism. Together with the Soviet New Economic Policy (NEP), the treaty made cooperation on a large scale possible. The Bolshevik leaders also cherished some hopes of revolutionary action in Germany. By the mid-1930s, the ideologization and radicalization of politics in both countries again made them antagonistic.[4]

Another surprise was the Hitler-Stalin Pact concluded in August 1939. However, this non-aggression treaty was a typical case of interest-sharing in an acute crisis situation, built on the basis of geostrategic circumstances and power political aims of two dictators. It is still difficult to decipher Stalin's thoughts in making the deal with Hitler. The treaty could just as well be a defensive move as one preparing for offensive action. Nevertheless, both Russia and Germany were challengers of the system created by the Versailles Peace Treaty, and their agreement was *de facto* one of the main preconditions needed for the German invasion of Poland and thereby for the whole Second World War.[5]

It is not easy to be sure about Hitler's aims regarding the Soviet Union. Obviously, he pursued ideas presented in his book *Mein Kampf* in the mid-1920s, but the decision to invade Russia was also a result of the strategic situation in the war. Hitler and the Nazis began, however, to wage the most destructive war explicitly against Bolshevism, but in effect against the Russian people. On the other hand, Stalin succeeded well in turning the German aggression from an ideological struggle into a total war against 'Mother Russia'. After this 'Great Patriotic War', it was natural to mix Communist ideological expansion with the imperialist goals of Russia.

5. SOVIET POLICY TOWARDS GERMANY AFTER THE WAR

For the future of Russo-German relations, the Second World War was crucial in many respects. First, the historical legacy of the war in Russia[6] and its aftermath in Germany[7] are to be viewed over a very long perspective. A generation change was needed before a settlement was possible at all. Second, the Soviet Union invested a large share of its resources in the Cold War strategy, and ruined its economy in this struggle - especially in Germany[8] - against the West. It ran into enormous difficulties in its disengagement from the Central European buffer zone created by the war.

Stalin's policy vis-a-vis Germany immediately after the Second World War was relatively pragmatic but ambiguous. Dealing with Germany as a whole (*'Deutschland als Ganzes'*) aimed, at least in practice, at the exploitation of the country's resources as war booty or reparations. Soviet propaganda also favoured old German national symbols and references to long traditions of Russo-German cooperation.[9]

After the formation of the two German states in 1949, Soviet policy distanced itself step by step from the idea of German unity and acceptance of the GDR as the only legal representative of the German nation. The apparent culmination point was Stalin's note of March 1952 proposing the unification of Germany through neutralization and de-militarization. The treaties on Germany in May 1952 then bound the Federal Republic to the Western bloc, although its realization had to be postponed until spring 1955.[10]

Between Stalin's death in 1953 and the Austrian State Treaty of 1955, Soviet policy kept to the old line of holding tight to the neutrality of a united Germany. The Soviet Union tried to build a large neutral zone through Central and Northern Europe. The Soviets knew, however, that the American 'roll back' policy could hardly be modified to accept this aim. The United States was then too powerful to be pressured to accede to German neutrality, and German public opinion was clearly pro-Western.

The Soviet policy-makers had to settle for the restriction

of their goals in Central Europe to Austrian neutrality and their protracted presence in East Germany. As an instrument for the consolidation of the socialist system and Soviet control in the GDR as well as in the buffer zone as a whole, the Soviet Union established in 1955 the Warsaw Treaty Organization.[11]

Both German states were after that members of antagonistic alliances, divided by a front line of increasing troop and fire-power concentrations. They were also participants in the economic integration in the respective blocs. Germany was yet without a peace treaty, and the German states lacked full sovereignty. However, the year 1955 stabilized the situation temporarily. The Federal Republic gained a declaration ending the state of war with the Soviet Union, and they were also able to establish diplomatic relations.

The German policy of the Soviet Union was based after 1955 on acceptance of the division of Germany. In its relations with the GDR, the Soviet Union aimed at concluding a peace treaty which could confirm the *status quo*. However, the Soviet Union allowed the government of the GDR to continue its explicit policy of German unification.[12]

6. THE GERMAN *OSTPOLITIK*

After the Berlin crises of 1958 and 1961, the Soviet Union accepted *de facto* the division of Germany into three parts - the German Democratic Republic, the Federal Republic of Germany and West Berlin. The West also went along with the Soviet view by, for example, delivering strong protests against the building of the Berlin wall in 1961 and the occupation of Czechoslovakia by Warsaw Pact troops in 1968.

After the normalization of Czechoslovakia and the declaration of the Brezhnev doctrine, an early détente phase ensued. At the end of 1969, the new coalition government of the FRG under the leadership of Willy Brandt initiated the so-called *Ostpolitik*, which recognized both the border of the Oder-Neisse line and the existence of the GDR as realities. The inauguration of Willy Brandt's policy, moreover, was marked by the signing of the German-Soviet treaty of cooperation in Moscow. It was followed by a long series of treaties with neighbouring countries. The basic treaty of the allied powers concerning the status of Berlin was one of the most important. The German *Ostpolitik* was also an important precondition for the CSCE process, which was basically an idea espoused by the Soviet Union and the WTO, but which was later put into practice by Finland and supported by the FRG.

A theoretical framework for *Ostpolitik* was 'conversion by rapprochement', launched by Egon Bahr as early as 1963. It was later accepted by the Social Democratic Party and was also supported by the Free Democrats. The theory of conversion, that is, the bringing together of the socialist and Western democratic systems as a result of common economic and technological needs, was seen as highly controversial. However, it did offer many practical benefits in the 1970s.[13]

The policy of détente lasted until the late 1970s. After the CSCE meeting in Helsinki in 1975, the Soviet Union may have thought that the position of the socialist community in Europe was secured at least temporarily and that it was time for its power projection in the Third World. The Warsaw Pact, however, continued with its large-scale military buildup at extremely high costs. This led to a Western reaction, resulting first in the decision on the INF nuclear forces in 1979 and then, especially during the Reagan administration, in extensive armaments programmes.

The new Cold War phase in the early 1980s froze both the German *Ostpolitik* and the Soviet political initiatives. The appearance of grave weakness in the economies of the socialist countries and the application of crude Soviet pressure in deloying new short-range nuclear weapons undermined support for the continuation of the old policy in the small WTO countries. By 1984, in both German states, new discussions were started on the means needed to overcoming that dangerous situation. Certain initiatives, aimed at improve the relations between East and West Germany, were squelched by the Soviet Union, but many private contacts were sustained.[14]

7. GORBACHEV'S NEW THINKING AND THE CHANGE IN THE GDR

The need for a new policy had been avowed in the Soviet Union soon after Gorbachev's takeover in March 1985. Economic and social - even moral - reforms were emphasized first, but after that the new leader undertook the revision of foreign policy as well.[15] A profound new strategic orientation adopted in about 1986 called for the withdrawal of troops, first from foreign continents and then also from the outposts in the buffer zone in Europe. The only problem was how to go about it.[16]

Obviously, the Soviet policy towards Germany was still rather obscure to the whole administration in Moscow.[17] The dilemma was quite well recognized: it would be disastrous to the country's image abroad and would undermine domestic support of the party bureaucracy if an initiative were taken that might lead to German unification and thereby to the disappearance of the GDR. Simultaneously, the country's economic problems were worsening and the only promising possibility for coping with them was increased cooperation with the Western countries.

The new thinking in Soviet-German relations emerged as early as during Kohl's visit to Moscow in October 1988. Kohl's dilemma was how to deal with the German question so as to avoid arousing Western suspicions of the 'special German way' towards neutrality and the Germans' own independent policy in Soviet relations. Gorbachev stated in an interview in *Der Spiegel* that they must see each other as potential friends and not as former foes. The visit to Moscow brought about a qualitative but not very clear change in the Soviet attitude towards Germany. The problem for the future was registered, however, in the GDR, which feared being pushed aside or being infiltrated by *glasnost*.[18]

The GDR government made some, though not very successful efforts to stop the liberalization process which came from the socialist 'fraternal countries' of Poland, Hungary and also the Soviet Union. Contacts with the West were increased, too. The security police, *Stasi*, was as effective as ever but could not prevent the growth of small opposition groups, particularly within the Church.

By early 1989, the Soviet leaders had apparently decided that rapprochement with West Germany was much more important than continuation of unconditional support for the GDR government. Their decision had become urgent because of the miserable state of the economy, but they had no intention of leaving the GDR or of opening the way to the unification of Germany.

The skilful policy of the West German government made this operation easier for the Soviet Union. Foreign Minister Genscher spoke against the plan to modernize the American Lance missiles and supported many ideas of the Soviet Union for the development of the CSCE process, which seemed to give an opportunity to manage the inevitably approaching change in Soviet policy towards Germany.[19]

President Gorbachev's visit to West Germany in June 1989 was a great success, with crowds cheering him 'Gorbi, Gorbi!' Nevertheless, he was cautious in his statements concerning Soviet policy vis-a-vis Germany. In the joint communiqué, however, the leaders of both countries supported the right of all nations to self-determination.[20] This was in principle easy to connect with the problem of German unification, although it was difficult to draw practical conclusions. Neither the German government nor the opposition had any clear unification policy. The major parties in Germany had to handle the problem very carefully and to take the concerns of the allied countries into account. In this respect, both the German and Soviet governments had analogous problems. For the small German opposition parties, for example, the Greens and the Republicans, it was easier to proclaim more radical programmes.[21]

In the celebrations of the 40th anniversary of the GDR in Berlin in October 1989, it was obvious that the Soviet Union had left Erich Honecker and his party leadership alone with growing refugee problems and mass demonstrations. President Gorbachev gave no public support to the GDR government.[22] During the power struggle in the GDR between October 1989 and March 1990, the Soviet comments were cautious. Almost all the Soviet diplomatic démarches concerned the Federal

Republic or generally the unification question, which the Kremlin tried to play down. The Soviet government had very few ties to the GDR leadership, with the exception of Minister Hans Modrow, who enjoyed support for his idea of a sovereign but internally reformed GDR. During Chancellor Kohl's visit to Moscow in February 1990, the possibility of unification was mutually recognized, but with many reservations.[23]

The Soviet tactic that winter and spring was to stick to the old line of demanding the neutralization of Germany in the future European system of peace and security. As a substitute for neutralization, the Kremlin promoted, for instance, the idea of Germany belonging simultaneously to both military alliances.[24] Fearing rapid collapse of the Warsaw Treaty Organization, the Soviet leadership decided to tighten its preconditions for German unification.[25]

The government of West Germany, headed by Chancellor Helmut Kohl, gained the support of its allies for unification by promising to remain a full member of the Western alliances - the most important of them being NATO and the EC. However, the 'Genscher plan', launched in January 1990, offered a useful compromise with the East. It was a very comprehensive programme for unification within the framework of the CSCE. The new united Germany would belong to NATO as an essential part of the European integration process but without NATO troops on the territory of the GDR.[26]

Quite soon after the GDR parliamentary elections in March 1990, it became obvious that the Soviet Union was in no position to resist the rapid unification process or therefore to put up any effective arguments against German sovereignty or to prevent the Germans from freely solving the problems of their political security. The majority of the GDR citizens supported rapid unification with the Federal Republic but had reservations regarding membership of NATO.[27]

The Soviet Union had, however, or at least seemed to have, an opportunity to delay the process. In fact, the Soviet military personnel and their families in the GDR were in a nearly catastrophic situation. There were 380,000 troops and 300,000 Soviet civilians waiting for instructions about what to do. Discipline among them was weak and the danger of severe clashes increased day by day.[28] Strategically, the Soviet army had lost its reason for staying in Germany. The place where the troops were really needed was the Soviet Union, to safeguard the population against uprisings and criminals.

8. THE NEW GERMAN *OSTPOLITIK*

The accord reached between Chancellor Kohl and President Gorbachev in Stavropol on 16 July 1990 was urgently needed by the Soviet government in its endeavour to prevent the threatening collapse of the morale of the Soviet troops in Germany and to secure favourable terms for their withdrawal. For the West German government, it was important to obtain an agreement without delay because of the need to accelerate the reunification process. Further economic cooperation with the Soviet Union was also sought. The agreement was therefore a model case of good timing and interest-sharing.

Earlier, the Kremlin had emphasized both the balance of power and stabilization as the cornerstones of Soviet foreign policy. In Stavropol, the Soviet side changed its announced policy, and a new set of more flexible and cooperative approaches was introduced. It accepted the advance of the Western zone of influence eastwards and in return received both money and a promise of further cooperation with Germany.

The atmosphere of Gorbachev's meeting with Kohl resembled in many ways the summits held earlier between the superpower leaders. Germany now took on the role of a European power on an equal footing with the Soviet Union. The reactions among the Western allies were restrained. Some British politicians could not hold back their comments on the 'Great' Germany that might soon dominate Europe by economic means, covered by the EC mantle.

The treaty, based on the so-called 'Two plus Four negotiations', was signed in Moscow on 12 September 1990, giving Germany full sovereignty. It was more an acknowledgment, however, of an inevitable development than the inauguration of a new phase. On the next day a more important document, 'Treaty of Good Neighbourliness, Partnership and Cooperation between Germany and the Soviet Union', was drawn up. It was a comprehensive and concrete agreement on future cooperation. It also had some articles that had already irritated both allied and other states.[29] The preparation of the treaty was quite expeditious and took place secretly.[30] It was also the first bilateral non-aggression treaty between the Soviet Union and a NATO country. The third article forbids each party to help an aggressor who has attacked the other.

This German-Soviet treaty was signed on 9 November 1990 in Bonn during the visit of President Gorbachev. Foreign criticism of some of the treaty articles grew louder, while the Germans were generally satisfied with the achievement of good relations with the Soviet Union.[31] The leaders in the Baltic republics argued that the treaty had the effect of consolidating the respective spheres of interest in the same way as the Hitler-Stalin pact of 1939.[32]

9. THE ACUTE SOVIET-RUSSIAN QUESTION

A serious problem which then faced the projected Soviet-German accord was the declining support for Gorbachev in the Soviet Union and the threatening total collapse of its federative system. It is therefore important to study also the attitudes of such Soviet republics as Russia and the Ukraine. We may assume that in principle they accept the cooperation with Germany.[33]

The Russian Federation, which intends to increase economic cooperation with Germany, has declared a free economic zone in the Kaliningrad region, formerly the northern part of East Prussia. This may be one of the most important test cases of German-Soviet cooperation. After the declaration of the Russian Supreme Soviet on 13 July 1990, there has been a power struggle concerning its implementation. The Soviet government has not so far accepted the declaration.[34]

Some arguments against the Russian declaration of the economic free zone have been military-strategic in nature, although they can no longer be regarded as entirely rational. The main military base of the Baltic Navy in Baltiskii (Pillau) would be an outpost of the sea defence against the West. In the new situation, a better location would be further north, i.e., in the Leningrad region.

Another aspect of the East Prussian question is the possibility of building a new settlement area for about two million ethnic Germans and their families in the Soviet Union. They are hesitantly waiting in Siberia and Kazakhstan for a decision by which they could receive a new autonomous region. There would naturally arise difficulties if immigration were to start to former East Prussia, where now about 900,000 inhabitants are living. However, before the war, 1.2 million people lived in the same area. The infrastructure there is also in relatively good condition in relation to the economic reconstruction and the population increase.[35]

The main threats to economic cooperation are now the internal struggles between the nationalist or separatist groups and, on the other hand, the measures taken by the Soviet government to contain, even by force, the rapid reformation of the Union structure. In this kind of a crisis, it is impossible to forecast the course of ideological developments. The German question has many mythical aspects, which can be used as one argument in the internal power struggle. Instead of an acute German question, we have a Soviet-Russian question, that is, the problem of how the nations of the Soviet Union can live with each other without a new form of 'Balkanization' and without a new civil war.

In a more pessimistic scenario, the reformation of the Soviet Union, leading to a civil war, radically changes the importance of the German factor as well. Although it is not very likely that Germany would fill the vacuum between Germany and the Russian heartland, a severe crisis could lead to the aggravation of such a fear. The very possibility of intervention could affect German-Soviet relations and make the security issues more important than economic and political cooperation.[36]

Soviet or Russian relations with Germany are further influenced by the reactions of the countries neighbouring Germany. The peaceful settlement of the border between Germany and Poland is a good sign for the future, but not a firm guarantee against further disputes.

The acute crises in the Middle East and in Eastern Europe are also aggravating the tensions in Soviet-German relations. The Baltic crisis especially affects the small ex-socialist countries of Poland, Czechoslovakia and Hungary, which are reacting to the developments involving the Soviet Union. The dynamics of those crises make all prophecies concerning Eastern Europe very uncertain and cause a postponement of cooperative efforts. The rapid withdrawal of Soviet troops is thereby endangered as well.[37]

10. CONCLUSIONS

In our present turbulent era, it is impossible to make concrete and far-reaching forecasts. Certain trends can be seen, however. First, Soviet policy vis-a-vis Germany has reverted to the long tradition of Russian cooperation with Prussia, or Germany. It was marked, most of all, by a rational interest in the sharing of political and economic means, but it was also affected by nationalist and ideological factors. Ideology can be understood as, for instance, imperialism, communism, fascism or liberalism. Second, in the current situation, the ideological factor has been put aside, but other factors are highly pertinent. There is no guarantee that some kind of an ideology could not become important again.

Third, the traditional course of policy can also survive a collapse of the Soviet Union. The direct relations between Germany and the Soviet republics aiming at separation could continue on the same basis. Internal struggles have, however, a negative impact on those relations. They can revive old fears of Germany or revive fears in Germany concerning chaos in the East. If Germany were to support some of the republics in their struggle for independence, this would provoke a serious reaction from the other side. In such an event, all the mythical elements of the German question would become alive as well.

Fourth, Germany constitutes an organic part of European integration, and this factor could melt down the most dangerous features of traditional power politics. In a positive scenario, the EC together with Germany could help Eastern Europe to overcome the crisis. Another bad scenario, however, could also become true. According to it, a new iron curtain might be erected, separating the prosperous from the poor Europe somewhere in the area between Germany and the Adriatic.

Nevertheless, Soviet policy vis-a-vis Germany is now at a crossroads. The future holds out many prospects for positive progress, but some of them are quite dangerous. We could try to influence the course of future developments. We cannot be sure, however, which is the best way. Further, we cannot, of course, fully control the turn of events in this European revolution.

NOTES

1. See, e.g., Wolfgang Seiffert, *Die Deutschen und Gorbatshow: Chancen für einen Interessenausgleich* (Erlangen-Bonn-Wien: Straube, 1989).
2. On the legacy of the Thirty Years' War and the Westphalian Peace Treaty for German nation-building and for the German question, see Michael Freund, *Deutsche Geschichte* (München: Bertelsmann & Goldmann, 1981), pp. 246-8, and a liberal positive interpretation by Günter Barudio, *Der Teutsche Krieg 1618-1648* (Frankfurt am Main: Fischer, 1988), pp. 585-95.
3. See, e.g., Gordon A. Craig, *Germany 1866-1945* (Oxford: Oxford University Press, 1981), pp. 103-39.
4. See, e.g., Manfred Messerschmidt, 'Aussenpolitik und Kriegsvorbereitung' in Wilhelm Deist *et al.* (eds), *Ursachen und Voraussetzungen des Zweiten Weltkrieges* (Frankfurt am Main: Fischer, 1989), pp. 678-81. Compare with the critique of Stalin's cooperative German policy by Leon Trotsky: Leon Trotsky, *The Struggle Against Fascism in Germany* (New York: Pathfinder Press, 1971).
5. On the interpretation problem, see Teddy Uldrichs, 'A. J. P. Taylor and the Russians' in Gordon Martel (ed.), *The Origins of the Second World War Reconsidered* (Boston: Allen & Unwin, 1986), pp. 163-86.
6. See, e.g., Michael Schneider, *Das 'Unternehmen Barbarossa': Die verdrängte Erblast von 1941 und die Folgen für das deutsch-sowjetische Verhältnis* (Frankfurt am Main: Luchterhand, 1989).
7. Wolfgang Benz (ed.), *Die Vertreibung der Deutschen aus dem Osten* (Frankfurt am Main: Fischer, 1985).
8. During the 28th Party Congress of the CPSU in July 1990, General Secretary Gorbachev said that the military expenditures of the Soviet Union had been 18 per cent of the GNP. According to Foreign Minister Eduard Shevardnadze, the real figures may have been as high as 20-25 per cent. Although the statistics are very vague, those figures mean that a comprehensive war economy had been prevailing over decades in spite of the absence of an open 'hot' war. Soviet troops in Central Europe, over half a million men, had been equipped with the most expensive armaments.

9. Wilfried Loth, *Die Teilung der Welt 1941-1955* (Nördlingen: DTV, 1980), pp. 64-9, 139. The National Committee of Free Germany (*Nationalkomitee Freies Deutschland*), consisting of POW-officers in Russia (in general, quite conservative) was used for Soviet propaganda also after the armistice. See Heinrich Böll and Lew Kopelew, *Warum haben wir aufeinander geschossen?* (Bornheim: Lamuv, 1981).
10. Andreas Hillgruber, *Deutsche Geschichte 1945-1982: Die 'deutsche Frage' in der Weltpolitik* (Stuttgart: Kohlhammer, 1983), pp. 51-4. The East German uprising on 17 June 1953 frustrated dramatically the efforts to have the Germans persuaded of the benefits of Soviet policy. See, e.g., Gerhard Wettig, 'The Soviet Union and German Unification', *Berichte des Bundesinstituts für ostwissenschaftliche und internationale Studien*, no. 38, 1990, p. 1.
11. After the Paris Agreements between the Federal Republic and NATO, the German question was an essential part of the speech by Marshal Bulganin in the founding conference of the Warsaw Treaty Organization. See TASS, 11 May 1955.
12. Seiffert, op. cit., p. 95.
13. Hillgruber, op. cit., pp. 82-4, 111-25.
14. Erich Honecker, for example, had to postpone twice his planned visits to West Germany (in April 1983 and August 1984).
15. See the statement by Mikhail Gorbachev on 15 January 1986 in Lawrence Freedman (ed.), *Europe Transformed: Documents on the Cold War* (London: Tri-Service Press, 1990), pp. 202-12.
16. On the doctrine discussion in the Soviet Union, see Pekka Visuri, *Sotilasliittojen piirissä käytävä opillinen keskustelu ja sen mahdolliset aseidenriisunnalliset vaikutukset* (The Doctrinal Discussion in Military Alliances and Its Possible Effects on Disarmament) (Helsinki: ARNEK, 1989), pp. 29-43. The declaration of the Warsaw Treaty Organization in Berlin on 29 May 1987 (published in for example *Europa-Archiv*, no. 14, 1987) on the defensive doctrine may have been understood in the West as propaganda, but in reality it was an important new orientation towards a defensive strategy.
17. During the initial phase of Gorbachev's policy (in 1985-88), the domestic *perestroika* and relations with the United States took first place. The German question became acute thereafter, owing to the worsening economic situation at home, in particular. See Hannes Adomeit, 'Gorbachev and German Unification: Revision of Thinking, Realignment of Power', *Problems of Communism*, vol. XXXIX, July-August 1990, p. 4.
18. Seiffert, op. cit., pp. 16-19.
19. In many NATO countries, this policy was named 'Genscherism'. It was already a symptom of a more independent German foreign policy. Genscher naturally acted in concert with the whole Christian-Liberal coalition government headed by Chancellor Kohl.
20. In the words of the 'Joint declaration of the Federal Republic of Germany and the Soviet Union', on 13 June 1989: 'The right of all peoples and states to determine freely their destiny and to frame sovereignly their mutual relations on the basis of international law in domestic and international politics must be ensured.' (Freedman, op.

cit., p. 317)

21. Seiffert, op. cit., p. 17. See also different approaches (traditionalist, Europeanist and universalist) to the unification problem in Germany, in Anne-Marie Burley, 'The Once and Future German Question', *Foreign Affairs*, vol. 68, no. 5, 1989, pp. 65-83. On the reservations in Gorbachev's announcements about the German questin during his visit to Bonn, see Wettig, op. cit., pp. 5-6.

22. It is not yet quite certain what the Soviet leaders said secretly to the GDR leadership, when they had refused to use Soviet troops in the internal struggle of the GDR. This was the decisive point. See also Adomeit, op. cit., p. 6.

23. See Hans-Peter Riese, 'Die Geschichte hat sich ans Werk gemacht', *Europa-Archiv*, no. 4, 1990, pp. 117-26 and the 'German-Soviet Joint Statement' in Freedman, op. cit., pp. 472-5.

24. See, e.g., 'Für militärische Neutralität', *Der Spiegel*, no. 8, 1990, p. 169 and 'Falin: Kein Beitritt Deutschlands zur NATO', *Süddeutsche Zeitung*, 4 July 1990. There was a variety of other proposals (mostly unofficial) as well (Adomeit, op. cit., p. 11).

25. On the Soviet policy concerning the unification problem in winter 1990, see Wettig, op. cit., pp. 13-26.

26. The programme can be found in, for example, the speech of Foreign Minister Genscher in the Evangelic Academy Tutzing (FRG) on 31 January 1990.

27. In spring 1990, the neutrality of Germany had many supporters in German polls. See, e.g., *Der Spiegel*, no. 17, 1990, p. 103. According to the results of the Usuma/Emnid polls, 23 per cent in the West and 53 per cent in the East favoured neutrality. Pro-NATO attitudes without reservations were registeted by 27 per cent and 15 per cent, respectively.

28. See, e.g., 'Das wird eine Gratwanderung', *Der Speigel* , no. 29, 1990 and *Die Welt*, 10 July 1990.

29. The treaty has been published *in extenso* in *Das Parlament*, 21 September 1990. On the circumstances during the preparation of the treaty in Moscow, see 'Das grosse historische Werk', *Der Spiegel*, no. 38, 1990, pp. 18-21.

30. The general situation in early September was rapidly deteriorating because of the Persian Gulf crisis as well as the internal power struggle in the Soviet Union.

31. See, e.g., 'Beziehungen zu Moskau auf neuer Grundlage', *Süddeutsche Zeitung*, 10 November 1990.

32. Interview with the Estonian minister Enn Lippmaa ('Unser Ressourcen abgezogen', *Der Spiegel*, no. 42, 1990, pp. 200-2). He and many other politicians in the Baltic republics criticized especially Article 2, which acknowledged all present European borders. They could not, however, accept the right of Germany to ignore the claims of the Baltic republics to independence.

33. The first poll on Germany in the Soviet Union, carried out during the autumn, showed positive attitudes towards Germany. See 'Bestätigung des guten Geistes', *Frankfurter Allgeimeine Zeitung*, 27 September 1990.

34. 'Königsberg - ein Tor zum Westen?', *Die Zeit*, 3 August 1990.

35. 'Ein russisches Königsberg unter europäischen Vorzeichen', *Süddeutsche Zeitung*, 6 September 1990), 'Ein weiter Weg bis Königsberg', *Die Welt*, 11 September 1990; and 'Wiederherstellung der Autonomie der Deutschen in der Sowjetunion verlangt' *Frankfurter Allgemeine Zeitung*, 27 September 1990.
36. The most alarming was the resignation speech by Foreign Minister Shevardnadze, held in the Congress of People's Deputies on 20 December 1990. During the congress, many conservative communists, among them the KGB chief Vladimir Kryuchkov, accused 'foreign powers' of intervention in the internal affairs of the Soviet Union and the Foreign Ministry of surrendering to the Western alliance. The loss of the GDR and the acceptance of German unification was also mentioned several times in criticism of foreign policy. Newspapers expressed concern over developments in the Soviet Union during the following month. See, e.g. 'Paukenschlag im Kreml', *Frankfurter Allgemeine Zeitung*, 21 December 1990 and 'Zurück zum Stalinismus', *Frankfurter Allgemeine Zeitung*, 15 January 1991.
37. See, e.g., 'Moscow Dragging Feet on Forces Pull-out, say Poles', *The Independent*, 26 January 1991 and 'Wie der grosse Bruder mit dem Kleinen: Warschau hat sich in eine prekäre Lage gebracht', *Frankfurter Allgemeine Zeitung*, 29 January 1991.

INDEX